THE GREATER GAME

THE GREATER GAME

Sporting Icons Who Fell in the Great War

CLIVE HARRIS
and
JULIAN WHIPPY

Foreword by Richard Holmes

First published in Great Britain in 2008 by
PEN & SWORD MILITARY
An imprint of
Pen & Sword Books Ltd
47 Church Street
Barnsley
South Yorkshire
S70 2AS

ISBN 978-1-84415-762-4

Typeset by Concept, Huddersfield, West Yorkshire
Printed and bound in England by Biddles Ltd

Pen & Sword Books Ltd incorporates the Imprints of Pen & Sword Aviation,
Pen & Sword Maritime, Pen & Sword Military, Wharncliffe Local History,
Pen & Sword Select, Pen & Sword Military Classics, Leo Cooper,
Remember When, Seaforth Publishing and Frontline Publishing

For a complete list of Pen & Sword titles please contact
PEN & SWORD BOOKS LIMITED
47 Church Street, Barnsley, South Yorkshire, S70 2AS, England
E-mail: enquiries@pen-and-sword.co.uk
Website: www.pen-and-sword.co.uk

Dedication

This book is dedicated to Lee Johnson and all men and women serving in Her Majesty's Forces around the globe.

Sergeant Lee 'Judo Jonno' Johnson
2nd Battalion (The Green Howards), The Yorkshire Regiment.
Killed on active service, 8 December 2007,
Southern Afghanistan.

'As a soldier he was the best and you would always want him at your side, due to his absolute professionalism and outright ability. With him around you always felt safe and that nothing could go wrong. As a sportsman he excelled in judo and in boxing and what he lacked in talent he made up for with courage and determination.'

C. Sergeant Elsdon
2nd Battalion, The Yorkshire Regiment

THE GAME

Come, leave the lure of the football field
With its fame so lightly won,
And take your place in a greater game
Where worthier deeds are done.
No game is this where thousands watch
The play of a chosen few;
But rally all! if you are men at all,
There's room in the team for you.

You may find your place in the battle front,
If you played the forward game,
To carry the trench and man the guns
With dash and deadly aim.
O, the field is wide, and the foe is strong,
And it's far from wing to wing.
But we'll carry through, and it's there that you
May shoot for your flag and King.

Will you play your part in the middle line
Where our airmen bear the brunt,
Who break the plan of the foe's attack,
And rally the men in front!
A bold assault, and a sure defence
In their game they well combine;
And there's honour too awaiting you,
If you will play in the middle line.

And, last of all, you may find a place
Perchance of less renown,
Where a willing arm may save the game,
If the first defence breaks down.
So while others serve in the far-off front,
Or out on the deadly foam,
Will you not enrol to keep the goal,
And fight for your hearth and home!

Then leave for a while the football field,
And the lure of the flying ball
Lest it dull your ear to the voice you hear
When your King and your country call.
Come, join the ranks of our hero sons
In the wide field of fame,
Where the god of right will watch the fight,
And referee the game.

A. Lochhead

Contents

Acknowledgements

There are a number of friends, colleagues and contributors without whom this book would not have been possible. First and foremost we would like to thank our wives Angie (Julian) and Ali (Clive) for supporting us on the all-consuming road to completion of the book. We would also like to thank our editor, Jon Cooksey, for his help and guidance and all the battlefield tour passengers and friends who have offered snippets along the way.

Valuable aid came from the men and women of the various museums and resource centres we visited around the country. These 'behind the scenes' people are genuinely passionate about their work and their praise is often under sung. We thank curator Jed Smith and his team at the RFU Museum of Rugby in Twickenham, staff at the Berkshire library and resources centre for their help with Poulton-Palmer, the patient librarians at Marylebone Cricket Club and Major Bob Kelly (retd.) who was extremely enthusiastic and helpful at the Museum of Army Physical Training in Aldershot.

Alan Little and Audrey Snell at the award winning Wimbledon Lawn Tennis Museum could not have been more helpful. Brian Belton, lifelong Hammer fan and West Ham history guru was a mine of information. We are grateful to Mike Sherrington, Harold Alderman and Harry Taylor for their generous help and contributions on boxing and cricket, while Michael Jones at the Leander Rowing Club archives helped us with F.S. Kelly's achievements along with Therese Radic of Melbourne University. In addition thanks go to Nigel Truman at www.rugbyfootballhistory.com for allowing use of rugby posters, and also to Ronny Biggs and Nick Eliason for use of their own archives and postcards. We are indebted to Sue Horton and her family for providing a treasure trove of information on Henry Berry and likewise thanks to Mark Wylie at Manchester United's Museum at Old Trafford for gems on Sandy Turnbull. Ron and Margaret Marks (Clive's in laws) spent many hours of holiday time in Australia tracking down the name of Arthur Jones on a long forgotten memorial. We are grateful to members of The Princess of Wales' Own Regiment of Canada whom, after allowing us the pleasure of guiding them around its Battle Honours on the Western Front, were most helpful with regards to the chapter on Frank McGee. Last but not least we extend our thanks to Ken Smallwood, Phil Bradley, Martin Purdy and Mark Gardiner who helped us with information and added personal anecdotes regarding their football clubs which helped us piece together the stories of other footballers who played in and gave their lives during the course of The Greater Game.

Foreword

I often feel haunted by the First World War: however much I promise that I will never write another word about it, somehow it elbows its way back into my life, and it is not hard to see why. Although the Second World War was a greater event in world history, for Britain and her empire the first was a unique experience. It saw Britain put her biggest-ever army into the field: not far short of 6,000,000 men served. Around 1,000,000 men were killed serving under British command, and 1 July 1916, the first day of the Somme, still has the dreadful distinction of being the bloodiest in British history.

I doubt if there will be one of you reading these lines whose family history was not in some way changed by the war. Perhaps you will have that trio of medals, unkindly called Pip, Squeak and Wilfred, tucked into a drawer, maybe with the bronze commemorative plaque, no less irreverently known as the death penny. If the war changed Britain, it is not too much to say that Australia, Canada and New Zealand saw their national identity crystallised by the conflict. That long slope between Delville Wood and High Wood on the Somme is crowned by the New Zealand memorial, with its unbearably poignant words 'From the Uttermost Ends of the Earth'. The Canadian memorial shines out on Vimy Ridge in newly-refurbished stone, and one does not have to be Australian to find the Lone Pine memorial on Gallipoli almost unbearably moving.

Although the war was so profoundly shocking that it would be optimistic to expect that we will ever be able to view it with any sense of balance, I applaud the way that its history is now being written. There are far fewer of those easy assumptions that gave us books such as *The Donkeys*, and greater recognition that, while some British generals were indeed out of their depth, much the same can be said for some of their allies and opponents too. Britain's over-riding task was the creation of the first mass army in her history, against a background of radical change in technology and tactics, as part of an alliance that was committed to attacking (for the Germans had seized almost the whole of Belgium and a great swathe of northern France) at the very moment that burgeoning firepower had made the defensive the stronger form of war. Expanding the army would have been difficult enough in itself, and doing so in the midst of a military revolution was challenge indeed.

Some historians maintain that even 1,000,000 dead are, given the size of the populations involved (46,000,000 for Britain alone), not really statistically significant – the influenza epidemic of 1918–19 killed more people. However, I maintain that the 'lost generation' thesis is no myth: what should concern us is the war's qualitative, no less than its quantitative, impact. Almost exactly half the men who joined the British Army in the war had volunteered, and it was not until the middle of 1916 that conscripts appeared at the front in appreciable numbers.

Clive Harris and Julian Whippy, both experienced battlefield guides, have chosen to explore one specific aspect of this impact by considering the sportsmen killed in the war. It is impossible to resist the conclusion that these were men of outstanding merit, whose character, courage and promise would be sorely missed, and whose physical and moral strength meant so much to their comrades. The rugby international Edgar Mobbs was killed as a lieutenant colonel, doing a job he could easily have delegated to a subaltern, the risk so obvious that one officer yelled, 'For God's sake, Sir, get down.' The rower and professional pianist Frederick Septimus Kelly had already won a Distinguished Service Cross with the Royal Naval Division in Gallipoli before being killed as a company commander on the Western Front. The footballer Donny Bell had joined up as a private soldier and been commissioned from the ranks to die on the Somme, winning a posthumous Victoria Cross.

Whole battalions were made up of sportsmen. 17th and 23rd Middlesex were recruited from footballers; 16th Royal Scots, drawn from Heart of Midlothian supporters, was bravely commanded by the club's chairman, and 13th Rifle Brigade contained many distin-guished golfers. The authors rightly include Arthur Jones, an

'Aussie rules' footballer, killed as a lance corporal when the Australian Light Horse made its impossible charge across the Nek on Gallipoli, and the Canadian hockey player Frank McGee, killed as an infantry officer on the Somme.

This is, as Shakespeare would have put it, 'a noble fellowship of death.' There will always be aspects of the war, like its capital courts-martial or some of its more unenterprising offensives, that rightly give us pause for thought. But the pages that follow illuminate the lives of decent men – spread across the social spectrum from Oxbridge to the ranks of the pre-war regular army – who deserve our admiration. I concluded my own book *Tommy* by saying that the sufferings of my grandfather's generation both lifted my spirits and broke my heart, and I can think of no more fitting tribute to the sportsmen who, in this timely and affectionate book, played the game up to the very last whistle.

Richard Holmes

Authors' Introductions

Buttoned up against a cold northerly wind, I walked slowly along the lines of headstones in Rue-de Berceaux Commonwealth War Graves Cemetery near Richebourg L'Avoue in Northern France reading each name as I went. Researching a future battlefield tour of the 1915 forgotten front had drawn me to this quiet, secluded French battlefield. In search of stories to tell, my eyes fell upon a headstone that stood out from the others. Surrounded by men from British Army Regiments, there, still proudly displaying his globe and laurel wreath badge, lay a Royal Marine. Why was this man buried here? The answer was revealed in the cemetery register. Captain Anthony Frederick Wilding, aged thirty-one, was a former Wimbledon Tennis Champion. Not only had I found my first story, the discovery had awakened in me a desire to discover more of these great sporting icons behind the headstones of Flanders.

The huge numbers killed in the Great War are difficult to comprehend but telling stories through the humanising medium of sport offers a common understanding and such stories are still there to be found. Amongst those many hundreds of thousands of lives cut short by the Great War were those of hundreds of young men who had demonstrated terrific athletic and sporting promise.

Coupled with my life long passion for history, especially of the two World Wars, I am a passionate and enduring fan of West Ham United. Standing recently at Upton Park cheering (and yes, sometimes groaning), I wondered if the highly rewarded players running around before me would hang up their boots if the country really was 'backs to the wall'? Would those stout hearted England 'fans' with three lions on their chest – some of them behaving so badly in Europe – answer the call of 'their' country and allow themselves to become moulded into the finest soldiers of the world, in the British Army? In answer to the last question I say 'yes' emphatically. The proof is out there today in the hot, sandy corners of the globe and in the obituaries of our young men and women being flown home in caskets draped in the Union flag.

Several books have been written on sport and sportsmen in war, but these have been written predominantly from a sports journalist approach, tending to focus on sporting achievements and often summing up their wartime roles in a short, often 'tragic waste of war' slanted sentence. The same writers fill our red top newspaper columns and act as pundits in radio and television studios, churning out sporting hero clichés, often with little thought of the realities of conflict and the effects of their comments on their audiences. In times of peace perhaps, sporting icons act for communities, almost as 'pseudo war heroes' fulfilling deep, primitive and tribal needs but they do not display heroism; for bravery must also be present alongside achievement over adversity for that accolade to stick. Once found though it will be lapped up by an eager public thirsting to read about real heroes in 'ripping yarns' in the *Boys' Own* style. As well as heroes, sport brings rivalries. Adversarial clashes between two great competitors can appear opposite and yet identical (Britain *versus* Germany?) and this can be echoed on the battlefield too. Some sport sociologists have even suggested that sport is 'war without weapons'– ritualised conflict minus the bombs, bullets and death.

Uncovering the stories behind these men who played 'the greater game' but who did not live to hear the final whistle and then writing about them, has moved Clive and I to become very fond of them. We are proud, therefore, to share their stories with you.

Julian Whippy.
Bedfordshire, December 2007

I can remember the Saturday well, it was March 1984 and I was given a clear choice; shopping in Stevenage with my Auntie Jo or football at the Valley with my Uncle Richard. The decision was an easy one. I had been to countless football matches before, Watford, Arsenal, Spurs, Chelsea and West Ham but none felt as comfortable as the minute I stepped onto the vast East Terrace and looked over an almost Peter Pan view of London. My uncle, seeing my awe swiftly announced, 'Your family hasn't always come from Hertfordshire you know, this place is in your blood.' At that moment, during a 3-3 draw with Grimsby Town, I became a 'pukka' football fan and remain one twenty-four years on.

My equal passion is history and in particular the Great War. From those precious times as a youth when I would visit numerous veterans who had retired from London to Welwyn Garden City, to my battlefield tour company today, the subject remains one of intense fascination and admiration. In researching this book Julian and I spent many a haunting moment on the 'old front line'; from The Nek at Gallipoli in search of Arthur Septimus Montague Jones or in treading in the footsteps of Alex 'Sandy' Turnbull at Cherisy our desire to tell the story of these remarkable men led us to write *The Greater Game* – our tribute to those sporting icons who fell in the Great War.

I can recall Bill Hay, a veteran of the 9/Royal Scots telling John Nicholls, 'We'd play whenever we got the chance; we had Bill and Jimmy Broad, two brothers who were professionals with Manchester City and that made us the best team in the division. Without doubt the most full bloodied games were friendly matches against 2 Platoon, I'd end up fighting with a stroppy sergeant called Wollocks, I would annoy him by spelling his name with a B!' This was but one memory of one man of the millions in khaki, but an indication of the relevance of sport as an oft – needed diversion from the wearisome rigours of trench life that existed for so many who served between 1914–1918.

My inspiration in life remains the countless men like Bill, ordinary fellows who served their country in an extraordinary time. I am sure, however, that were he around to read this book today he would agree that many of the characters that feature within its pages were extraordinary men in extraordinary times and that is exactly what makes them so interesting to us all almost a century on.

Clive Harris
Hertfordshire, December 2007

Chapter 1

Ronald Poulton Palmer

'His presence was like a gleam of sunshine'

Swerving and dodging as he carved his way through the French back line, the crowd cheered then laughed as first he feigned a drop kick and two of the French team crashed into each other comically before he sprinted through the resulting gap to score his fourth try of the game. There was little doubt that 'Ronnie' Poulton Palmer was on fine form again.

France had scored first and were still in the game until half-time when England led 13-8 but England ran away with it in the second half and won convincingly 39-13. England had won the Grand Slam; the year was 1914. Just a year later Poulton Palmer was dead; killed whilst fighting for his country rather than merely playing for it.

Ronald Poulton, as he was christened, had developed an ability to read the opposition in rugby matches and mount darting runs at lightning speed. As early as 1907 *The Meteor* reported that he was 'a really good three-quarter, with plenty of pace; has an excellent swerving run and makes good openings, but is sometimes inclined to pass somewhat wildly; a good tackle and a fair kick.' It lists him then as being '18 years old, 5 foot 11 inches and 10 stone 6 pounds' and goes on, 'he gathers the ball beautifully, holding the ball with both hands at arms length, swerving forward, combining excellently with those around him, seldom without success. If his tackling improves he will become a truly great player.' Clearly the slightly deformed little finger of his right hand, which had troubled him in his early years, was no hindrance in top flight sport.

In the pre-war Edwardian era Ronald played alongside the influential Adrian Stoop. Many have said that Stoop's style of rugby football back play was a revolutionary approach to the work of the 'backs' and led to the modern era in terms of rugby three-quarter tactics. Stoop played for Harlequins and England as did Poulton Palmer, so no doubt the two friends influenced each other and perhaps some of Stoop's work was inspired by the handling and creativity of 'Ronnie'.

Stoop went on to become captain of Harlequins, won fifteen caps for England and was later President of the RFU. Now, in the shadow of the huge Twickenham complex, Harlequins' home at the 'Stoop Memorial Stadium' is named after him.

It was only when he had reached the age of twelve that Ronald started to shine in athletics and ball games; this was in his fourth year at the Oxford Preparatory School. It is clear from the school records that he was a bigger than average pupil and his height and weight were about average for a boy two years his senior. Perhaps it was this sudden growth spurt that allowed him to excel in classes and matches on the fields. This was also his first year of playing rugby and he caught the eye of those recording the match. An after school match report records that, 'he was the best of the three-quarters on the day, however sometimes less effective in defence and was seen to "scoot away" from the enemy.'

Pupils of the Oxford Prep School are known as 'Dragons' and on leaving naturally become 'Old Dragons'. In his last year at the school, Ronald's Headmaster paid tribute to him by writing, 'his presence was like a gleam of sunshine.' Sporting achievements had continued to accrue as a Dragon and he was top scorer in hockey, good at gymnastics and played cricket for the School XI. It is thought he was the best all-round sportsman that the school has ever produced. His academic prowess was also evident and he submitted an essay on Mary Queen of Scots which won a top prize. Often the centre of attention and much liked by his fellow pupils he was seen as the 'life and soul' of many teams. If there was one possible drawback to his personality it was that he seemed a terrible chatterbox and bets were often laid, whilst on train journeys to other schools for away matches, that he could not stay silent for at least five minutes! Apparently Ronald never won the bet. Ronald left Oxford Prep in 1903, thereby becoming an 'Old Dragon'. Seventy-four other Old Dragons were to fall in the Great War.

Ronald Poulton had been born on 12 September 1889 at Wykeham House on the Banbury Road in Oxford, a house which would be his childhood home. He was the fourth child to parents Edward and Emily Poulton. Edward Poulton MA was a lecturer at Jesus College, Oxford and his wife Emily was a daughter of the wealthy Reading family behind the Palmer biscuit empire, a firm which later became better known to all biscuit lovers as Huntley and Palmer.

Their first born, a boy six years Ronald's senior, was named Edward and there then followed two girls, Hilda and Margaret before Ronald came along. In 1891, two years after Ronnie's birth, came child number five, Janet.

The family were reasonably wealthy and employed a nanny named Edith from South-West Africa who recalled that, 'even before he [Ronald] could talk we were good friends; he was always smiling and seemed a very happy baby.' By the time he had reached the age of five his kindergarten teacher, Ms Cobbs, described him as, 'full of energy with a long attention span, bright, merry and often with a sunburnt smiling face.' Two years later his friendship with his cousin Miss Eustace Palmer began and many have remarked that had he survived the Great War, the pair would have controlled the great biscuit and cake business together.

Despite his later fearless play on the fields of Oxford, Twicken-ham and Flanders, death and suffering clearly upset him in his early years. When playing with model toy soldiers with his brother he often got frightened when they were lined up, knocked over and 'killed' and Ronald would run from the room. Similarly the two brothers chased and caught butterflies in the garden of Wykeham House but Ronald cried when his brother killed one accidentally. These are perhaps early signs of compassion in a man who was often described in later years as kind and gentle to his friends and to the soldiers under his command. His sense of humour was also noteworthy and he frequently joked and poked fun, usually at himself. He enjoyed the humour of words and once wrote, on his Oxford college wall, 'The more I see of some people, the more I like my dog!'

Following Oxford Prep School came five formative years at the famous Rugby School in Warwickshire from 1903 to 1908. In 1823 a local lad called William Webb Ellis had first picked up and run with a football and so had invented the game of rugby football. Players on the pitch in those days were somewhat more numerous and in

1839 one match had boasted nearly 300 players! Today, innumerable tourists visit the 'home of the game' and rugby teams from all over the world can be seen training against the distinctive backdrop of the school buildings. The memorial chapel walls boast tablets in memory of renowned Rugbeian writers like Lewis Carroll and also the Great War poet Rupert Brooke, who also has a school 'House' now named after him.

Brooke, who was known to Ronald, was the author of a series of poems, the best known being *The Soldier* in 1914 which begins, 'If I should die, think only this of me: that there's some corner of a foreign field, that is for ever England.'

Moving back to his home town of Oxford for his university years in the autumn of 1908 took Ronald to Balliol College where he had digs in Oriel Street just off the High Street. As might be expected he joined all manner of sporting clubs, teams and associations swiftly but also enjoyed academic debate and joined the debating society. His first motion read, 'This house views with alarm the increasing luxury of the age.' Perhaps similar motions are still echoing at Balliol today? Academic study took its toll and some sporting activity had to be curtailed. Rugby was a passion for Ronald, so tennis was dropped. In fact the year he arrived at university, Ronald was invited to trial for the Harlequins Rugby Club and only a few months later that which he had yearned for finally arrived; a letter inviting him for a trial for his country. What is also of interest here is that Poulton is one of a very select band of players who were invited to play for their country, before they had played for and thus earned their 'Blue' cap at university level. The university clearly believed that, 'the arrival and presence of an exceptional genius in a team does not immediately improve the combination.' He did go on to play for Oxford in the Varsity match against Cambridge in 1909, scoring five tries. In 1911 he hobbled into the game injured but with the help of some characteristically low, searching kicks over the scrummage he got forward to score twice.

Whilst sharing digs he met and became great friends with a man called Keith Rae. They remained friends after university and Rae, like Ronald, also joined the Army in the Great War and served in a different regiment but near to Ronald at Ypres. They spent many happy hours 'messing about in boats' on the Thames backwaters during weekends and holidays. Both a humorous and sporting moment took place one year at college when Ronald and his rugby chums spontaneously challenged the Football XI at their own game. Ronald, Keith and Neville Talbot all played and, annoyingly for the football players, disregarded all pretence of tactics and simply chased the ball *en masse* wherever it went; first up at one end then down at the other. The footballers lost and it was a sore subject for some time.

The free spirit and healthy, outdoor lifestyle he enjoyed at university had first been experienced during earlier holidays when Ronald had been introduced to the Boys' Camps at New Romney on the Kent coast. Known as the Rugby Mission, from their association with his school, these Boys' Camps were an introduction to a form of social work which he was to enjoy when later employed in Reading. Much physical activity was enjoyed on camp and after one such excursion to the Lake District Ronald wrote a letter to his sister Janet:

> We have just come back home after a very long day, but it has been a glorious day-the only day in fact that we have been dry and warm. We first biked six miles then we walked nine miles to Scawfell Pike, where people climb, and back down to a beautiful lake called Wast water, six miles, then a hard uphill walk of nine miles. We then biked home. After dinner we walked in the perfect moonlight for five miles. It has been the day we have been waiting for.

They thus covered twelve miles cycling and almost thirty walking. He continued:

> I am absolutely dog tired and my feet have nearly given way with blisters and bruises. Tomorrow we have a slack day with breakfast at 9, which is a great thing.

Such adventurous activity was certainly good training both physically and mentally and no doubt stood him in good stead when he answered the letter to appear for his country as a three-quarter back in January 1909 against France then again two weeks later against Ireland. He did not score any points in his first two matches but performed well enough to catch the eye of coaches and team selectors to assure himself a place in the starting line ups when his studies would allow. For the following three years his appearances seem somewhat sporadic but this can perhaps be explained by the pressures of study and examinations. His first ever run out must have been exhilarating as the teams played in front of 15,000 spectators at the Welford Road Ground and England beat the French 22-0. His modesty is exhibited, however, when he replied to a letter from a young boy who had asked for an autograph by telling the young fan 'not to be a little idiot, and to spend his time better than worshipping athletes.'

Ronald was always a sensible man who preferred to live simply and in inexpensive surroundings. He would have wanted paid work quickly and having left Oxford University in 1911 a position was offered with his uncle George Palmer at the cake and biscuit business in Reading. He saw himself as an apprentice to the entire biscuit manufacturing process and, under the guidance of his uncle, studied much of the business including management and accounts in addition to the manufacturing processes. He was sent to Manchester where he underwent training in engineering in the factory and whilst doing so with the real 'working man' his skills in social work, learned earlier, came to the fore. He cared for the men and understood that many had little option but to work long hours and do overtime whilst juggling the needs of wives and children at home. Ronald set about helping with the establishment of evening clubs for the children of the factory employees, so that their parents could do overtime. Thirteen of the twenty-nine lads from the Reading clubs of 1913–14 later lost their lives in the Great War. It was during this pre-war period that his close friendship with Eustace Palmer and his untiring work at the business of Huntley and Palmer led to Ronald taking the name 'Palmer' as a suffix to his existing surname. There is a suggestion that George Palmer made him an offer of inheritance, with the condition that he took the surname too. Ronald was now known as Ronald Poulton Palmer (not hyphenated). George Palmer did indeed die shortly afterwards in 1913.

Holidays, though rare, were taken with the family on the Isle of Wight where they owned a small cottage in St Helens not far from the harbour. Ronald would always be busy with 'projects'; often up at dawn to carry out repairs, build garden walls or decorate. This was mirrored during the war when he wrote home to his father from the front in 1915 saying, 'you would simply love all the schemes for improvements and dugouts with drainage.'

In 1912 Ronald joined the British Army with a commission in the Royal Berkshire Regiment following his previous service with the Oxford University Officer Training Corps. His service began on

30 April as a Second Lieutenant in the 4th Battalion, Territorial Force. On attestation he listed his address as Portland Place, Reading, which was only 800 yards from the Huntley and Palmer factory. He clearly accepted that he was the commander of his men with some hilarity as many of them had seen previous service in the South African Wars, had Regular Army experience over many years and at least one had a medal for gallantry! He revelled in the role, however, and after his death it was reported in a Reading newspaper that Poulton Palmer had said, as early as 1912, to his employees at Huntley and Palmer that they should all join the Territorial Army as he was sure that Britain would be at war with Germany within two years! Ronald now managed to balance his busy life of work at Huntley and Palmer, assisting with the boys' clubs and playing for the England Rugby Team.

This was a golden era for English rugby and Ronald was part of a winning squad. In the squad of the era were other rugby greats such as Edgar Mobbs (winger and soldier) and Norman Wodehouse (played as a forward with England on fourteen occasions, six of those as captain). He, like most rugby players, joined the colours and became a sailor in the Great War. He was decorated for self-lessly diving into the sea to save a drowning sailor who had fallen over board in the dark. He survived the First World War only to perish in the Second. In 1941, whilst serving as a Vice Admiral aboard HMS *Eaglet* at the age of fifty-four, his Atlantic convoy was attacked and his ship was sunk by a U-boat.

Ronald Poulton Palmer, often shortened to 'RPP', gained seventeen caps for his country and only experienced defeat three times, once against South Africa in 1913 and twice at the hands of Scotland. He never lost his down-to-earth, approachable character, however, and when he arrived at Cardiff Arms Park the day before a match against Wales he and a friend started to kick a football about. Before long a large group of boys on their way to choir practice had been invited to join in and have a proper game. Realising who they were being invited to play with the boys jumped at the chance, before being called in to church thus having to leave the game reluctantly.

The new ground at Twickenham had increased capacity and in front of a 25,000 crowd Ronald scored his first try for his country against Ireland. Others followed and so did drop goals against Wales. His finest sporting hour must have been against France in Paris in the Five Nations Cup where our chapter began, and Ronald

7

scored twenty of the thirty-nine points to secure a famous victory in his last sporting appearance for the national side.

The magazine *British Sports and Sportsmen* of 1914 recorded that, 'Ronald Poulton Palmer was the most conspicuous figure in the Rugby world at the close of the 1914 season immediately before the War. In addition to his great personality as a player he had just captained the England team victoriously in all its four International matches.' *The Rugby Football Annual* recorded, 'As a Three Quarter back he is unique and his name will be handed down as an epoch maker in that part of the game. He is a born leader never over confident and never flurried.'

Just before the outbreak of war in August 1914 Ronald, like many other Territorials, was at summer camp. He spoke of the camp as one 'that brought us very close to each other and taught us that after all one of the best things in life is a true and real friendship.' Clearly well prepared for war it came as no surprise to Ronald when the declaration came just as camp finished. His mother and father were away in Australia at the time and set sail for home via Suez when they heard Ronald was committed to serving overseas. Like many men Ronald kept a journal of events and wrote frequently to family and friends. These records provide an insight into the chaotic days of August 1914 when hysteria swept the nation and many thousands were being mobilised. Typical of this period was the Army 'hurry up and wait' scenario, played out hundreds of times. The 1/4 Royal Berks mobilized 930 men out of a possible 1,000 and on 4 August were ordered to march to Marlow, twelve miles away, then on a further two miles to a camp for only three hours sleep before being sent back to Reading. Ronald explained, 'we were then locked in the drill hall until 0900 and then dismissed to our homes!' News arrived of the men going to camp for extra training, 'I expect we will train hard, but know no more. All my 35 lb of kit is ready. Now I must stop and go to drill.' He wrote to his mother on 7 August, 'The papers are heavily censored and no news leaks out. There is sure to be a big naval engagement soon. It is a terrible thing but some good may come as it may put an end to armed enmity in Europe.'

The battalion spent several days near Portsmouth as part of the area defences and he saw some anti-airship guns being positioned, 'They seem awfully frightened about airships.' Camp was to be near Swindon and it was here that his Division, 48th (South Midland), was addressed following Kitchener's appeal for 100,000 volunteers to serve overseas. Interestingly enough, the call up was not answered with 100 per cent success, at least not to begin with:

The General wants his whole division to go together. The Colonel paraded the Battalion and gave a very unbiased speech saying no one would be thought the worse of for refusing and gave us 5 minutes to think about it. Result – 14 Officers and 214 men. Disappointment as 75% is needed for the Battalion to go. Meanwhile the Colonel got news that all the other Battalions have volunteered almost complete, so we are paraded again! Great Speech – 'If you refuse to go you never hold up your heads among the Oxfords, the Gloucesters and Warwicks again. Follow your Colonel and your Company Commanders'. Result – Over 70% so it is likely we shall now go!

Edward, Ronald's older brother asked him if he volunteered at the first request or the second, 'He seemed rather surprised at the question and said that it was at the first opportunity of course.'

The next seven months were spent at camp in England training and preparing for the move to France. Finally, in March 1915, the order for France arrived. In a letter to his father Ronald wrote:

We are definitely off at 7pm Tuesday. The transport arrives at 3am so we are all pretty busy. Now goodbye dearest and say goodbye to mother and Janet. Don't worry about me especially if you don't hear regularly. I'll write as often as I can, but I may not always be able to.

Some letters survive that were also sent to Ronald, where, for obvious reasons, he could not keep them all. One, very upbeat, from his great friend Keith Rae ran:

I believe very firmly that there will be a Bright beyond after this war. How lucky it is that we can go out knowing both that we ought to go and that we could never forgive ourselves were we not to go. There is such tremendous spirit among everyone. My Love to you, and God bless you, always your affectionate friend, Keith Rae.

Shunted on troop trains down from London the battalion was loaded aboard a traffic steamer at Folkestone and cast off under clear skies at 11.00 pm on 30 March. Ronald remarked that it was the same ship he had travelled on to go to his last international rugby match against France the year before. He also said that the ship was very quiet all the way; the men hardly speaking to each other. Following a few days at camp in a snow-covered Boulogne the battalion began the slow move through more camps and along hard congested *pave* roads to billets closer to the front line.

Ronald seemed very impressed with 'the whole scheme' of supplies and movements of men through busy junctions and rail heads. He found the food plentiful, though largely of the tinned variety with, ironically, the addition of large quantities of biscuits! Bread and eggs were frequently purchased from local farmers to supplement the diet.

Ronald was at ease with his men and found it somewhat humorous to receive unofficial compliments when tasked with 'censoring' men's letters.

Having been inspected and complimented by General H. Smith-Dorrien at Steenvorde the battalion was tasked with going 'up the line.' Two Companies at a time were to go forward for forty-eight hours and receive 'instruction' in trench routine from some more experienced troops of the 1/7 Battalion, Argyll and Sutherland Highlanders (4th Division). The line to be held here was just north of Armentieres, very close to the Franco-Belgian border.

The 1/4 Royal Berks consisted of four companies lettered A-D. Ronald was in command of 13 Platoon, D Company. A and B Companies were to go first but D Company had to form working parties as was the norm when not in the line. Having been promoted to Lieutenant, Poulton Palmer led his platoon to the trenches for the first time on 10 April 1915, for a forty-eight hour tour of instruction alongside the Royal Dublin Fusiliers also of 10 Brigade, 4th Division, 'The atmosphere was tainted with the smell of death and occasionally bullets flew over us on the approach.' He saw the ground was pitted with shell holes and broken by trenches half-full of water. The trenches were only dug to a depth of about a foot into the ground and then had to be built up with breastworks of earth filled sandbags:

The men carried out sentry duty and repairs before I was sent out on a listening patrol. Carrying a rifle and 15 rounds we climbed through the wire after dark and went perhaps 100

10

yards out and lay doggo close to a decomposing cow for over an hour.

On the morning of 11 April, Ronald and his men experienced their first bombardment. Around ten German 6-inch shells landed on the line causing damage but no casualties. Ronald noted that some men were frightened and unnerved, others prayed and counted rosary beads, whilst others simply continued to cook breakfast. After a quiet afternoon the men watched as several Royal Flying Corps aircraft flew about over the German lines, being shot at furiously from the ground. None were hit and the day ended peacefully. The next day was at rest and the Division organised a rugby match against their trench hosts of 4th Division which was played near Bailleul. Numerous well known rugby players were present from domestic clubs and international teams. There is no mention of Ronald scoring but his 48th Division team won 17-0. Such short interludes away from the trenches must have been welcome but surreal when only hours later they went back to the business of war.

Late on 15 April D Company went back up the line to a wooded area, 15 km south of Ypres, called Ploegsteert; better known affectionately to the British Tommy as 'Plugstreet'. Ronald wrote of the place, 'It is full of wire and seems impregnable. You can move about because of the cover of the wood, except in the front advanced posts, where there is a little sniping. But mostly it is peaceful as I sit and write my letters.' He goes on to describe the awful smell in the wood due to partially buried and decomposing bodies; one body sticking out of the ground just in front of the British wire. Their position at this time was just north of Le Gheer on the eastern side of Plugstreet Wood. This area had become popular as a reasonably quiet area for the Army to acclimatise newly arriving battalions to the realities of trench warfare. Yet despite the 'quietness' the battalion suffered its first fatality and several other casualties in mid-April. Many a young soldier succumbed to the inquisitive urge to peer over the parapet and have a peek at 'the Hun' only to fall prey to a sniper's bullet. Behind these advanced posts was a series of trenches in the wood known as 'Tourist lines' owing to the frequency of visitors, reporters and staff officers being shown around. Later in 1916, two future British Prime Ministers were stationed in the wood: Winston Churchill with the Royal Scots and Anthony Eden with the Kings Royal Rifle Corps.

During the very dark and wet night of 16 April, Lieutenant Poulton Palmer led a Lance Corporal out to an advanced listening post in front of the British line as a relief. When Poulton Palmer returned to the post later he found the NCO asleep at his post. Despite feeling sorry for the man and feeling that he was suffering because of shelling, he had the man arrested as was his duty. He wrote in his journal that he feared for the man as he might face a Court Martial. When out of the line the next day at the village of Romarin, Ronald attended the funeral of one of his soldiers accidentally shot by his comrade whilst in the trenches the previous day. He was also called upon to attend a court of inquiry for the NCO found asleep at his post. Ronald wrote to his sister, 'I slept like a log on a bed of straw at billets in Romarin' – this despite the continuous gunfire and sounds of battle from the heavy fighting only a few miles to the north at Hill 60.

Ronald took pleasure in dealing with the engineering aspects of his trenches and often wrote of ideas for improvements and schemes for dugouts and parapet strengthening in his journal. His company commander gave him control of all aspects of field works being undertaken by other platoons nearby. Sniping was the main concern for everyone and often the habit was to give a nickname to an enemy sniper. One active German sniper close to the Prowse Point area (named after Brigadier General Prowse of 4th Division) of the wood was nicknamed 'Sir Charles' whom, despite strenuous efforts, was not located but whom thankfully did not hit very much either; 'We cannot locate the brutes yet and they keep knocking down our periscopes. When we do find them we shall have them.'

Ronald was very proud of his men and expressed to his father that they worked harder than regulars and do not moan as much either, 'except about the lack of biscuits, and no H & P's.' He also comments in a letter home, 'the war is a farce, both sides have working parties only a hundred yards apart, talking, laughing, smoking and making a hell of a row, but no one shoots! Sometimes there is silence and you would not know the War is on.' Letters and parcels were also arriving at the front on a frequent basis. Socks, chocolate, almonds and raisins were much coveted by Ronald when they arrived from his aunt and sister. Also in one parcel was a cap sent by his mother which he wore despite it not being regulation attire.

The Old School House in Ploegsteert village itself provided a draughty but dry billet for four days at the end of April 1915, during which time the Court Martial concluded of the sleeping NCO. He was found guilty and sentenced to five years penal servitude but this was commuted to three months Field Punishment. Ronald, however, noted that, 'he was taken straight off to Hospital with his nerve quite shattered.' As the sun set on one Sunday afternoon, Holy Communion was held in the shattered church with an altar built out of old ammunition boxes covered in a ground sheet. The men were unable to kneel due to the rubble and debris under foot and Ronald for one thought it would have been wiser and more comfortable to take the service across the road in a pasture. Companies were either now in the line close to Antons Farm on the north side of the wood or in reserve near the Piggeries on the Messines road in what had been named Hyde Park Corner.

During a day at the advance line on 28 April 1915 Ronald was watching some 'bomb throwing', when suddenly a man next to him (Private F. Giles) was shot by a sniper and fell backwards into Ronald's arms. Badly wounded, the man was carried away on a stretcher and died soon afterwards. Ronald describes this in his last letter to reach home as well as the slightly comical sight of their drunken cook being blown bodily out of his dugout but otherwise being completely unhurt.

At 6.00 pm on 6 May 1915 there came a knock at the door of Wykeham House in Oxford. When answered, the Poultons saw a young telegram boy on the step. On opening the telegram they read, 'Regret your son killed last night. Death instantaneous. Colonel Serocold.'

In fact Ronald had died just after midnight on 5 May. He was, as usual, supervising working parties repairing dugouts and trenches next to Antons Farm. Several accounts relate that Ronald had climbed out onto the roof of a dugout to better see what progress was being made as the night was particularly dark and a mist was beginning to form above the damp ground. A single shot came from the German lines and hit Lieutenant Poulton Palmer in the right side of the chest. He was heard to mutter 'Oh!' quietly and then fell into the arms of Sergeant Brant. Lowered gently down into the safety of the trench by his men he was seen by Captain Thorne and a doctor who arrived quickly and both agreed that death was instantaneous. His expression in death was said to be peaceful and happy. Later that morning Ronald's body was carried to the Royal Berkshire Regimental burial plot near to Hyde Park Corner at the rear of the wood on the Messines road.

The death of such a popular officer and sportsman cast a deep gloom over the whole Division. One man from the Warwicks wrote, 'It cut me up terribly, the more so that we saw him carried back through our lines.'

Strangely, the telegram to Oxford was being read at precisely the time a burial service was being held at Ploegsteert. Visiting the area was the Bishop of Pretoria who presided at the ceremony and later wrote to the Poultons describing the event, which was attended by his company and a few other fellow officers, 'Before the simple service I consecrated the plot of ground which is now being fenced off. We sang *Let Saints on Earth* as the coffin was taken from the motor ambulance and finished the service with *Abide with Me*. The company then presented arms and the officers saluted. Many then went to the grave individually to pay their last respects. The Bishop continued, 'Our hearts were heavy and our eyes filled with tears' and he concluded, 'May God help you and yours to carry your load and make your sacrifice in the same spirit of forgetfulness of self as your boy made his – and it is a bigger one for you, but God will see you through, and it is all worth it.' A simple wooden cross was placed over the grave bearing the inscription:

RIP

Killed in Action

Lieut. R.W. Poulton Palmer. 1/4 Royal Berks.

5.5.15

His was only the second burial in the plot; alongside lay Private Giles whom Ronald had caught as he fell when sniped the week before.

Numerous letters were sent in condolence over the next few years to the Poultons and several recounted incidents of soldiers visiting the grave and actually helping to replace the cross which had become damaged and weather beaten. One friend of Ronald's, Army Chaplain Dick Dugdale wrote home, 'You know I loved him more than anyone else.' Dugdale used to say to his sister that, 'each year passing merely means one year less to wait for Ronald.' Dugdale did not have many more years waiting to 'meet' Ronald again as he too was killed by enemy fire in 1918. Letters also came from close friend Keith Rae, by then serving at the front, asking for a location of the grave in order that he could visit. In mid-July 1915 he wrote again thanking Mr Poulton for the description of where the grave was but stating that he was, as yet, still unable to visit due to pressure at the front lines. He said he would continue to try and get there and promised to try and follow in the footsteps of Ronald. He agreed to write of his recollections but only when away from the arduous distractions of war.

His letter concluded, 'the clouds will lift and the sun will shine forth again.' Keith never got to the grave. Two weeks later Second Lieutenant Rae was listed as 'missing presumed killed' after the ferocious German flamethrower attacks at Hooge on the Menin road. His body was never found and he is commemorated on the magnificent Menin Gate Memorial to the Missing at Ypres and also with a private memorial now located in Sanctuary Wood.

The hurt continued for Ronald's parents when, tragically, they lost their daughter Hilda in 1917 to a rare disease contracted when she was a child, followed two years later by the youngest, Janet, who was killed in a fall from her bicycle.

A memorial service for Ronald was held in Oxford several weeks after his death at which one person said, 'His football [rugby] career was a mere fraction of his activity and had he lived I am sure he would have been known for far greater things.'

With the lack of surviving film footage and action photographs from the Edwardian era, it is almost impossible for us modern day fans to imagine what Poulton Palmer was like as a player. We are, however, left with snippets such as this match report from *The Times* after the epic 10-9 victory over Wales at Twickenham in 1914:

> In the circumstances of this game England's victory was alone made possible by the soundness and resource of the greatest three-quarter back that this country has had for a quarter of a century ... did ever man do so much for his side as Poulton? When over and over again England looked to be 'in extremis' it was some wonderful kick by Poulton, some electrifying cut through, some steadying influence amongst the backs that kept the fifteen together ... Wales, the better team of the day, retired beaten by fate and Poulton.

But perhaps most fittingly, and probably as Ronald would have wanted, the last word should go to a private soldier who served with him: 'We would have followed him into the jaws of death for he was a brave soldier and a gentleman.'

Sitting on the N365, 15 km south of the martyred Belgian town of Ypres, is the village of Ploegsteert where Ronald was billeted for a short while. Further north on the road which leads back to Mesen (Messines) is Ploegsteert Wood and Hyde Park Corner. This spot is easy to find as there are cemeteries flanking both sides of the road.

Hyde Park Corner (Royal Berks) Cemetery was begun in April 1915 by Ronald's battalion, the 1/4 Royal Berks, and was used at intervals until November 1917. The cemetery now contains eighty-three Commonwealth burials of the First World War and four German war graves. Ronald is buried in plot B11. Across the road, on the west side is the far larger Berks Cemetery Extension. The extension cemetery was begun in June 1916 and used continuously until September 1917. At the Armistice, further plots were added and in 1930 more graves were brought in from Rosenberg Chateau Military Cemetery about 1 km to the north-west, when it was established that these sites could not be acquired in perpetuity. The Berks Cemetery Extension contains 876 burials and also houses the sizeable and striking Ploegsteert Memorial, which commemorates more than 11,000 men who died in this sector and have no known grave. Most named on the walls were killed in the course of the day-to-day trench warfare which characterized this part of the line or in small-scale set engagements, usually carried out in support of the major attacks taking place elsewhere. The cemetery and memorial were designed by H. Chalton Bradshaw. One can easily walk around 'Plugstreet Wood' and the excellent book by Tony Spagnoly of that name details how best to do so. Several more cemeteries mark out the battlefield around the wood, including Strand, Mud Corner and Prowse Point cemeteries. It is close to and just north of the latter where Ronald Poulton Palmer – one of the finest exponents of free-flowing English rugby – met his fate.

16

Chapter 2

Tony Wilding

Tennis star, Heart Throb and 'Motor Bandit'

Had Anthony 'Tony' Wilding been born 100 years later he would have been the subject of huge media attention, sure to have graced the columns of glossy magazines and television sport shows studios. Today you will find his name recorded in all manner of places as his short but very full life catapulted him into record books, the Tennis Hall of Fame and also, sadly, the registers of the Commonwealth war dead.

Most will come across the name 'Wilding' in the annals of tennis greats and Grand Slam winners but will probably pass over it easily in deference to the more familiar names such as Borg, Federer, Connors and Laver. A dip into the history books, however, reveals that Tony Wilding deserves more of our attention and was a true sporting icon of his time.

Born in Opawa, Christchurch, New Zealand on 31 October 1883, Wilding was christened Anthony Frederick by his parents Frederick and Julia. His mother was the daughter of the six times Mayor of Hereford and his father was a lawyer. In 1879, just four years before his birth, his family had moved to New Zealand where his father had started a law firm – Messrs Wilding and Acland – in Christchurch. The young Tony grew up in comfortable surroundings with two sisters and two brothers in the family home called 'Fownhope', named after the small West Country village from whence they had come. Set in many broad acres, the home had wide verandas surrounded by evergreen hedges festooned with sweet peas and scarlet poppies.

The more important facilities for a growing lad, however, were the presence of a tennis court, croquet lawn, cricket wicket and a small, crystal clear, freshwater swimming pool fashioned in shining white marble. This healthy environment enabled young Anthony to excel at athletics and he soon represented New Zealand at junior level at cricket as well as showing a great aptitude at rowing, football and horse riding. Indeed long pony rides were common place, on one occasion, aged eleven he rode fifty miles in one day on his favourite pony 'Jack'. Perhaps some of Anthony's extrovert nature came from his father, who would often shoot birds on his lawn, betting with visitors as to who would hit the bird first. Anthony also became an accomplished shot with both rifle and shotgun at an early age.

Wishing to gain a higher education he set sail for England to study for a law degree at Trinity College, Cambridge in 1902. He had hoped to become a professional cricketer whilst at university but he found himself playing more and more tennis. During his first summer break in 1903 he began to play on a tour circuit. There he met people who had earned enough money to pay for their competition lifestyles and this led to Tony himself turning professional. He continued to study hard for his law degree and intended to return to his father's law firm when his education was completed. His fun loving nature was never far from the surface, however, and on one occasion at his digs in New Court, the police were called to a rag caper which ended with a whole tub of water being thrown from a fifth storey window over some less than amused passers by. Thankfully, for the high spirited Wilding and his friends, no charges were laid.

He was called to the Bar in England in 1906 having qualified as a barrister but never actually practised, preferring instead to play his games on court rather than in one. Later he also qualified as a solicitor and barrister for the New Zealand Supreme Court. It was during his frequent long voyages to and from New Zealand that he worked to perfect his backhand stroke and service.

Wilding first visited Wimbledon as a spectator in 1903. He watched H. Mahony and was most amused at his blazer – obviously borrowed according to Wilding – and his odd socks! A year later Wilding was back, this time as a player at the All England Club, at that time located in Worple Road. To his great amusement he was drawn against none other than 'Odd Socks' Mahoney in the second round.

Not only was Anthony now playing his tennis at Wimbledon, he was also on the 'circuit' in France, Norway, Serbia, Hungary and Germany. In 1905 he played for the Australasian team in the International Lawn Tennis Challenge which later became known as the Davis Cup after one of its Harvard founders Dwight Davis. The competition was then only five years old and 1905 was the first year it had been expanded to include countries other than Great Britain and the USA. The following year brought Tony his first Grand Slam win at the Australian Open. Played at Kooyong Lawn Tennis Club, Melbourne, he beat Francis 'Lefty' Fisher in straight sets 6-0, 6-4, 6-4. He also won the doubles with Rodney Heath, the competition's inaugural winner, beating Messrs Cox and Parker. At the age of twenty-three Tony was well and truly on the path to tennis fame and was to dominate male tennis across the world for almost a decade, a feat emulated by the likes of Borg and Federer decades later. So whilst it is not the purpose of this volume to catalogue Wilding's lawn tennis successes, suffice to say that by 1913 they were spread all over the globe. Championships had been won at Wimbledon, Melbourne, Johannesburg, Bad Homburg, Nice, Christchurch, Prague and Brussels.

Travelling to and from these tennis competitions was a race in itself, but Tony had developed a liking for fast motorcycles and was often seen arriving at the tennis matches on his Bat Jap motorcycle, with his suitcase strapped to the back. One summer he joined in, and won, a race from Land's End to John o'Groats on his motorbike. He had in fact developed a liking for all things mechanical and petrol driven, which was later to take him on to an unlikely and obscure military posting.

Blond, six feet two inches tall and extremely fit, Wilding was every inch the sportsman. He was renowned for his vigorous training regime, recognized as being revolutionary for its day. The regime included, running, distance walking, skipping and punch-ball workouts. He also concentrated on the self-confessed weaknesses in his game such as his backhand and a tendency to lob the ball. With a combination of flawless defence and a strong attacking drive he made use of superb pace and top spin. Picking his shots carefully, almost with the ability to slow the game down, he was able to temper his opponent's speed and daring from the baseline.

He finished many gruelling matches as 'five setters' proving his stamina over his opponents. His tenacious side was illustrated in a match against Bill Clothier (USA) when he was two sets down, losing by five games to two in the third and at match point. He fought back, taking the final set 10-8 and winning the game. In an era of long white trousers and shirts, white balls, wooden racquets and a single umpire to call all line shots, Wilding was a shining light of panache and a *bon vivant* in a world of serenity and decorum.

As if motorbikes and fast cars were not enough, he also learned how to fly before the war, financing his lessons in France from his match winnings, of which, by 1907, there was a steady stream. His French flying instructor at Mourmelon Le Grand near Rheims spoke virtually no English, his repertoire reportedly extending only to saying 'goad-bye' in different tones. Wilding simply referred to him as Monsieur Pilot! Despite engine failure and some bumpy landings he described his first flight as 'very fine'. Tony also noted, rather ironically, the presence of several German trainee pilots at the school.

In 1907 a packed Wimbledon Centre Court, in which spectators paid 2s 6d to have a seat, saw Wilding's first win at the All England Club as doubles champion with his partner, Australian Norman Brookes. Fellow Antipodean Brookes was the son of a rich gold miner and went on to be president of the Australian Lawn Tennis Club and worked for the Red Cross in the Great War. Singles success at Wimbledon was achieved in 1910 when Tony captured the men's title, defeating Arthur Gore, 6-4, 7-5, 4-6, 6-2. He was to retain his crown in 1911, 1912 and 1913, his last being remembered as perhaps the greatest of all these victories in the Challenge Round against the American Maurice McLouglin, known as the 'Californian Comet'. After his 8-6, 6-3, 10-8 win Tony was described as being, 'in prime physical condition, all his best fighting instincts were aroused, his tactics were as sound as his strokes.'

Described as dashing, handsome and 'gentlemanly', women flocked to see him on court and many fainted in the rush at the end of the 1913 Wimbledon final, some having to be laid out on the court itself to recover. The British public loved Wilding in much the same way as they have done more recently with Connors, Becker and Henman. Traffic chaos, long queues and security searches of bags are not a new phenomenon at the All England Lawn Tennis Club in Wimbledon either. The meteoric rise of Wilding on the tennis scene from 1911–13 and the resultant attraction of thousands of spectators, coincided with Suffragette arson attacks at the tennis courts which inevitably gave rise to security checks.

Wilding's sporting, academic and social standings were enhanced when, in 1912, he published a book on his experiences entitled *On the Court and Off*. He also became engaged to the Broadway actress Maxine Elliot, described as being the most beautiful woman in America, this union simply added to his public appeal. Alongside Wimbledon success there was continued good form in the Davis Cup when, in 1914, at his last doubles match in Pittsburgh, Wilding and his long standing partner Brookes played and beat the German duo Otto Froitzheim and Oskar Kreuzer. The match was played on 1 August, the day Germany declared war on Russia. The match organizer heard of the declaration mid-way through the game but promptly cut the telegraph wires so that this game at least could be finished in peace. The German duo raced for home aboard a cruise ship but were intercepted mid-Atlantic by the Royal Navy and both were interned. Wilding had partnered Brookes for the last time. Both these remarkable men would go to answer their call to duty but only one would return.

After war was declared Anthony returned from America in September 1914 and the question appears not to have been whether he should he join the military, but rather how quickly this could be accomplished? With his love of all things petrol driven and the need to avoid long dreary training periods in a Foot Regiment he spoke to his friend Winston Churchill, First Sea Lord who eased his acceptance into the Royal Naval Air Service, Armoured Car Section as an officer of the Royal Marines.

Wilding's earlier loves of motorcycles and mechanics, meant the technical side of this almost unofficial, fledgling unit would have appealed to his sense of adventure. Having passed the strict mechanical exams and rigorous fitness test Wilding would have revelled in the opportunity of being part of a unique team.

Still in its infancy, the task of this innovative naval branch was to secure landing grounds ahead of the Royal Naval Air Service establishing a shore base for its 'string bag' aircraft. As naval personnel they came under the command of the Admiralty but evolved to be equally, if not more useful, to the Army and thus the Navy began to distance itself from their existence.

Equipped with a variety of machines, the crews were essentially pioneering a form of mobile, armoured warfare and perhaps can be seen as forerunners of the tank crews which first appeared on the battlefields of the Somme in 1916. The first 'armoured cars' were based on Rolls-Royce Silver Ghosts. The vehicles, with a speed of up to 45 mph, had a Vickers .303 machine gun fitted in a revolving turret. They were first used in Belgium in 1914 when the squadron was charged with searching for and rescuing downed pilots. The need for the vehicles to be armoured was quickly recognised, hence an initial batch being converted with 'boiler plate armour'. The Squadron was withdrawn to Dunkirk in the autumn of 1914 under Squadron Commander Samson who reported that the machines were giving a good account of themselves. This also gave Winston Churchill good reason to keep a Royal Navy presence on mainland Europe. Further experimental vehicles arrived on various chassis including the 'Seabrook Armoured Lorry' which Wilding was subsequently given command of. Fittingly enough, the Seabrook looked more like a boat washed up on land than a sleek armoured car. Fitted with a machine gun and a three-pounder gun it was intended to carry a heavy punch in support of the lighter, swifter Rolls Royce's.

Despite the disinterest setting in with the Admiralty as to the longevity of the armoured car squadron, the Army took a different view on the use of Naval Armoured Cars. They had shown their worth in the Dardanelles, where an officer and one other rank had been recommended for the Victoria Cross during the tragic landings of April 1915 – not awarded subsequently – and in East Africa where they were found invaluable for reconnaissance purposes with the British fighting a guerrilla style war over open country. In France and Flanders, where Anthony was to serve with No. 2 Squadron, the slog and stalemate of trench war was beginning to restrict such opportunities.

Within six weeks Lieutenant Anthony F. Wilding had arrived in France with his unit. In a letter home dated October 1914 he describes, 'motoring as close to the German lines as possible to report all information to Headquarters.' He was now living at the Headquarters with the intelligence staff, they having realised that Wilding's insight into European geography and the road network gained during his travels on his tennis tours, was most valuable. A further letter talks of him shooting at aeroplanes and states, 'I find it the most intensely interesting work I have ever done. I am afraid the War will be a big business.'

During the long, harsh winter of 1914–15 the unit moved around behind the lines and attracted comment from various quarters. A flavour of the unit's rather eccentric identity can be discerned from the following remarks of Commander Charles Risk from April 1915:

> From their appearance, their apparent discipline, and the variety of so-called uniform as worn by both officers and men, and their unshaven appearance, I am not surprised to learn that the Armoured Car Force is still known as 'The Motor Bandits.'

In the light of such comments it is hardly surprising that the Sea Lords and staff at the Admiralty developed strong views about the unit's perceived shortcomings and began to view it with a mixture of indifference and inconvenience. An example of this can be found in a report, dated April 1915 and received by the Admiralty, with regard to the setting up of a permanent, recognised unit within the Navy and of promotions for its leading members:

> I cannot concur with these proposed promotions. I do not think they have been earned – on the contrary the so called naval cars have gained an unenviable reputation in and around London. Neither Lt. Commander Gregory nor Major Risk has shown any marked ability. As regards Lieutenant Nickerson there are no (prize) funds here of any gunnery work earned out of Royal Navy Cars. It appears an entirely military service provided and will perhaps be better administered by the War Office as opposed to us.
>
> First Sea Lord.

Wilding, however, had by that time already achieved two rapid promotions and by April 1915 held the rank of Captain. He frequently showed frustration at the apparent inability of the unit to 'have a go' at the enemy and when given command of around thirty men and two seven-ton Seabrook Gun lorries he motored off to the front and fired off some 500 rounds at a house hiding a German machine gun crew. He describes bullets whizzing around him all night but no one getting hurt – at least not on his side of the lines.

The section of twenty-four 'cars' was hence attached to the Indian Corps whose officers he found 'thoroughly agreeable' and with whom he would often mess with, trying his best to ingratiate himself in order to be given a task. He told a companion he really 'hated war' and found 'the slaughter abominable' but was always looking for his next job. His inventive mind led to his developing a trial weapon. A three-pounder gun was mounted on two large wheels and a trailer so that, towed behind one of the armoured cars, it could cross rough ground and add weight to the fire power of the squadron. Captain Wilding did not have many opportunities to use the new weapon before the squadron was called to assist in the action which was, up to that point, the largest British set piece attack of the war. The British Expeditionary Force (BEF) was to assault the Aubers Ridge in northern France; an area little travelled by battlefield visitors today. Cooperating with the French to their right, First Army, under Sir Douglas Haig was to attack on either side of Neuve Chapelle village. The village was already largely destroyed after the failed attack by the British two months earlier in March. This time the British 1st Division and the Indian Corps were to form the southern arm of the assault while 8th Division attacked in a pincer movement 5 km away to the north-east.

The plan involved an artillery bombardment to cut the barbed wire and destroy defences before an infantry advance on 9 May 1915. It is here that the Royal Marines of the Royal Naval Air Service Armoured Car Squadron found a niche. They were attached to the Indian Corps as additional mobile 'fire support', both in the bombardment and in the follow up advance. The legendary Indian Meerut and Lahore Divisions comprised both Indian and British soldiers and arrived in France from India in October 1914. Commanded by Lieutenant General Sir J. Willcocks KCB, DSO, the soldiers were of mixed background coming from both Indian and British Regiments. The Ghurkhas, The Black Watch, Dogras, Suffolks, Jats and Seaforths were all represented. They were really in the centre of the battlefield plan and attacked across the old battlefield of March 1915, near the crossroads called Port Arthur and towards the Bois de Biez. In this central area Wilding and his new trailer gun were asked to position themselves just behind the British breastworks. The ground was so wet here that trenches could only be dug two feet deep, so the soldiers built sandbag walls to shelter behind. Wilding's job, commanding the gun, was to direct fire on some particularly troublesome machine gun nests. In true Wilding style he left nothing to chance and on 8 May went forward to the area to help prepare the position and used a periscope to look at the targets

24

for the next day. He annoyed a staff officer who kept ducking with the periscope whilst Wilding stood bolt upright and laughed at him.

During the quiet hours before the attack he wrote two letters, which were to be his last. One was to his mother the other to his old commander, Chilcott. The tone of each is very different; to his mother he writes, 'We are off directly to take part in a very difficult job. I think my guns will do great work and help the Infantry a good deal ... The General [Anderson] is most helpful with our Task,' and to his senior officer, 'I have a job in hand which is likely to end in gun, I, and the whole outfit being blown to hell. However it is a sporting chance and we will help our Infantry no end. From my study I know the task exactly for it is the only way to play business or war. What I write to you about is this ....' There then followed several lines about the disposal of his motor car and other property in the event of his death.

As all armies march on there stomachs, it is right that Anthony declared his last supper the best he had consumed at the front. Pea soup was followed by roast lamb, fruits and white wine. Then the journey – three miles up to their forward positions – began; Wilding and his Chief Petty Officer (CPO) taking it in turns to walk in front of the machine to guide it in the dark. On arrival at his gun position he was delighted to find two old acquaintances, Lieutenants Milburn and Barnes, both of the 1/4 Suffolk Regiment who had been lawn tennis players. Sharing a dugout with a sleeping officer of the Seaforths they reminisced over old lawn tennis stories as sporadic German shellfire interrupted their preparations above. By the early hours all was set for the morning attack. As Captain Wilding curled up in his great coat to catch a nap, Barnes said to him, 'well old man, you were in rotten form when you last met Brookes', Wilding shrugged his shoulders and, smiling, said, 'One can't always be at one's best.' It was his last reference to the game he had so loved.

Dawn crept across the clear skies just after 0400 hrs on Sunday, 9 May 1915, and the whole battlefield was quiet. Wilding's dress was reported as being anything other then 'regulation' in regard to his breeches, the dashing young officer choosing instead to opt for slacks and low shoes as if popping out in his car for a few rubbers before lunch at Wimbledon.

The battlefront erupted at 0500 hrs with 600 guns firing onto the German lines. The infantry just in front of Wilding were of the 1st Battalion, Seaforth Highlanders. Climbing over the breastworks they were soon pinned down by heavy return fire and many fell just yards ahead, hit by machine guns and shrapnel from German artillery. Captain Wilding's 'trailer gun' crew fired like demons; the heat of the barrel setting fire to the sandbags under the gun's barrel more than once. Wilding directed fire throughout the next few hours, moving from the gun platform to the breastworks ahead in order to gain a better view. Shrapnel burst around his crew and it was miraculous that there was not a direct hit. His attitude remained cool and calm and this undoubtedly had a good moral affect on his men.

The work done that day did not go unnoticed, earning the praise of his commander the Duke of Westminster who submitted a dispatch, 'Sir, I have the honour to report that the 3pdr trailer was in action at Neuve Chapelle the afternoon of May 9th under the command of Captain Wilding and under the orders of General Anderson of the Meerut Division. Captain Wilding was to shell certain houses and also the parapet of the enemy trenches. This operation was carried out under a heavy fire with successful results at a range of 500 yards.'

By 4.30 pm, after nearly twelve hours in action, Wilding's men had fired over 400 rounds and all needed a rest as, indeed did Wilding himself. They stood in the trench behind the breastwork wall and Captain Wilding said he was going to take a short nap in a dugout. He was advised against it due to the fact that this particular dugout was poorly positioned in the rear of the trench and therefore exposed to greater risk of being hit. Laughing this off he crawled inside and sat talking to another officer, Lieutenant Don Pretty, a fellow tennis player from Suffolk, in the doorway.

At 1645 hrs there came a heavy burst of laughter from the dugout and immediately afterwards a large shell hit the roof with an enormous explosion. The destruction was complete and the dugout collapsed. CPO Robbins and four men dug furiously to get the men out. Two privates were found first, both killed. Then Lieutenant Pretty was dug out alive but badly injured. He was to succumb to his injuries two days later and is buried in Bethune Town. Finally, amid the earth, torn sandbags and twisted iron, they found the remains of Captain Anthony Wilding. With the body was a gold cigarette case (although he did not smoke he carried them for those gentlemen that did!) presented to him by a friend after a tennis success on the French Riviera in the summer of 1914. As darkness fell

CPO Robbins broke the news to the other officers, all of whom had great admiration and affection for 'Tony'. At dawn on 10 May his remains, wrapped in an army blanket, were taken reverently to a small orchard, just yards from the position and buried along with several other soldiers. His grave was marked with a temporary cross, made from wooden packing cases. This small burial plot became known as Edgware Road Cemetery.

The British attack was a dismal failure, poor quality ammunition, inaccurate artillery fire and good German defensive actions had served to stall the attack. Small numbers of determined Indian and British troops had reached the German lines in places but these were never seen again. Casualties were over 11,600.

The Duke of Westminster's report of the actions on 9 May concluded, I regret to report that after the gun had ceased fire, a shell exploded in Captain Wilding's dug out killing him instantly. The conduct of the men under this heavy fire was excellent – CPO Robbins especially so.'

Hundreds of letters were written following the death of Captain Wilding, both to and from his family and also to the various clubs and associations at which he had played and competed. The Duke of Westminster also wrote to Julia Wilding saying, 'He was one of my finest officers and had done very good work.' The Viscountess of Grosvenor also wrote saying, '... he was so loved and spent many happy days in England with his friends and now he is among the band of heroes who have paid the great sacrifice and that will be your comfort dear Mrs Wilding.' Anthony's father wrote to a friend, '... better for Anthony to have fallen in the manful discharge of his clear duty than to have remained in safety in England ... done very good work.'

Obituaries and tributes appeared in the press very quickly, too quickly in fact as the *Lawn Tennis and Badminton* periodical had to apologise for an article dated only four days after his death when it stated erroneously that he had died in Gallipoli. Other stories were in the *Telegraph*, *The Field*, *The Bystander* and *Manchester Athletic News*.

So ended the life of one of Wimbledon's greatest stars. Anthony Wilding never did anything in life by halves, whether it was preparing his motorbike for tours, playing on the green lawns of Wimbledon or reconnoitring his gun position in France, he gave every task his utmost in both mind and body. One can also see an echo of the rapid rise in his tennis playing career in his military promotions. Perhaps we can assume that if it was not for that fatal shell on 9 May 1915, he would have gone on to gain longer lasting higher honours in the field than those which befell him in the mimicry of warfare on the lawn tennis courts of the globe.

In this modern era of hero worship for our sporting greats, Anthony Wilding stands out as an icon for all that came after him, especially in his native New Zealand. Not only did Wilding 'play the game', he also made the supreme sacrifice. Today he lies under the exemplary care of the Commonwealth War Graves Commission in the beautiful Rue de Berceaux Cemetery and, to amend a line from his Great War naval contemporary Rupert Brooke, 'there is some corner of a foreign field that is for ever "All England".'

As the war finished, moved on or at least entered a quiet phase, field burials such as Captain Wilding's were moved to larger cemeteries for easier upkeep. After the Armistice his remains, along with all the others from 'Edgware Road', were taken to Rue-de-Berceaux Military Cemetery, Richebourg L'Avoue, about a mile to the west and placed in Plot II. D.37. There are 450 burials in this cemetery but only 243 are identified soldiers.

This is an area rightly referred to as 'The Forgotten Front'. Very few battlefield visitors arrive here despite it being so close to the channel ports only seventy miles distant. Yet that fact really adds to its attraction for here the coach loads are never jockeying for position. In many spots locals still give you a second glance and are pleased to welcome you to their quiet villages. Not the most attractive area in France, it is a predominantly flat, agricultural area between the Belgian border near Ypres to the north and the Loos battlefield with its slag heaps to the south. Further south still is the rising mass of Vimy Ridge. The ridge of Aubers is barely discernible as a rise in the otherwise flat landscape, criss-crossed with drainage ditches and still dominated by isolated farms and dark, substantial woods. In fact little has changed since 1915.

The *Auberge de la Bombe* café at Neuve Chapelle – the site of Port Arthur crossroads – stands opposite the far grander Indian Corps Memorial. This fine circular memorial is one of the most striking on the Western Front and the 5,000 brave soldiers whose names are etched into its stone panels deserve more visitors than they get today. A column, fifteen metres high, is guarded by two snarling tigers which seem to be shrugging off the scars of shrapnel damage suffered when armies clashed here again during a Second World War which also passed this way twenty-two years later. A description of the area is not complete perhaps, without also mentioning the magnificent memorial to the missing of this area and cemetery at Le Touret just about three miles west of Neuve Chapelle on the D166. This memorial bears the names of 13,375 men who fell near here but have no known grave, including three Victoria Cross winners and, of no consequence to the reader, but of enormous significance to one of the authors, is the name Private Albert Whippy, Northamptonshire Regiment, killed on 9 May 1915 – the very same day as the legendary tennis ace Anthony Wilding.

Chapter 3

Henry Berry

'A fast and clever forward'

Pressing hard, the 'Dukes' forced their way towards the line but Berry ran across and collared Wilson in the nick of time to avert a certain score. A foul against Ryan for an illegal tackle relieved the pressure temporarily and then Lieutenant Tweedie drove on and looked around in vain for support whilst being 'grassed'. By sheer hard tackling the Gloucesters' defence forced the ball to the sideline. Attempting an overhead pass the 'Tykes' looked dangerous on the break but Berry came to the rescue again to touchdown behind his own posts. Half-time arrived shortly afterwards with neither side putting points on the board. The second half seemed to follow the pattern of the first; the Gloucesters having to touch down frequently to save the day. A temporary cessation of hostilities occurred while Hyland was laid out by a kick to the head, followed by a terrific burst by the Yorkshire forwards who dribbled the ball down the field with determination as the Gloucesters' three-quarters misjudged the situation. With the ball bobbling just beyond the Gloucesters' line, Sutcliffe went for it like a greyhound but Berry arrived first and judiciously hoofed the ball into touch to the surprise of the former, who fell without the ball under him. Soon afterwards Mr Martinelli whistled for time.

And so ended the contest for the 1908 Calcutta Cup. Made from melted down silver rupees and with its famous three handles the Calcutta Cup was the most coveted item of silverware for rugby sides playing on the Indian subcontinent. The final of 1908 was described as 'a sensational draw' and was played out between the West Riding Regiment, perhaps the most succesful all-round rugby team in India and the Gloucestershire Regiment then unbeaten for three seasons. The Gloucesters were captained by the often match winning, or as was evidenced in that 1908 final, match saving, Henry Berry – 'Harry' to his family and friends.

It was on 31 January 1883 that James and Hannah Berry gave birth to their ninth and final child Harry. James an ex-printer and builder had by then found work at the then prosperous Gloucester docks. Life was hard for the family and both parents were to die prematurely, Harry losing his father when he was ten and his mother in 1897 when he was just fourteen. Harry left school – St Mark's Church School conveniently located on Sweet Briar Street, Gloucester, the street on which he lived – the same year.

Two years later, in November 1899 and aged just sixteen, he enlisted in his local militia unit the 4th Battalion, The Gloucestershire Regiment. A tide of patriotism was sweeping the country at the time as the Boer War raged in South Africa. The successes of the year, notably at Paardeburg where Lord Roberts had captured a large contingent of Boer forces, belied the fact that the war was not going exactly to plan. As a result UK based militia units were given special dispensation to serve overseas. Within weeks of Harry enlisting in the army and being issued with his service number (5711), his battalion volunteered en masse for service in 'South Africa or anywhere'.

As the RMS *Goth* slipped anchor from Queenstown in Cork on 2 April 1900, Harry and the men of the 4th Gloucesters on board were not embarking on a voyage to South Africa to wage war against the Boers, for a far less glamorous role was awaiting them on the small South Atlantic island of St Helena. Just as Napoleon Bonaparte has seen out his days under guard on the island many decades earlier, thousands of Boer prisoners found themselves similarly incarcerated and it was fate of the Gloucesters to guard them for the duration of hostilities.

The island was described by one member of the battalion, in a letter home to the *Western Daily Press* as, 'a very undesirable residence, except for people who wish to die and be buried peacefully, to be forgotten by the world in general.' The soldier went on to explain that during his stay between May 1900 and January 1901 he witnessed no more than twenty-five days in total that were not subject to incessant rain and wind.

Deadwood Camp offered a monotonous routine of duty where fifty men daily were employed guarding the Boers who were relatively well cared for in terms of rations – some would say better than the guards! The remainder of the battalion were employed on fatigues and drill, there being no formal entertainment ashore. The officers of the battalion set about changing this and in the following weeks, rugby, cricket and hockey matches were organised at inter-company level. More 'glamorous' opposition could also be found from amongst the crew of HMS *Niobe*, a cruiser stationed on the island and a link to the outside world. It was during this time that Harry began to excel at sport.

In February 1901 the battalion returned home to a different country. Queen Victoria had died and her son Edward had become King heralding the Edwardian era. Harry, however, had grown accustomed to military life overseas and stayed on, transferring to the 1st Battalion of his regiment. This saw him serve briefly in South Africa as the war came to a close in 1902. Remaining overseas, 1/Gloucesters escorted more Boer prisoners to Trincomolee, an important naval port in eastern Sri Lanka. Here they took up guard and garrison duties for a short period before embarking for India on a seven year tour. Whilst in India the pace of life was dictated by the seasons. Units often moved every six months, a rotation system that kept men fit and broke the monotony of colonial postings. Between 1903 and their return to the UK in 1910, 1/Gloucesters served in Lucknow, Umballa, Lahore, Dalhousie and finally Bombay before setting sail for Portsmouth.

Harry eventually established himself in the Gloucesters successful rugby team, playing as a three-quarter. He even captained the side for five unbeaten seasons. The regiment had a tradition for rugby football dating back to the 1898 season when it had been the first winner of the Calcutta Cup. For Harry Berry to captain his regiment as an 'other rank' was testament to his ability as a player and gentleman.

In November 1909 Harry had completed ten years' service with the colours. During his time in India he had contracted malaria and would suffer with recurring bouts throughout his life. He arrived back in the UK almost a year ahead of his regiment and found work almost immediately with the Great Western Railway Company as an apprentice steam engine driver. His training often took place on quieter branch lines and for Harry Berry the Gloucester Railway and

Carriage Company in Bristol Road provided his place of work. Rugby remained his off-duty passion and the Kingsholm Rugby Club was exceptionally fortunate to secure his services before he was snapped up by Gloucester Rugby Club whose coaches thought his future lay as a forward in the 'pack'. One team mate described him as a, 'fast and clever forward, who shone in the lineout and in loose footwork.'

County honours followed and this alerted the national team selectors who chose Harry as one of no less than five Gloucester players as the backbone of their side. These were golden days for English rugby what with the successful move to Twickenham and improved facilities beginning to bear fruit. The 1910 Five Nations tournament was the first following France's entry into what had previously been a domestic competition. England were due to play their opening two fixtures at home against Wales and Ireland. The captain for both matches was the legendary A.D. Stoop, a Harlequin whom, as we have seen in an earlier chapter, was later to give his name to their home ground. The first game was an 11-6 victory over the Welsh, England's first in eleven years. A week after making his international debut Harry Berry rounded off the perfect January by marrying Beatrice Arnold, whom, at the age of twenty-three, was three years younger than Harry. It is uncertain how they met although records suggest that Beatrice was lodging alongside Harry at No. 3 Upper Church Street, Gloucester, the home of Harry's sister Alice.

The daughter of a blacksmith from Chepstow, her father too had died when she was three years old. At their wedding, Beatrice was given away by her brother Arthur at the ceremony held in St Catherine's Church, Gloucester, the newlyweds soon moved into a home of their own at 12 Vine Terrace, Kingsholm Road, Gloucester.

Returning to rugby, the Five Nations tournament was spread over two months, and it was almost a month after the win over Wales that the Irish came to Twickenham and fought out a grinding 0-0 draw – shades of the Calcutta Cup two years earlier for Harry. Harry was again selected for the side that travelled to Paris to face the passionate and enthusiastic French, this time the captain was a certain Edgar Mobbs who features elsewhere in this book. Harry scored in an impressive 11-3 victory, a result that set England up nicely for the championship if they could defeat their arch rivals

Scotland in Edinburgh. Once again the captaincy changed, though the results didn't and it was J.G. Birkett who led them to a 14-5 victory with Harry scoring again.

It was to be a successful but all too short international career for Harry Berry. Malaria bouts continued to plague him at irregular intervals and his family life also took centre stage with the arrival of a son, Henry George, on 19 August 1911. A brief change of vocation may also have been as a result of ill health as Harry was recorded as being the innkeeper/licensee of the Red Lion Inn, Northgate Road, Gloucester in 1914, by which time pub talk would have been dominated by discussions of the storm clouds of war that were gathering over Europe.

Harry was still a reservist and accordingly mobilized on 4 August 1914, age thirty-two, by the end of the month he had left his family for Bristol, unaware that his wife was expecting their second child. His battalion came up to strength at Tidworth, near Andover and was destined for France before the year was out, so along with a number of fellow reservists he was posted to Woolwich where he joined the 3rd (Reserve) Battalion. Primarily assigned to fortress duties at the Woolwich Arsenal, Surrey Docks and Thames fortresses there were no shortages of submarine sightings and regular reports of German agents operating in the vicinity. His wife, now three months pregnant, took over as licensee of the Stags Head in Alvin Street, Gloucester whilst Harry was recorded as being both a soldier and wagon maker for his original employees at the Gloucester Railway and Carriage Company.

The BEF's long retreat from Mons had been punishing both in terms of the distance it had had to travel and in the continual fighting of rearguard actions. Most of the units which had landed in the August and September of 1914 were severely depleted of both men and materiel by the year's end. The retreat ended with the fighting on the Marne and after the Allies drove the Germans back in a brief advance to the line of the Aisne, both sides dug in for winter. Subsequent attempts to outflank each other led to the establishment of a continuous trench system that stretched from the Swiss border to Belgium.

The BEF headed north to Flanders and took up the line from Ypres to Armentières, closer to the channel ports that were vital in resupplying them. The Germans attempted to force the channel ports once more in late October but the British, backed by the timely arrival of the Indian Corps, held the line. Whilst ground was given around Ypres and a dangerous salient was beginning to form in the British northern sector by mid-November, the First Battle of Ypres, whilst costing both sides tens of thousands of casualties, had ultimately ended in defeat for the Germans given their objectives. Between August and December 1914 the British casualties are accepted as being 57,000 killed, wounded, missing or taken prisoner and whilst Kitchener set about raising the first 100,000 of his citizen army, territorial soldiers and reservists began arriving in France to fill the depleted ranks. Harry Berry was about to leave England for the last time in early February 1915.

In early February 1/Gloucesters moved into the village of Marles-les-Mines just west of Bethune after a long spell in the firing line. Today the countryside of this industrial area remains littered with numerous slagheaps interspersed with dense copses and large woods as it rolls along south of the Franco-Belgian border. As the battalion took over the village, billeting themselves in the loft of the local school, the station goods yard and an assortment of tumble-down barns, they set about cleaning themselves up and training in the latest infantry tactics. The men of the Gloucesters forged cordial relationships with the villagers and before long most of the men were housed in the more comfortable surroundings of family homes where hot coffee, rough wine and plentiful eggs could be purchased from their hosts to supplement their army rations. On 7 February a draft of 202 officers and men arrived to reinforce the battalion; the war diary described them as being 'good material' and it is very likely that Harry was amongst them.

Once the battalion was bought up to strength the new arrivals set about embedding themselves with the 'old sweats'. As was the fashion in early 1915 an inordinate amount of time was spent digging, both in practice trenches and in reinforcing the existing line. Digging trenches became second nature to the infantryman of the Great War; the sheer weight of earth shifted from one hole to fill another via sandbags and trench building per month was stagger-ing. Overhead cover was, however, a vital component for survival and in the lines of the time, dominated as they were by German snipers, the ability to construct a trench system at short notice was a key role for a battalion or company on the Western Front. Not all people saw it that way, however, Captain Pagan of 1/Gloucesters felt that it took up too much training time when out of the line and prevented them from becoming an efficient fighting machine, one capable of breaking the trench systems that they seemed so determined to perfect.

The nearby wood, Bois de Dames, was an excellent space that could be used for inter-platoon training and also sporting events, a pre-war French shooting range even providing the scope for rifle practice. Organised sport was such a vital element of army life during the Great War – a period of military history where men were cooped up in trenches and prevented from taking part in healthy exercise for long periods of time. It was also a period of military history in which civilians who might otherwise have been turned away for failing to meet the fitness levels required in peacetime, joined the ranks and it was a period during which military rations often improved a soldier's diet from that he was used to at home, although soldiers were always complaining of being hungry. These three elements raised a fitness issue that, by 1915, needed to be addressed and sports such as football, rugby, hockey and cricket provided the answer when troops were out of the line.

For Harry Berry this presented an ideal way of settling into his new surroundings. He was already well known for his sporting prowess both at club and county level, and would certainly have been seen as an asset to whichever company he played for in battalion competitions. It should also be remembered that his previous service with the battalion would have meant that he would have known a number of the senior NCOs who had been his fellow soldiers on the dusty plains of India five years earlier.

In late February the battalion were inspected by the Corps Commander, Lieutenant General Munro, along with the Divisional Commander Major General Haking and the Brigadier General Butler. This display of gratitude from the top brass, who commented that the standard of drill and appearance was excellent, also heralded the end of their period in rest. When the Corps Commander added that he felt sure he could rely on the old 28th Foot to perform any task required of them many of the more experienced soldiers present would have interpreted his speech as meaning, 'you're heading back up the line boys'! The old sweats did not have to wait long to test their theory.

On 24 February 1915 1/Gloucesters marched via Bethune, Labeuvriere and Annazin to spend the night in a derelict Girls' School just behind the firing line. The following afternoon the Royal

Inniskilling Fusiliers were relieved in the trenches with A and B Companies in the front line and C and D in reserve. Running from north to south and reached by the La Bassée canal bank, the stretch of line garrisoned by the Gloucesters formed part of the Festubert defences and was sited 500 yards east of Le Plantin. The battalion had already served in the same sector where the close proximity of the canal meant that flooding was a continual problem. Almost as soon as the men had settled into their new abode the training in digging was put to good use as sandbags were filled, trench walls revetted and breastworks rebuilt. For the next eleven days the men of the Gloucesters lived in conditions described as being like a 'sea of slush, the roads were morasses.' Snow and frost brought some relief from the wet and occasional shafts of sunlight brought a spring like feel to proceedings whilst some comfort was drawn from the fact that just 200 yards away the enemy were living in the same conditions and nightly working parties from both sides would turn the usually silent and deserted no man's land into a hive of activity. A live and let live policy naturally evolved after dark, yet rifle and artillery fire would return during daylight hours at any sign of activity from either line.

The numerous bodies of men that had fallen in the attacks of the previous December presented some of the foulest features of no man's land. Occasionally one or more of these were brought in for burial. The nearby cemetery – continually expanding – contained the body of Sergeant Major 7866 James, a rugby player of some distinction for the 2nd Battalion of the Gloucesters. He had scored the winning try in the 1910 Army Cup. A rotation system amongst the companies meant that forty-eight hours were spent in the firing line followed by forty-eight hours in the cottages of Le Plantin just to the rear. These were often subjected to shellfire and although provided less comfort than the trenches themselves, they nevertheless defended the road leading to a section of trench known, due to its shape, as the 'Tuning Fork'.

On 7 March the 2nd Battalion, The Royal Munster Fusiliers, famous throughout the British Army for its gallant rearguard action at Etreux in August 1914, and the 4th Battalion, The Royal Welsh Fusiliers relieved 1/Gloucesters, which returned to brigade reserve near Gorre. Although the accommodation was awful, a pleasant walk along a peaceful stretch of canal bank would lead them to Bethune where hot baths and estaminets were located. Just three days later the Battle of Neuve Chapelle began and the battalion were put on ten minutes notice to move should a breakthrough occur. Initial successes were not turned into anything more substantial, however, and the battalion were stood down the following day, by 14 March the entire brigade moved back to the more comfortable surroundings of Hinges, a delightful hilltop village reminiscent of England and free from enemy shelling.

The weather was also now warming up nicely and the men soon slipped into a routine of bathing, relaxing, training and being inspected by high ranking officers. Much sport was played including rugby and, notably, a boxing competition which was delayed as a lack of knowledge amongst the battalion to find the correct French word for 'scales' meant that fighting categories were difficult to sort out!

After a week of rest the trenches beckoned again and an exhausting march took them into the line east of Neuve Chapelle where they relieved a battalion of The Royal Berkshire Regiment. This sector was dominated by extremely active snipers located on the edges of the Bois de Biez, a large, dense tract of woodland that looks as intimidating today as it did in 1915. British sniping was yet to be organised under the guidance of the famous Major Hesketh Pritchard, whose efforts and training methods in later months would eventually help win the sniping war along the Western Front. In early 1915, however, retaliation was arranged on an enthusiastic, if local level, a number of casualties were inflicted on the battalion – including Captain Pagan who was shot in the arm – as men showed their heads above the parapet or dallied past low sections of the breastworks. Though Pagan would return in time to be killed in the Hohenzollern Redoubt near Loos in October 1915, his loss to the men of C Company at that time was felt immensely. Throughout his period of leadership he had displayed continual gallantry and shown an intense care for the welfare of his men. Harry Berry did not fall prey to a sniper's bullet during this two week period in the line but forty-five of his colleagues did, five of them with fatal results. Whilst battalion headquarters was located in the northern houses of Neuve Chapelle all four companies were positioned in the fire trenches. Once more the weather turned and cold snaps brought the return of frost; the stretch of line they inhabited, however, was an improvement on their previous tour of duty in front of Le Plantin.

On 26 March saw Harry and his colleagues relieved once more to the support lines behind Neuve Chapelle. These were in fact the old German trenches captured in the advance of 10 March. They had been heavily shelled and abandoned and although there was many a deep dugout to be found, the majority were wet, lousy and full of German dead. The hard frost that followed hardly improved conditions and to obtain water for washing and cooking meant a sortie out into the old no man's land where, armed with an entrenching tool, ice could be broken and water collected from the numerous shell holes. Three of four times a day the lines were subjected to heavy shelling, the German gunners having the exact coordinates of their old front line. This meant the furnishing of continual working parties at night to repair broken dugouts and breastworks.

Relief was eventually found when the battalion advanced to the forward positions in the vicinity of Port Arthur on 31 March. Here the newly dug positions were deep and dry, the dugouts being very habitable although lice were everywhere. Men not on guard duty spent time 'chatting'; the affectionate term that remains in use to this day originating from the sound a lice makes when cracked open as men gathered to 'de-louse' and at the same time pass around news from home.

It was during this time that the 47th London Division arrived from the UK. These territorial men from across the capital were attached to more experienced troops for trench training. The 22/ Londons, the men of which originated mainly from the Croydon area, relieved the Gloucesters who remained in close support. A bizarre order was issued on 3 April when every man in the firing line was ordered to open up with three bursts of rapid fire towards the German lines; this display of offensive spirit appeared to do little more than upsetting the enemy guns which shelled the British trenches in retaliation wounding fourteen men of the battalion.

After a further four days at the front the 1st Battalion, The Northamptonshire Regiment relieved Harry's unit and a weary march back to the village of Locon followed. This was made worse for one company as their relief got hopelessly lost en route to the front meaning it did not reach billets until 0845 hrs on the morning of 8 April, the two week spell in the trenches around Neuve Chapelle had cost the battalion forty-five casualties.

Fine weather and pleasant fields full of wild flowers were compensations for crowded billets in Locon and the lack of bathing facilities. When the unit returned to the front between Neuve Chapelle and Richebourg they found the new line far from complete and the next eight days were spent in building and improving on a forty-eight hour rotation system between the forward trenches and a pleasant orchard in reserve. These positions were subjected to daily shelling from the Germans in retaliation for the fire of British trench mortars. The newly returned and ever outspoken Captain Pagan described this mortar fire as the work of two lunatics – one infantryman and one gunner – who descending daily on their positions to fire a few rounds and then retreat leaving others to reap the dreadful consequences of their actions. In total four men were killed and twenty-three wounded during this position. On 22 April the Gloucesters were relieved to brigade reserve where comfortable billets were found in neighbouring farms and buildings, although these were still within earshot of the guns.

The increase in troops and materiel in the rear areas told anyone willing to pay attention that a new offensive was being planned and when, on 24 April, the battalion returned for a prolonged rest in the old billets of Hinges the term 'fattening up before the feast' was on many soldier's minds. Gentle training and recreational sport filled the men's lives for the next ten days. This was to be the final opportunity for Harry to play his beloved sport of rugby and it was also during this spell that he would receive the splendid news from home that his wife Beatrice had given birth to their second child on 14 April; a daughter named Phyllis Irene whom he would never see. On 6 May the officers of the battalion went forward to Richebourg to reconnoitre the ground to be attacked on 9 May and a regimental concert in Locon on the same day offered some light relief and diversion from the impending assault. Harry and his battalion set off on the evening of 8 May 1915 reaching Windy Corner at 1130 hrs after marching a distance of eleven miles. On occupying support trenches at Rue du Bois they drew rations, bombs, respirators and additional ammunition then settled down for an all too brief sleep.

Sunrise was at 0406 hrs on Sunday 9 May 1915 and the whole front line was in silence. It was a delightful spring morning with a cloudless sky, the Battle of Aubers Ridge was about to begin, whilst secrecy had been paramount in the preparations, rumours abounded that the enemy had been heard shouting across no man's land that they were ready and waiting for the attack. At 0500 hrs the artillery barrage of field guns cutting wire and howitzers pounding the German front lines erupted. A severe shortage of ammunition meant that the barrage would last no more than forty minutes and that only 8 per cent of the shells fired were high explosive; exactly the type of ordnance required for the job. German records recount that their trenches received shells that were filled with sawdust as opposed to high explosive. Further examination of the shells revealed their country of origin to be the USA, where profiteering arms manufacturers were unlikely to be wringing their hands over the effectiveness of their wares and the impending fate of hundreds of British infantrymen waiting to climb over the top.

The bombardment intensified momentarily and the leading waves emerged to take up a position just eighty yards from the German front line. When the barrage lifted and the smoke began to clear German histories reported that, 'there could never before in war have been a more perfect target than this solid wall of khaki men, British and Indian side by side. There was only one possible order to give – fire until the barrels burst.'

Some men were killed before they even left their own trenches but others continued to press forward and soon the support lines and communications trenches were crowded with dying and wounded men. Those that reached the enemy lines found the barbed wire uncut and many were forced to bunch up around the obvious gaps, again creating an excellent target for German machine gunners and riflemen. After the cessation of a further British barrage of no man's land, which killed many of its own men who had sought shelter in shell craters, a general retreat back to the British front line was hastily arranged (although not ordered) and this led to the Germans firing into the backs of the retreating soldiers. Due to the fact that in some cases German prisoners were at the head of the returning columns, British troops holding the line believed that a counter attack was in progress and they also opened up on the unfortunate souls withdrawing to seek refuge. Few men survived to tell the tale of this withering crossfire.

The bigger picture, however, brought news of a French break-through on the important Vimy Ridge spur, the main objective for this offensive some way to the south. A second attack was ordered on the strength of this piece of information. Most commanders felt that a further attack across the same ground could not succeed; General Haking of 1st Division remained confident, however, and as a result Haig accepted his judgement. Initially timed for twelve noon, this attack was delayed so that a further forty minute bombardment could take place. Confusion in the assembly trenches caused by the many wounded men from the earlier attack, induced a further delay before The Black Watch eventually emerged at 1557 hrs to attack again led by their pipes. They were joined by the Cameron Highlanders and within a few minutes only fifty survivors remained pinned down on the edge of or just inside the German front line.

At 1600 hrs the Gloucesters and the South Wales Borderers, the remaining reserves of the division, entered the fray. They were immediately exposed to intense machine gun fire and the leading companies found they could advance no further than 100 yards. There they found what cover they could and began to dig in.

An item which appeared in the *Gloucester Graphic* a few days later read:

Letters from The Front
1st Gloucesters in Desperate Fighting
Casualties Rather Heavy – Harry Berry Reported Killed

That the 1st Gloucesters have been again hit badly in the desperate fighting near Ypres is evident by a letter received from Private George Young.

'I have been in the thick of a big fight and pulled through safe. I must not describe the fight as the censor says we are not to do so until the battle is over. The fight is still in progress. Harry Berry the Gloucester and International footballer was killed and several other local men were killed and wounded. Our casualties are rather heavy.'

The fate of Harry Berry – the report that he has been killed is not officially confirmed – will be received with great regret by footballers in Gloucester. Berry was a reservist when called up at the outbreak of the war, but still did not go out to the front with the regiment at the start. For some time he was on military police duty at Woolwich, but subsequently proceeded to France with a draft. Car Cummings, C. Rose, F. Goulding and others went about the same time. Berry had finished playing first class football but his valuable services to the City and County teams will be ever remembered. In 1910, Berry gained International honours, playing for England against Wales, Ireland, Scotland and France and scoring in two matches.

Between them two proud battalions had lost 495 men in that second attack and amongst them was Harry Berry, the thirty-two year old who had served his country loyally in India, South Africa, Ceylon and St Helena, represented his regiment, county and country at rugby, worked as an engine driver, wagon maker and pub landlord and had a wife and two young children. His body was never recovered and he is today commemorated on the Le Touret Memorial to the Missing very close to where he fell during his final charge towards the 'line'.

Chapter 4

Arthur Montague Septimus Jones

Making his Mark

Sixty-seven top class 'Aussie Rules' footballers fell in the Great War. The sport, a mutation of Gaelic football played on cricket ovals, first spread with the early convict inhabitants to Australia and was then developed into a competitive sport by later fortune seekers during the Victorian Gold Rushes.

Today huge local support can swell attendances to 90,000 for major games like the ANZAC day clash or Grand Final at the Melbourne Cricket Ground (MCG). These fixtures, alongside huge domestic television audiences, are on a par in both spectacle and tradition to the English FA Cup Final. With two sides of eighteen players and three umpires, the object is to get the ball through the opposing team's four posts; between the middle two will earn a goal or six points, a similar kick between the outer posts is recorded as a behind and is worth one point. Scores of over 100 points per side are not unusual and players can make forward progress by handballing or punching, kicking and even dribbling the oval ball along the ground. Today's game is still dominated by Victorian sides – it was known as Victorian Rules Football during the Great War – although franchising has taken the sport nationwide with the Sydney Swans enjoying particular success in recent years.

Amongst the earliest of the sport's casualties was Rupert Balfe, a medical student at Melbourne University which was then a leading Victorian Football League side. It was there that he became a good friend of the future Australian Prime Minister Robert Menzies. An all round athlete; at his 1906 school sports Balfe recorded victories in the 100, 200 and 400 yard races, the long jump, high jump and

44

120 yards hurdles, all this in addition to starring in the school football team. He was a Grand Final participant in 1908 for Brunswick when he lined up alongside his two brothers Harold and Stan. Harold broke an arm early on and the game was lost by twenty-four points to a side from Footscray in front of 40,000 spectators. Balfe played a further season at the highest level for his university in 1911 before concentrating on his studies and athletics activities, most notably the long jump. Shortly after Australia joined the war he was commissioned into the 6th Battalion, The Australian Imperial Force (AIF). At the time his father was the Mayor of Brunswick. After a voyage to Egypt his unit were involved in the initial ANZAC landings at Gallipoli on 25 April 1915. Balfe and a small group of his men fought their way to Pine Ridge where ahead of their lines they were soon unsupported and overwhelmed by the Turkish defenders. In 1919 an official Australian Historical Mission uncovered the graves of some men of the 6th Battalion AIF, still identifiable from their cloth insignia. From the location of the bodies it was believed to have been the final resting place of Rupert Balfe and his platoon. They were all re-interred in Lone Pine Cemetery where their names adorned the adjacent memorial as no individual identification was possible.

A university colleague of Balfe's was Cyril Seelenmeyer, a veterinary student when he turned out for the first XI in the 1914 season, *The Sport* said of him in April 1914:

> Seelenmeyer is a fine player from Caulfield whom University is likely to find a place for this season. He is a solid chap, and besides being able to play in the ruck, is a hand man amongst the forwards.

Commissioned into the Army Veterinary Corps in 1914 he first served in Egypt and then France from 1915 onwards. He was decorated with the Military Cross in April 1918, the citation reading:

> For devotion to duty and most efficient service during the period 22 September 1917 to 24 February 1918, and including all the operations leading up to the capture of the Broodseinde Ridge, he performed his duties in a most efficient manner, not withstanding shell fire and aeroplane bombing attacks to which animals under his care were frequently subjected. It was largely down to his ready assistance, care and skill that the

pack animals were enabled to keep the batteries supplied with ammunition, not withstanding their heavy expenditure during the above operation.

This was a rare decoration for the veterinary services during the infamous Passchendaele offensive; in addition a later Mention in Despatches was recorded by General Sir Douglas Haig as well as a personal letter from the Australian Commander General Birdwood. Just two months later, on 8 August 1918, in one of the most spectacular actions of the war, the Battle of Amiens, Cyril was mortally wounded by a passing shell at Fouilloy near Carnoy and is today buried in the local communal cemetery.

A further top class footballer who fell was Arthur Montague Septimus Jones; his obituary in a major sporting paper, *The Football Record* (4 September 1915), broke the news of his death:

> Arthur Jones, the Fitzroy follower, has been reported among the fallen at Gallipoli and the news was received by his old club mates with deep regret. He was a fine stamp of a man and stood over six feet in height, of a bright and cheerful disposition, he was one of the most popular of young fellows. He went away to do his duty to his King and country, and died like a hero. His name will be handed down as one of the athletes who served as a true patriot against the German ruffians and savages.

Arthur had enjoyed just one year of top flight Victorian Rules Football. During the 1914 season he had made seven appearances scoring three goals. His opening game in the colours of Fitzroy came in a second round match against Richmond and his promising debut led to the influential *Football Record* to comment that:

> Fitzroy's new player, Jones from Tasmania, shaped well on the back line on Saturday, and the critics consider that he will be of great service to the club. He has weight, pace and youth on his side.

His second match against Collingwood Magpies proved a tougher outing for Arthur and by the end of the season he had moved positions into the forward line. In this new role he excelled and the strong centre half forward scored twice against St Kilda. Following this performance *Sport* reported that:

> The ex-Tasmanian, Jones, thoroughly justified his inclusion in Fitzroy's team last Saturday. Not lacking anything in the

manner of height he brought down several great marks, but did not kick up to practice form. An injury caused through a collision with one of his own men in the third quarter, kept him quiet for the rest of the game.

This proved to be Arthur's penultimate appearance at the highest level. Just weeks later in a one-sided semi-final against Carlton, his Fitzroy side was defeated by a clear twenty points. By now, however, most people in Australia had one eye on events in Europe.

Unlike many popular sports of the day neither the players nor supporters of Victorian Rules football were swept along by a jingoistic fever to the nearest recruiting office. It has been suggested that the Irish working class origins that still dominated the sport found it less alluring to rush to serve the old country of 'Mother England'. There is little documentary evidence to support this and certainly the 10th and 16th Kitchener Divisions then being recruited in Southern Ireland were not struggling for recruits. It is known that in one Melbourne based match a recruiting sergeant and his staff were chased from the field by an angry mob during one half-time rally although at Fitzroy's home ground this was not the case.

In all, seven of the first team enlisted at the outbreak of war, Arthur being amongst them. The twenty-two year old had been born on 12 October 1891 in Mersey, Tasmania. His parents Henry and Martha had christened him Arthur Montague Septimus and he was soon to move to Railton, a suburb of Launceston. Though showing a talent for football from an early age he took up the family profession of farming. His first break in sport came in 1911 when the then nineteen year old was signed for Lefroy, the largest and most successful side in Tasmania at that time. He made his debut the following May against Cananore, scoring twice as his side swept to a comprehensive victory. The dream start continued for Arthur as he topped the Tasmanian Football League scoring table with fifteen goals. His Lefroy side won both the League and State Premiership titles and in addition he played in four touring matches for a Tasmanian League representative side, scoring four times.

This proved to be a short-lived affair with Tasmanian football fans; they were surprised when the following season he moved across the Tasman Sea to New Zealand. This decision appears most likely to have been for employment rather than sporting reasons although his exile would last just a year before he returned to the game in the Maroon strip of Fitzroy. Alas the impending war was once again to cut this promising sporting career short.

On 21 October 1914, Trooper 828 A.M.S. Jones was enlisted into the 8th Australian Light Horse. He reported to Broadmeadows camp in Victoria where the battalion was being formed as part of the 3rd Light Horse Brigade. These mounted infantry soldiers performed heroically in the Boer War and were held in high regard by Australians and the world over. With their impressive ostrich feathers adorning famous slouch hats they were not only fine horsemen but exceptional infantry soldiers, excelling in rifle skills and fieldcraft. Although unsuited for the original landings at Gallipoli they were soon to be landed at ANZAC Cove in a dismounted role.

After enlistment, Arthur remained at the depot for three months until being drafted for overseas service on 9 February 1915. He set sail from Melbourne on the HMAT A18 *Wiltshire* in mid-April bound for Egypt where the ANZAC contingents were preparing for the Dardanelles campaign. Whilst his unit sailed from Alexandria on 15 May bound for Gallipoli, Arthur arrived two weeks later as part of a fourth draft of reinforcements commanded by Captain Hoare. The 8/Light Horse had relieved the Wellington Mounted Rifles for their first spell in the front line and the thirty new soldiers joined them in No. 4 section of trenches on Walker's Ridge. Within hours a Turkish attack was launched on nearby Quinn's Post and a number of casualties were reported within the battalion including one man 'accidentally shooting himself in the foot.'

When the unit was relieved a week later their reserve positions were just 300 metres behind the firing line in Mule Valley; indicating just how precarious the situation remained at ANZAC until the eventual evacuation in December. They returned for a spell in the trenches on Walker's Ridge between 12 and 27 June and four men were killed in the day-to-day war against the nearby Turks, although losses through illness were far more common than those wrought by enemy action during this time.

On 27 June a hurricane bombardment of six-inch howitzer and 77 mm field gun shells rained down on the battalion and caused great damage to the trenches, killing five and wounding sixteen. Amongst those killed were Charles Trethowan King, his service number (830) was only two away from Arthur's. They had joined up together and were in the same draft. Today King lies in the peaceful Ari Burnu Cemetery on the shore of ANZAC Cove. The following day the whole of the ANZAC front opened up with 'a demonstration', this was a common tactic of the campaign with every available rifle and gun joining in together with some localised grenade throwing; another indicator of how close the opposing lines were. A member of HQ Company was killed in the retaliatory Turkish barrage.

In what was fast becoming a 'tit-for-tat' war, 29 June saw a Turkish barrage on 8/Light Horse positions between 2100 hrs and 2230 hrs, closely followed by an infantry attack. Forward outposts in the ANZAC line were able to negate any element of surprise and by firing from concealed positions ahead of the main trench were able to force the attackers to the battalion's left flank. Here they were met with a withering enfilade fire. The few unwounded Turks who pushed on then ran into a 'secret sap' manned by men of 9/Light Horse. Localised fighting continued until daybreak when casualty returns were submitted and it was found that 8/Light Horse had lost six men killed and twelve wounded. It was estimated that 250 Turkish bodies lay in and around the ANZAC positions with a further 250 wounded.

This was to prove to be the last action that Arthur Jones would see for some time as his unit was relieved in the early hours of 1 July and moved into a rest area at the foot of Walkers Ridge. On 11 July Jones reported sick to the battalion medical officer Captain Sidney Campbell and was diagnosed as suffering from acute gastritis. He was evacuated from ANZAC Cove later that day to Mudros via the hospital ship *Draickren*. In a sad quirk of fate it proved to be one of the final acts of duty for Captain Campbell; he was killed whilst swimming off ANZAC Cove in an artillery strafe of the beaches just two days later and is today commemorated on the Lone Pine Memorial alongside Arthur Jones. Whilst recuperating in the 24th Canadian Casualty Clearing Station on Mudros he was able to catch up with news from home and relax, free from the attentions of the Turkish guns for the first time in months. The *Football Record* kept him abreast of football stories including the sad demise of the University Club who were forced to drop out of the Victorian Football League through a lack of players.

He was deemed to be fit to return to active service on 29 July 1915 and rejoined his battalion, then occupying No. 1 and No. 3 outposts of Walker's Top, two days later. As August progressed, it was clear to all that a major attack was planned to coincide with a further allied landing at Suvla Bay to the north. On the evening of 6 August a bombardment opened up along the ANZAC front concentrating on the Turkish held, 'Baby 700' positions. In reply, 8/Light Horse were shelled whilst forming up in their forward trenches. At 0430 hrs they left their line to assault the Nek; the commanding officer, Lieutenant Colonel A.H. White, led the first wave over the top consisting of 150 men, they were closely followed by the second wave of equal strength, the battalion war diary simply records that, 'Owing to deadly machine gun fire, the attack failed to get home ...'

The losses were severe, six officers and sixteen men killed, six officers and 121 men missing – the 'missing' were later corrected to confirmed as 'dead' – and a further four officers and seventy-two men were wounded. Of the 300 men who left their trenches that fateful morning, 225 had become casualties. Star footballer Arthur Montague Septimus Jones lost his life in one of the most dramatic and seemingly senseless charges of the ill-fated Gallipoli campaign.

The moment was captured on canvas by the war artist George Lambert in 1924 and the iconic image is now housed at the Australian War Memorial in Canberra and the charge was later re-created with dramatic effect by Peter Weir in the Golden Globe nominated 1981 film, *Gallipoli* starring Mel Gibson.

News of the attack filtered back to Australia where next of kin waited patiently for news of the casualties. Whilst it was common practice to update family members, a rather sad note is included in Arthur's service records. It consists of an enquiry direct to the Secretary of Defence for St Kilda from Arthur's fiancée, Nita Wertheimer, dated 29 August. It reads:

> Dear Sir,
> Could you please, of your goodness, give me any information about No 828 LCpl Arthur M Jones, B Troop, 8th Light Horse, 3rd Light Horse Brigade who was posted missing since August 8th ... We are engaged so you can understand how deeply grateful I would be for any definite news, the uncertainty is un-endurable. Thank you so much in anticipation, yours sincerely
> Nita Wertheimer.

Whether a reply was ever despatched is unknown. Arthur was confirmed as officially killed in action as early as 15 August and his family were advised of this fact. His effects were received by them some months later in December and consisted of a pair of field glasses, a military book, a Bible, postcards, a letter and some photographs.

On hearing the news his football club, Fitzroy, included a short obituary in their 1915 annual report that read:

> In the list of players who enlisted and went to Gallipoli, was Mr Arthur Jones. He attained the rank of Corporal, and gave promise of further promotion. It is with great regret that the committee has to announce that he was killed in action, and adds to the many Australians who have offered up their lives for the preservation of the Empire.

> He sleeps far away from the land of his birth –
> But the night dew that falls, though in silence it weeps,
> Shall brighten with verdure the grave where he sleeps;
> And the tear that we shed, though in secret it rolls'
> Shall long keep his memory green in our souls.

Today Arthur is commemorated in three separate places; the Lone Pine Memorial on the Gallipoli Peninsular along with over 4,000 of his comrades; the Australian War Memorial in Canberra where his name can be found in Bay 6 as part of the Roll of Honour of over 102,000 Australians and finally on the often forgotten memorial arch that once formed the entrance to Fitzroy's football stadium, the Brunswick Street Oval. Somewhat sadly in the modern world of sporting franchises and economic pressures, July 1996 marked the end of an era for Fitzroy, a club that had been formed in 1883 and held numerous premiership titles, when it merged with the Brisbane Bears. Today the memorial bearing the name of Arthur Montague Septimus Jones stands half-remembered to the rear of a modern electricity supply station. It should be noted, however, that 'Aussie Rules' football stars like Jones are not forgotten, for a fresh poppy wreath is laid every ANZAC day by those who have not forgotten.

Chapter 5

Donald Simpson Bell

'One of the best types of the professional footballer ... scrupulously fair in his play'

When the battalion went over, I, with my team crawled up a communication trench and attacked the gun and the trench and I hit the gun first shot from about 20 yards and knocked it over. The G.C.C. has been over to congratulate the battalion and he personally thanked me. I must confess it was the biggest fluke alive and I did nothing. I only chucked one bomb but it did the trick. The C.C. says I saved the situation for this gun was doing all the damage. I am glad I have been so fortunate for Pa's sake; for I know he likes his lads to be at the top of the tree. He used to be always on about too much play and too little work, but my athletics came in handy this trip. The only thing is I am sore at the elbows and knees with crawling over limestone flints. Please don't worry about me, I believe that God is watching over me and it rests with him whether I pull through or not.

So wrote Second Lieutenant Donald Simpson Bell on 7 July 1916 from his front line dugout near the village of Contalmaison on the Somme. They were to be the last words he ever wrote and he was never to learn that the actions he described would earn him a Victoria Cross.

Life had begun for 'Donny' Bell on 3 December 1890. One of seven children, including five sisters, he grew up in the comfortable surroundings of No. 87 East Parade, Harrogate. It was whilst at his first school, St Peters, that he began to excel at sport; fortunately he was able to concentrate on his schooling at the same time and gained a scholarship at the nearby Knaresborough Grammar School. At Knaresborough he won colours in rugby, swimming, cricket and hockey but his first love was football and as a keen amateur he turned out for Starbeck, Mirfield United and Bishop Auckland; the high standard at the latter club making the teenage Bell's achievements all the more remarkable. His father, however, extolled the virtues of Donny succeeding academically, unconvinced that sport could provide the lifestyle he would wish for his youngest son. Fortunately Donald was able to combine his studies alongside displaying his sporting prowess. It was during this time that he met and became friends with Archie White, a fellow Yorkshire lad from Borough Bridge and another sporting schoolboy. He, like Donny, would earn a Victoria Cross on the Somme. White survived the war and later wrote of Bell:

> He had the build of a hammer thrower; he could never have been a runner. Yet he had a unique gift of acceleration; he could start from zero on the centre line, be in top gear in two strides, and cover thirty, forty and fifty yards at the speed of a sprinter on a running track. That is what made him so valuable as a footballer.

He was indeed a strapping lad in excess of six foot tall with a physique to match and by his eighteenth birthday Donny had made the decision to venture to London. There he attended the Westminster Training College where he embarked on a career in teaching. In his first year he was posted as one of the first division of trainee teachers excelling at geography, English, maths and modern history. His love of sport continued, however, and whilst not attending lectures he had trials with and later turned out for Crystal Palace, then in the Southern League First Division and attracting crowds of over 15,000. That season ended with Palace finishing seventh in the table. Donald turned his attention to rugby a year later and after lining up in the back row for Westminster College caught the eye of a number of top amateur sides. His accommodation during this period was in a north London suburb and as such he played for the Hertfordshire County XV, to the envy of many of his college friends who recognised the honour of doing so.

In 1911 Donald completed his education and returned to his home town of Harrogate, where he had secured a place as assistant master at Starbeck Council School, in a village he had played for when a schoolboy himself. In his first year he won the hearts of his pupils when he turned out as an amateur for Newcastle United, a top side of their day which had lifted the league title three times and appeared in five FA Cup finals in seven years. Their appearance in the 1911 Cup Final was notable in that although they lost 1-0 to Bradford City, the winning goal was scored by Scottish international Jimmy Speirs. Speirs would go on to win a Military Medal in France before being killed at Passchendaele in August 1917 and is today buried in Dochy Farm New British Cemetery, 7 km north-east of Ypres.

Whilst at Newcastle Donny tried a move from defender to forward; perhaps his electrifying pace had caught the eye in training. The switch was a near disaster when he squandered chance after chance, the trial ended at half-time and in a post-match interview with a local reporter Donald conceded, 'Until I returned to the defence we never looked like getting a goal, afterwards we got several.'

His defensive performances for Newcastle were quite sound and during the summer he was approached by local side Bradford Park Avenue to join them for the 1912–13 season. Whilst they were a Second Division side they offered more 'boot money' than Newcastle and in addition the switch also enabled Donny to play local rugby and cricket whilst still teaching at Starbeck. With a monthly income of £10 the sporting spin-offs were a welcome addition. It was a fairly successful season for Bradford as they finished mid-table but for Bell, however, the opportunities to play had proved limited. At a time when the club really decided to push for promotion to the 'big league' Donald, at the age of twenty-two, decided to leave his teaching position and turn professional.

Prior to the start of the 1913–14 season Donald seized the chance to improve his match fitness by touring Denmark as part of a Yorkshire representative side. On his return, however, he soon became understudy to the impressive Watson at right back but three months into the season he got his chance against Leicester Fosse on 3 November. Bradford ran out 3-2 winners and leapt to fourth in the table; Bell being particularly effective against Leicester forward Tommy Benfield. Benfield, an ex-soldier of The Leicestershire

Regiment, would sign for Derby County the following year and score fifteen times in their Division Two championship side. With the coming of the war he rejoined the colours in 1916 and was killed serving with 6/Leicestershire Regiment in September 1918. Today he lies in Varennes Cemetery north of Albert on the Somme.

Donald Bell retained his first team place in a vital away game against Wolverhampton Wanderers a week later. The Wolves were widely tipped for promotion and had built a side around a number of internationals. Although the Midlands side would finish a disappointing ninth, when Donny and his Bradford team mates arrived they were facing the league leaders and little hope was given as to their chances of success.

Only an undeserved eighty-first minute goal by the Wolves striker Sam Brookes separated the sides and again Donald's own performance caught the eye; the influential *Athletic News* reported:

> Mason was very solid in the visitor's goal, but his work was not of a most difficult character for he had in front of him two sterling backs in Bell and Watson, who kept their rivals so well at bay that most of the shots which came in were from a fairly lengthy range.

His appearances then tailed off as regular players recovered from injury. He played twice more for Bradford which continued to push for a promotion place. Donald was then selected to play in a crucial away game to league leaders Notts County in January 1914. That game ended in a draw and also in frustration for Donny as he picked up a bad injury in the closing stages that would mark a premature end to his season. Ultimately it proved to be a successful campaign for Bradford Park Avenue despite Bell's injury as they finished runners-up to Notts County but ahead of Woolwich Arsenal on points and as such secured promotion to the First Division. Bell's performance over the season was reported in a Bradford paper:

> Bell is one of the best types of the professional footballer, broadminded in outlook and scrupulously fair in his play. Had it not been for an accident he would probably have secured a regular place in the side. Indeed, some of his displays, particularly those in the matches with Notts County at Trent Bridge and Wolverhampton Wanderers at Molineux, were good enough for any team in the country.

The reference to Trent Bridge refers to the fact that Notts County played at the county cricket ground for a spell before moving to Meadow Lane, this may be an error on the reporter's behalf as the side had moved into their new ground in 1910, three seasons before the game was played.

That summer a chance meeting with Rhoda Margaret Bonson and events in far off Sarajevo would change his direction entirely; the first he would marry and the second lead to the Great War. When war became inevitable Donald had reported back to Bradford for pre-season training, despite now having the opportunity to play against sides like Sheffield Wednesday, Aston Villa and Manchester United, his responsibility to do his duty for his country was always at the forefront of his mind.

As early as late August he wrote to the club requesting they release him to serve with the colours:

> I have given the subject some very serious consideration and have now come to the conclusion I am duty bound to join the ranks. Will you therefore kindly ask the directors of the Bradford Football Club to release me from my engagement?

Mr T.E. Maley responded with positive news that they would allow him to leave their employment to join up, he would later say of Bell:

> He was about six feet tall and when fit about 13 st. 8 lbs. With it all he was most gentle. He played many fine games for our team. At Nottingham against Notts County he played grandly but the best of games was against the Wolves, when he completely eclipsed Brooks and Co.

The club set about replacing Donald at the back, signing Billy McConnell the Northern Irish international from Bohemians and Donny set about enlisting as soon as possible.

On 24 October 1914, Lance Corporal 15722 D.S. Bell joined A Company of the 9th Battalion, The West Yorkshire Regiment, and in so doing he became the first professional footballer to leave their career and enlist.

Initially life was dreary with a routine of training and drill at his unit's base in Wisley, Surrey. Like thousands of men who had answered Kitchener's call he longed to get to France and teach the Hun a lesson. In May of 1915 he bumped into his old school friend

Archie White. White, then an officer in The Yorkshire Regiment (Green Howards), was quite astonished to find Donny serving in the ranks and enquired as to why he hadn't been commissioned. Bell was said to have replied 'if only' and, like a shot, Archie introduced him to his own CO Lieutenant Colonel E.H. Chapman. Chapman was a good judge of character and within minutes realised Bell's potential and agreed to support his application to become an officer in the Green Howards.

This was duly applied for on 10 May 1915 and he was commissioned into the 9th Battalion, The Yorkshire Regiment (The Green Howards) in June of that year. His unit, now part of 23rd Division, embarked for France two months later in August 1915. By now he had proposed to Rhoda and planned to marry on his first spell of home leave.

On arrival in France the battalion was afforded a spell in the rear areas where its training intensified. Route marches became a regular feature, many of the men from poor urban backgrounds were not as athletic as Donald and the divisional history notes one particular march being tough on the New Army men:

> This two days march, carried out in oppressive heat, proved the division to be still somewhat raw. There was a good deal of straggling and lack of the march discipline on which the division in later days was to be congratulated on more than one occasion. But the test was severe, some units covering as much as twenty-one miles a day in full marching order, and much of it pavé roads.

The first taste of trench life came under the instructions of troops of the 20th Light Division which had been in France for a number of months and these were able to convey the lessons of camouflage, blackout discipline and keeping one's head down to the newly arrived Yorkshiremen. The sector chosen had so far been a quiet one, known as the Armentières front.

Things were to change in late September when 9/Yorkshire Regiment were ordered to hold the line whilst the regular soldiers of 8th Division attacked in support of the Loos offensive further to the south. After a four day bombardment a smoke barrage was laid down in front of the British lines. This primitive affair was conducted with the use of hand-thrown smoke canisters, large candles and Roman-style catapults! Although Donald's unit had only played a bit part in the battle that ultimately ended in stalemate with little ground taken, it marked the first occasion that the battalion had 'hopped the bags' and provided them with some vital battle experience for future operations. Despite the hazards of the hand made catapults no fatal casualties were experienced by the battalion.

The next episode of excitement for Donald came during a raid on New Year's Eve 1915. Accompanying a raiding party of the 10th Battalion, The Northumberland Fusiliers, 100 men of 9/Yorkshire Regiment raided the German lines at Rue du Bois. Although Donald remained in his own trench they were subjected to a heavy counter bombardment throughout the action; the men who stayed behind suffered heavier casualties than the raiders themselves with four men killed and twenty wounded. With charcoal blackened faces and armed with the password 'Charlie Chaplain' the raiders returned to their lines triumphant only after the barrage on Donald's position had lifted.

The third year of the war started quiet enough for Donald Bell. In March his unit transferred to the Souchez sector further south and overlooked by the vital Vimy Ridge. Here they relieved the French troops holding the Notre Dame de Lorette spur. The ground in front of the Yorkshiremen's front line was littered with French dead from the costly attacks of the previous year; one of them, never to be identified, was François Faber, the Tour de France winner featured elsewhere in this book.

Compared with the dreary, wet Armentières front the previous winter, the new sector was much more pleasant as spring gave way to summer. One of Donald Bell's fellow officers described the scene:

As I came down the wooded slope on the north side of the Notre Dame de Lorette Spur I could see the whole plain as far as La Bassée. Lens was quite distinct, and the flash of a gun firing near Loos was visible, though the report could not be heard. Birds all round were singing, and but for that one gun, the only sign of war, all seemed perfect peace. Very pleasant it was, too, to reach the village as the men's breakfast was being cooked. The whole village was fragrant with the aroma of frying bacon, and I reflected that at that hour a similar fragrance must exhale from the whole British line. The scent of honeysuckle or wallflower may bring a pang to the heart of a British exile, but there is a poetry in the smell of frying bacon more potent to stir the heart of the British soldier than can be found in any garden.'

For Donald Bell some welcome news punctuated this quiet spell when he was granted ten days leave in the last days of May 1916. On 5 June, as promised, he married his sweetheart Rhoda at the Wesleyan Chapel at Kirkby Stephen in Yorkshire. There was little time for a honeymoon but after a few days at home Donald returned to his unit which had moved further south and were busy preparing for their part in the great Battle of the Somme.

On the opening day of the battle the 23rd Division was in reserve with 9/Yorkshire Regiment resting in St Sauveur in the pleasant Somme valley, although the distant guns could be heard clearly. That evening a night march brought the battalion up to a wood on the outskirts of Baizieux. There the men came into contact with witnesses of the first day's fighting for the first time and rumour and counter rumour abounded as to how the fighting had gone. By 3 July the battalion moved up to the firing line over the shell-torn ground of the Tara-Usna Ridge and onto a crest overlooking La Boisselle. The following day a bombing raid was launched by Donald's battalion, although it proved largely unsuccessful when it met with fierce German counter attacks. Ahead lay a locally important, tactical position known as Horseshoe Trench; a long feature, some 1,500 metres long that stood on a curve in the high ground between La Boisselle and Mametz Wood and ran between two strong points known as Scots Redoubt and Lincoln Redoubt.

At 1800 hrs on 5 July 1916, 9/Yorkshire Regiment attacked the position again. All went well at first with nearly 150 prisoners and two German machine guns being captured as the men reached and occupied Horseshoe Trench. Donald and his men were consolidating their newly-won position and collecting German wounded and dead when they suddenly came under heavy machine gun fire from their left flank which caused numerous casualties. On their own initiative and without instructions, Bell set out to locate the gun position with Corporal Colwill and Private Batey. Creeping up a communication trench they reached a position almost thirty metres from the still active machine gun. All three men were armed with Mills bombs and Bell carried his service revolver. Assessing the situation Bell calmly informed the two men with him that he intended to rush the gun and deal with it.

Colwell and Batey agreed to accompany him and, after shaking hands and checking and rechecking their hand grenades, they waited for the moment. In less time than it takes to read this short passage, all three broke cover and hurled themselves towards the enemy position as the German machine gun traversed to greet them but it was too late. Donald Bell had shot the gunner with his revolver and thrown his grenade with the accuracy of a first class cricket fielder silencing the machine gun for good. He had left his two younger colleagues in his wake but within seconds they had landed in the trench alongside him and then all three went off in search of further targets.

They returned to the battalion to hearty congratulations and talk of honours and awards; Bell himself alludes to this in his letter quoted at the start of this chapter written on 7 July as well as one written to a friend and fellow teacher in which he states:

> There is talk of me getting a military cross or something of the sort, talk about luck! Fancy, just chucking one's bomb, even if it was a bull's eye.

His school friend Archie White saw it differently and long after the war wrote in the *Regimental Gazette*:

> At Contalmaison the problem was to cross no man's land, badly cut up by shell fire. Probably no one else on the front could have done what Bell did. Laden by steel helmet, haversack, revolver, ammunition and Mills bomb in their pouches, he was yet able to hurl himself at the German trench at such speed that the enemy would hardly believe what their eyes saw.

Just five days later, on 10 July, the battalion was defending the newly-captured village of Contalmaison when it was subjected to a determined counter attack by strong German forces. The 8/Yorkshire Regiment, sister unit of Bell's battalion, broke up the initial attack at 1930 hrs with the skilful use of captured German machine guns. Just over an hour later a second attack developed to the south of the village and a hasty barricade was thrown up as a protective screen. Donald Bell and a number of bombers were sent to assist 8/Yorkshire.

On arrival he immediately led his party past the barricade and without thoughts for his own safety with the intention of driving the

Germans back he dashed forward into a fusillade of fire. One of his fellow officers in the battalion described his final moments:

> Bell dashed forward with an armful of bombs, and started to clear out a hornet's nest of Huns who were ready to take toll of our advancing troops. He advanced with great courage right up to where the enemy were posted. He took careful aim, and bowled out several of the Germans. Unfortunately he was hit ... for a while he fought on, but was hit again. He got weaker and weaker, and had to relax his efforts. He collapsed suddenly and when we reached him he was dead.

The spot where his body was found became known as Bell's Redoubt and a rough wooden cross was erected by members of the battalion who carved the words, 'he gave his life for others' upon it. The helmet Donald wore in the action that led to his death was pierced by a German bullet and is today on display in the Green Howards Museum and in recent years a more permanent memorial has been placed on the site of Bell's Redoubt.

News of his death reached his family around the same time as his last letters arrived, Donald was never to learn that he had been awarded the Victoria Cross for his efforts, the citation published on 9 September 1916 hints that both actions had been taken into account:

> For most conspicuous bravery, during an attack a very heavy enfilade fire was opened on the attacking company by a hostile machine gun. 2nd Lt. Bell immediately, and on his own initiative, crept up a communication trench and then, followed by Cpl. Colwill and Pte. Batey, rushed across the open under very heavy fire and attacked the machine gun, shooting the gunner with his revolver and destroying the gun and personnel with bombs. This very brave act saved many lives and ensured the success of the attack. Five days later this gallant officer lost his life performing a very similar act of bravery.

Amongst the letters of condolence that reached his family, his Commanding Officer Lieutenant Colonel H.G. Holmes wrote:

> He was a great example, given at a time it was most needed, and in his honour, the spot where he lies and which is now a redoubt, has been officially named: Bell's Redoubt. He is a great

loss to the Battalion and also to me personally, and I consider him one of the finest officers I have ever seen.

The news of his death was also recorded at Westminster College where today a stained glass window stands, having survived the *Luftwaffe* bombings a generation later. His principle the Rev. Dr H.B. Workman wrote:

Lieutenant Bell possessed a wide circle of friends, whose sympathies go out today to his young bride, to whom he was married on his last leave only a few weeks ago, and to his sorrowing parents, who are closely and honourably associated with our Church in Harrogate ... 'Don' was surely one of the finest representatives of Westminster ...

Perhaps the most memorable tribute, however, came from his batman, Private 11495 John Byers who replied to Rhoda's query for further information regarding her husband's death:

I would to God that my late master and friend had still been with us, or, better still, been at home with you ... The men worshipped him in their simple wholehearted way and so they ought, he saved the lot of us from being completely wiped out by his heroic act ... We have lost the best officer and gentleman that ever was with this battalion and we have lost some good ones. He was called to go to the 8th Battalion of this regiment that was just on our right, so that we heard nothing of his death until the next day. The last time we were on the Somme, some of the lads came across Mr Bell's grave and they told me that it was being well cared for and that there is a cross erected over it ... I am very pleased his valise arrived to you and that you think it was alright. You would find in the souvenirs that we got on the 5th July in the first great attack, a Prussian helmet, bayonet and pair of boots. I packed them all in it but I cannot quite remember whether his little toilet bag was packed or he carried it with him at the time of his death ... You ask me if I smoke, yes but not cigarettes, only a pipe and tobacco so if you will send some, I will be very grateful to you. Believe me, wishing you the best of health and wishes.

On the news that his Victoria Cross had been awarded Donald's father decided that Rhoda should receive the award personally from the King at Buckingham Palace, she was by now staying with relatives at Charlwood on the Altringham Road, Wilmslow, Cheshire. A first class rail warrant enabled her to travel to London Euston and she was presented with the medal by King George V on 13 December 1916. With the medal came a widow's pension of £100 per annum and she also received a gratuity of £100 from the *Daily Mail* as she had been a registered reader with the paper.

Rhoda had been married for just over a month when her husband died and most of that month had seen Donald on active service. She never remarried. Her husband's body was moved after the war and is today buried in Gordon Dump Cemetery. There is no doubt that Donald Bell and Sandy Turnbull, another footballer mentioned in this book, came from very different backgrounds and lived very different lives yet both gave their lives in extreme acts of personal gallantry. The final tribute to Donny came from Bradford Club Secretary T.E. Maley who wrote:

> He has triumphed, and if a blameless and unselfish and willing sacrifice have the virtue attached with which they are credited, Donald is in the possession of eternal happiness, and in his glorious record and great reward there is much to be envied.

Chapter 6

Frank 'One Eye' McGee

'You don't see many like him'

In the early hours of 16 January 1905, players, supporters and officials of the Ottawa Senators, known throughout the ice hockey world as the 'Silver Seven' were celebrating as their side had just recorded their sixth straight defence of the Stanley Cup. The victory party was held at 185 Daly Avenue, Ottawa, the home of their star player, Frank 'one eye' McGee. Incredibly McGee had just scored fourteen goals in the previous night's 23-2 rout of the Dawson City Nuggets, a record that stands to this day.

Frank Clarence McGee had been born on 4 November 1882. His father John James had moved to Ottawa from Kingston, Ontario and had set up the family home in Daly Avenue. The McGee's were a prominent Canadian family of the time; Frank's father held the office of Clerk of the Privy Council, one of the highest civil service positions of the day.

Frank had a famous ancestor in Thomas Darcy McGee, an Irish immigrant, notable poet and staunch Republican. Initially a supporter of Canadian annexation to America, Thomas's view changed as his political career took shape in Montreal. After being elected to parliament in 1867 he publicly denounced his Irish Republican views following the Fenian Raids of 1866. Two years later he was assassinated in Ottawa in an alleged Fenian plot. Patrick Whelan was tried and hanged for the crime and Darcy McGee, a pioneer of a Canadian confederation, rights for the aboriginal population and supporter of railway networks, was afforded a state funeral.

As Frank went through his education in Ottawa he would have been surrounded by constant reminders of his uncle; three schools, a government building, a popular drinking establishment and two villages bore his name. On leaving school Frank followed in his father's footsteps in the civil service being employed in the Canadian government department for Indian affairs and a position with the Canadian Pacific Railway. Alongside this promising career his emerging talent as an athlete was flourishing in a number of sports. A talented half back at rugby and grid iron, he played for Ottawa City, winners of the Dominion Cup in 1898. He was a useful lacrosse player but was first and foremost an exciting, young ice hockey prospect turning out for both the Ottawa Canadian Pacific Railway (CPR) team and local amateur side the Ottawa Aberdeens.

His first taste of hockey glory came in 1900 when he led the Aberdeens to success in the Quebec intermediate hockey championship and his CPR side claimed first place in the Canadian Railway Hockey Union. This achievement was made all the more unique given the events of Wednesday 21 March the same year. Whilst Frank concentrated on his hockey his elder brother Charles McGee was serving with the Canadian contingent in the Boer War then raging in far off South Africa. The Canadian Patriotic Fund were at that time an active organisation raising funds to support the war effort with flag days, parades and occasional sporting exhibition games.

A game between the Ottawa CPR side was arranged against a local Hawkesbury side raising $120 for the cause; Frank's side struggled on a tiny rink lit only by oil lamps, the puck being barely visible in some of the darkest recesses. The final result was a 10-4 defeat but a cut over the eye late on in the game meant that he missed out on the banquet and the series of speeches that followed the game. As the season drew to a close his eye failed to heal and in the following weeks it became apparent that he would lose half his sight permanently and the next two seasons saw him pull out of the game as he came to terms with the injury. During this period he began to referee hockey matches and at the age of just twenty-one it seemed his promising career as a player had reached its end.

In a somewhat bizarre 'Boys-Own' twist, he was approached in January 1903 by a prominent backer of the Ottawa Senators, who wanted Frank to come out of retirement and step straight into senior hockey, a level at which he had yet to play. Continuing the comic book come back the 'one-eyed' Frank McGee made his debut against reigning Stanley Cup Champions, Montreal AAA, on 17 January

1903. Ottawa trounced their auspicious opponents 7-1 with McGee netting a brace. Subsequent victories over the Montreal Victorias and the Rat Portage Thistles – notable for a puck which disappeared through the ice never to reappear – saw McGee net a further seven times and, by the end of the year, the Stanley Cup heading to Ottawa. It is reported that each player was given a silver nugget as a souvenir; one of the theories for his side's nickname the Ottawa 'Silver Sevens'. In an often changing line up of twenty men, Frank McGee would keep his place consistently as the side went on to dominate first class hockey for the next four seasons.

The 1904 season saw two major changes to the Stanley Cup challenge competition, it now became a 'best of three' tie and goal lines were drawn across the ice from post to post. Amongst Frank's team mates for the season was Harvey Pulford, a defensive Hall of Fame player who was also in the championship winning Ottawa football and lacrosse sides and held the amateur heavyweight boxing belt for Eastern Canada for two years. An active member of the Ottawa Rowing Club he won numerous Canadian and US titles and rowed at Henley in 1911.

To the frustration of fellow Canadian Amateur Hockey League (CAHL) members challengers from the Western Canada Hockey League again emerged to strip Ottawa of their Stanley Cup. This continued interruption of their own league season led Fred McRobie, the President of the Montreal Victorias to claim that, 'the matches for the cup have simply paralyzed the game here.' Despite these and similar views the proposed series against the Winnipeg Rowing Club was authorised by the Stanley Cup trustees and the three game series took place in front of a packed Aberdeen Pavilion in Ottawa in early January. The venue, which stands to this day, is a structure steeped in military history in that it witnessed the departure of Lord Strathcona's Horse for the Boer War and was the muster point for Princess Patricia's Canadian Light Infantry in 1914. The first game ended in a 9-1 victory for Ottawa and the series was taken 2-1 after a setback in game two.

An interesting controversy took place when the Senators travelled to Montreal in a CAHL league game in late January. A late start saw Frank's side take a 4-1 lead but at midnight, with the game still in play, local curfew laws led to the match being abandoned. As a result of the ensuing debate the Senators withdrew from the league for the remainder of the season and concentrated on their defence of the Stanley Cup.

The following month saw blistering victories against the Toronto Marlboros with Frank scoring a then record five goals in a match in the 11-2 victory in game two. An alternative challenge had been received from Ontario in the shape of the Berlin Union Jacks – from a town whose name would be changed to 'Kitchener' during the Great War – but the challenge never materialised. Frank repeated the feat against Brandon Wheat Cities in March as his side continued its unbeaten run. By the end of 1904 Frank had become a scoring sensation who would elicit the following from the sport's legendary Frank Patrick:

> He had everything, speed, stick handling, scoring ability and he was a punishing checker. He was strongly built but beautifully proportioned and he had an almost animal rhythm. When he walked around the dressing room you could see his muscles ripple, they weren't blacksmith's muscles, either. They were the long muscles of a great athlete. You don't see many like him.

1905 witnessed the pinnacle of Frank's career and his team's domination of first class hockey. The year started in strange fashion when a challenge for the Stanley Cup from the Dawson City Klondikers or Nuggets was accepted, despite their lack of genuine hockey credentials. The side was put together and backed by the multi-millionaire entrepreneur Joe Boyle; he would later see action in the Russian Revolution fighting the Bolsheviks. What followed was one of the strangest episodes in hockey history as the Yukon adventurers set off on a 4,000 mile trek on dog sled, boat and train that would last for a gruelling twenty-three days. Arriving just twenty-four hours before the first game, having brought only their skates, the challengers had to purchase uniforms and equipment locally; unwittingly they had caught the imagination of Ottawa as the national press had reported their progress. The gate was expected to be so large that a request was made for spectators to refrain from smoking during the game should the high attendance and large tobacco consumption dim the lights by half time in a fog of smoke! The anticipation was not matched on the ice and in a woefully unequal contest a 9-2 opening victory for the Senators was followed by an astonishing 23-2 victory in game two. During this match Frank McGee scored an incredible fourteen goals, four of them in a space of

140 seconds. His team finished the season as champions of the Federal Amateur Hockey League and with the Stanley Cup firmly in their grasp.

McGee had a reputation amongst his team mates and friends as a prankster, the jokes often being played at their expense. On one occasion the Silver Seven dined at Government House with the Governor General following a cup victory. Given his social background he alone had a grasp of etiquette at such functions and so, in order, so he claimed, to spare his teammates' blushes, he simply advised them to copy whatever he did. On the arrival of finger-bowls he picked his up and slurped the water. His teammates copied him forcing the Governor General to decide it was appropriate for him to follow suit, fortunately all those present saw the funny side of his antics.

By now Frank McGee was regarded as the finest player of his generation but he was sidelined with a wrist injury when the Rat Portage Thistles renewed their challenge for the cup in March under their equally famous player Tom Phillips. Things did not look good for his team. The opening game saw Phillips grab five goals as Ottawa were thrashed 9-3 at home. In Montreal and Winnipeg neutral fans crowded the streets outside the newspaper offices and celebrated whenever Ottawa conceded a goal.

Just as the Senators' grasp on the Stanley Cup seemed to be slipping, McGee returned for the second game in front of a record 3,500 crowd. With his damaged wrist encased in a steel cast and then both wrists wrapped in bandage to camouflage which was injured (such were the dirty tricks of the day), he took to the ice and the spectators 'went into a frenzied delight.' It had the desired effect for although Frank failed to score himself the game was won 4-2. Two nights later the deciding match was played out in front of 4,000 with a further 1,000 being turned away and, with just a few minutes remaining, the game between the country's two best sides with its two best players opposing each other was balanced on a knife edge at 4-4.

Up and down the country hockey fans again packed the streets to hear telegraph announcers provide a running commentary from the upper floors of buildings. An estimated crowd of 4,000 gathered in Montreal and heard the following unfold:

Ottawa takes desperate chances to score now. Pulford is up on the firing line. The line Smith, Westwick, McGee, Gilmour,

Pulford continue the bombardment. It is Ottawa now with the Thistles' defence fighting desperately to hold them off. Phillips and McGimsie work down as far as centre but Pulford makes another of his rushes. He and McGee close on the nets. Frank gets the puck. Brown comes at him but McGee sidesteps and drives the puck into the nets between the legs of Giroux. The rink had been in a furore but it bursts into a veritable Niagara of sound now. Young and old weep with joy.

They had done it again. The Stanley Cup was retained for a third straight season and although no one present could have predicted it then, the 'Silver Seven' would not hit the same dizzying heights again.

The following season started promisingly enough with straight-forward defences of the cup against Queens University and Smiths Falls supported by an equally impressive league record. Montreal Wanderers were now also emerging as a force in the game and both sides reached the end of the regular season with 9-1 records. It was decided that the two should meet in a two-game series with aggregate scores counting to determine the league and cup champions. As expectations in both Montreal and Ottawa reached fever pitch the search for tickets provided a field day for touts charging five times the face value for rink side seats at the Westmount Arena for game one. Uncharacteristically the Silver Seven failed to turn up in sporting terms. The game was a disaster for Frank and his team mates as they were beaten 9-1. Surely the return game in Ottawa four days later was no more than a formality for the new champions elect?

Over 1,000 Montreal fans swelled the crowd to 6,000 in the Deys Arena on 17 March 1906; few could have anticipated the events that unfolded before them. The game was tight and scoreless for the opening ten minutes before Lester Patrick scored for Montreal putting them 10-1 up in the series, the away fans erupted in celebration then the Silver Seven awoke.

Ottawa replied with nine straight goals as they besieged the Montreal goalmouth. With just two minutes remaining the score stood at 10-10 for the series, there would, however, be no repeat of the previous season's heroic climax as Montreal broke away in the dying minutes to score two goals. The Stanley Cup had passed into the hands of new champions who were carried aloft from the ice by their fans.

Defeat saw an exhausted and battered McGee retire at the age of just twenty-three. In a short, but exciting career he had scored 135 goals in just forty-five games and been a focal point of his side's domination of hockey between 1903 and 1906.

Frank settled down into his career with the civil service for the next eight years and the 'Silver Sevens' were never to be as successful again. Working in various government posts he took an active role in the militia enlisting as a Lieutenant in the 43rd Regiment, The Duke of Cornwall's Own Rifles. On Canada's declaration of war he enlisted for overseas service joining the 21st (Eastern Ontario) Battalion of the newly formed Canadian Expeditionary Force on 9 November 1914.

Family legend suggests that when asked to cover each eye up during the sight test of his medical he simply switched hands and not eyes, fooling the doctor who then signed his examination sheet 'vision – good'. After a period of training at Kingston the battalion proceeded overseas to England on 5 May 1915. They arrived in Devonport ten days later and proceeded to West Sandling Camp in Kent to continue their training. Garrison duties followed in Ashford before Frank attended a machine gunnery course on Hythe Ranges. Having qualified in the art of this new weapon he proceeded across to France with the battalion on 14 September 1915. His first taste of trench life came alongside the 2nd Battalion, The East Surrey Regiment in the line near Dranoutre. By December a system of trench rotation in the La Clytte sector was taking shape for Frank and his men. On 17 December Lieutenant Frank McGee was in an armoured car putting a machine gun to good use near Piccadilly Farm, it was struck by an high explosive shell and the vehicle was blown into a nearby ditch. The eight foot deep ditch caused Frank to strike his right knee whilst falling which immediately became swollen. He reported to his medical officer at Dickebusch who diagnosed synovitis and he was evacuated further back to 1st British Red Cross Dressing Station (The Duchess of Westminster's) at Le Touquet. He remained there until being evacuated back to England on 27 December 1915 aboard the hospital ship *Brighton*.

Back in 'Blighty' he was housed in an officer's hospital with Mrs Arnoldis at No. 47 Roland Gardens, South Kensington until his discharge on 8 January 1916.

Still unfit for active service he was attached to the Canadian Training Headquarters at Shorncliffe where he instructed in machine gunnery. This period of his service saw frequent trips to the RAC Club in Pall Mall – where the Canadian Medical Board had set up its office – for progress reports on his injury. He was granted a month's leave to recuperate and after four more medical examinations he was finally passed fit for overseas service, though not for strenuous marches. He arrived back in France and rejoined his battalion on 16 March 1916 and at that time the battalion was back in its old stretch of line based at Piccadilly Farm near La Clytte.

This was a very active sector for the Canadian Corps and Frank had clearly not fully recovered from his earlier wound as his spell at the front was short lived. By 1 April 1916 he was posted back to England where he was added to the general list of officers under the newly formed Director of Railways and Ordnance. Given Frank's previous experience with the Canadian Pacific Railway this is not surprising. At that time the British began a massive railway construction programme across France and Flanders, enlarging the existing system by a third. The legacy of that expansion programme can still be seen today in the French and Belgian rail networks.

Frank remained in this post as the Battle of the Somme began on 1 July and when the Canadian Corps were earmarked for participation he returned to his old unit on 29 August 1916. The 21/Battalion CEF had re-equipped with the SMLE rifle having discarded the Ross ready for the new attack. They trained intensely for the first two weeks of September and this time the attack would feature a new secret weapon; the tank.

Over a frontage that stretched from Combles in the south to Courcelette in the north, and employing 8th British, 2nd Canadian and 1st New Zealand Divisions, the plan was to smash through the German defensive line in the south of the Somme battlefield. The Canadian Corps objective was the important village of Courcelette along with its well defended Sugar Factory. Frank's 21/Battalion was to attack astride the Albert-Bapaume Road in an effort to reach and capture Candy Trench before finally digging in on the junction with the north-south road that lead to Martinpuich.

Between them and their final objective stood the ruins of the Sugar Factory, bristling with barbed wire and well concealed trenches containing machine guns. The battlefield fell eerily silent at 0615 hrs on 15 September 1916. The previous night had seen heavy German bombardments on the Canadian rear areas causing numerous casualties amongst the infantry forming up. A raid on

71

Dot Trench had been launched by 211th Prussian Infantry and although it failed to disrupt or delay the planned advance, it was suggested by prisoners collected during the main attack that the strange sound of tank engines had been heard from the German lines causing a degree of panic about what was in store.

Frank's battalion made its way to their jumping off positions north of the Albert-Bapaume Road having passed up the line via 'Happy Valley', a west-east re-entrant that provided welcome shelter for passing troops and acted as the location of numerous Canadian field ambulances set up in readiness to receive the wounded of the attack. Overhead, contact patrols of the Royal Flying Corps buzzed in and out of patches of clear sky above the low-lying mist that wreathed the battlefield.

As they passed the ruins of Pozieres to their left they caught their first glimpse of the new weapon. Six of the steel monsters belonging to C Company of the newly formed Heavy Section Machine Gun Corps, were attached for operations with the division These were named after French drinks: C1, *Champagne*; C2, *Cognac*; C3, *Chartreuse*; C4, *Chablis*; C5, *Crème de Menthe*; and C6, *Cordon Rouge*. C1, C3 and C5 were male tanks carrying six-pound guns whilst C2, C4 and C6 were the female variety with Vickers machine guns. A contemporary description of the tanks in action on that day comes from Donald Fraser in *The Journal of Private Fraser*:

> Away to my left rear, a huge grey object reared itself into view, and slowly, very slowly, it crawled along like a gigantic toad, feeling its away across the shell stricken field. It was the tank *Crème de Menthe*, the latest invention of destruction and the first of its kind to be employed in the Great War. I watched it coming towards our direction. How painfully slow it travelled. Down and up the shell holes it clambered, a weird, ungainly monster, moving relentlessly forward. Suddenly men from the ground looked up, rose as if from the dead, and running from the flanks to behind it, followed in the rear as if to be in on the kill. The last I saw of it, it was wending its way to the sugar refinery. It crossed Fritz's trenches, a few yards from me, with hardly a jolt.

It was 0624 hrs when the 21/Battalion crossed its start line. A whirlwind artillery bombardment of every calibre available roared overhead slamming into the collection of brick dust, shattered timber and chalk which had once collectively formed Courcelette village and its adjacent sugar factory. There was a degree of retaliatory German fire but the infantry, advancing well ahead of the tanks and behind a tremendous barrage reached, the German front line – its initial objectives – within minutes. Little mercy was shown to Germans as they appeared dazed from their concealed dugouts as momentum gathered en route to Candy Trench. Small patches of opposition were met as they approached, in one instance thirty Germans were seen retiring in disorder along the Bapaume Road; all were accounted for by the rifles of the battalion. Now almost an hour into the battle casualties mounted within the 21st, notably from an isolated but still active machine gun position on its left flank. Once this had been dealt with by men of the neighbouring 27/Battalion CEF the men pressed on to the remnants of the Sugar Factory.

Here they found the enemy resistance lighter than anticipated, perhaps because they had now been joined by the tank *Crème de Menthe*, and 125 men of the garrison surrendered on their arrival. The battalion cleared cellars and dugouts with 'P' Bombs, a form of white phosphorus, and by 0700 hrs had consolidated its position and pushed forward an advance party of men with Lewis guns to defend a sunken lane 150 yards ahead. Numerous deep German dugouts and field gun positions offering ample cover were located there and the position was soon named Gun Pit Road. It was defended by approximately 200 men with four machine guns, this number doubled to eight on the capture of some captured German ones. Isolated and alone they held this line until 0610 hrs on 16 September.

Frank McGee had spent the day back at battalion headquarters as part of the reserve and it was now, as numbers dwindled, that his part in the battle began. At 1100 hrs on 16 September he reported to the Sugar Factory with a collection of men to reinforce the newly captured line. From there he proceeded to Gun Pit Road, where, including his draft, roughly seventy-five men now garrisoned the position. Throughout the day the position was subjected to a continual bombardment and a counter attack developed after a party of unarmed Germans had been allowed to cross the battalion frontage under the cover of a Red Cross flag. It was initiated by enemy artillery turning its guns on the group who were obviously attempting to surrender and under the cover of this further Germans attempted to bomb their way towards the position. Whilst this was eventually beaten off the bombardment intensified and among the casualty roll when his group were finally relieved later that day, was Lieutenant Frank McGee. His body was never identified and is amongst the 11,285 names listed on the Vimy Ridge Memorial, the majority having been killed at Courcelette.

News of his death was received first by his uncle Darcy McGee before he then broke it to Frank's next of kin; this arrangement had been requested by the family and agreed by the military in advance. Of the items which were later presented to the family his sister Lillian took possession of his medals, his father John his memorial plaque and his mother Elizabeth his Cross of Sacrifice. So ended the life of a sporting legend in Canada. As the town of Ottawa learnt of his death tributes appeared in the local press, perhaps the most moving of which appeared in the *Ottawa Citizen* on 25 September 1916, just nine days after his death:

> Canadians who knew the sterling stuff of which Frank McGee was made, so often proven on ice or gridiron, and they were not confined to Ottawa alone – were not surprised when he donned another and now more popular style of uniform and jumped into the greater and grimmer game of war. And just as in his sporting career he was always to be found in the thickest of the fray, there is no doubt that on the field of battle Lieut. McGee knew no fear nor shunned any danger in the performance of his duty. The sympathy of his thousands of admirers in Ottawa and the big hockey centers of Canada will be extended to his family.

Chapter 7

Frederick Septimus Kelly

'His boat a living thing under him'

With London due to host the 2012 Olympic Games it is illuminating to reflect that the Games held in London in 1908 was the first and only time that Britain won more medals than any other nation in the Olympics. Swimmer Henry Taylor picked up an impressive three gold medals, and George Larner triumphed in two walking events. British teams dominated rowing and sailing, winning three and four gold medals respectively and there were notable victories in tennis, shooting, football, and boxing. Britain even pulled its way to Gold in the Tug of War!

The Games were a triumphant success, although not without controversy. In what later became known as the 'Halswelle Affair', British runner Wyndham Halswelle was impeded by one of his American rivals John Carpenter as they rounded the last bend and turned into the home straight in the men's 440 yards, to shouts of 'foul'. When the judges disqualified Carpenter and ordered a rerun, the other two Americans promptly withdrew, leaving Halswelle to race alone for gold in a 'walk over'. This incident led to all future Olympic races being run in marked lanes. Halswelle took a commission in the Great War rising to the rank of Captain in the Highland Light Infantry. On 31 March 1915 he was organising the defence of a sector near Laventie in France when wounded by rifle fire. Once bandaged and given medical attention he rushed back to his position only to be struck again by a sniper's bullet and killed.

It had been the first Olympic Games where all the competitors had marched into the new Olympic stadium following their nation's flag patriotically. This heightened sense of patriotism was perhaps at the root of several disputes which somewhat marred the Games. The Finns refused to march under a Russian banner and the American discus thrower, Martin Sheridan, refused to dip the standard on passing the Royal Box.

The British Olympic Committees of 1908 were faced with a truly momentous task as they had just less than two years to get the Games ready. Rome was due to host the games but when Mount Vesuvius erupted near Naples in 1906, the Roman purse was suddenly emptied of available funds and diverted to Naples' regeneration. A new stadium was erected at White City in West London – where now stands the BBC TV Centre on Wood Lane – to host athletics, swimming and cycling with a 68,000 spectator capacity. Twenty-two nations took part with 2,008 athletes, in twenty-two sports across 110 events. Britain cleared up with over fifty Gold medals, more than twice that of nearest rival USA.

Rowing made its first appearance as an Olympic sport in Paris in 1900 and in 1908 the rowing events were held at Henley-on-Thames, thirty miles west of central London. Rowing has been an event in which Great Britain has excelled since its first inclusion in the Olympics, with well over 100 medals in total and gold medals won in each of the last five Olympiads. Rowing has also given us the man whom many regard as our athlete of the century in the form of Sir Steve Redgrave, winner of six World Championship and five Olympic gold medals. Back in 1908, one of the first ever rowing gold medals for Britain hung proudly around the neck of twenty-seven year old Frederick Septimus Kelly. Not perhaps the same Kelly which might immediately spring to mind when that name and rowing are mentioned; that particular 'Kelly' was Jack Kelly, the great American rower of the 1930's and father of actress, later Princess, Grace Kelly.

A strong, individual rower, Frederick Kelly, born in 1881, was a welcome addition to the coxed eights in what was to be his only Olympic appearance. In the 1900s club teams such as New Oxford and 'Leander' represented their country. The Leander Club of Henley-on-Thames was, by the turn of the nineteenth century, the world's oldest and most renowned rowing club. It provided the gold medal winning team for Great Britain in 1908 with a time of 7 minutes 52 seconds, one and a half lengths clear of the Royal Club

76

Nautique of Gent, Belgium with a joint team from Toronto and Cambridge Universities landing the bronze medal.

For Frederick the path to the winning of that coveted gold medal had begun when he was introduced to rowing at Eton College. In 1899 he stroked (set the pace) in the school eight Ladies Challenge Plate at the Henley Regatta and led the team to his first nautical win.

Juggling his normal academic studies with rowing for club and country is quite an achievement but Kelly had more, much more, to offer and he really blossomed in several areas, emerging not only as a gifted rower but as a musician and composer. It is in this latter field that Kelly is now most fondly remembered today.

Kelly's father had been a wealthy wool trader in Sydney, Australia and Frederick had been educated at Sydney Grammar School before being sent to England to complete his education at Eton. In 1901 Kelly made a sad return to Australia for the funeral of his father, after which he inherited a sizeable fortune which he duly brought back to England, along with his sister Maisie, and together they shared a home at Bisham Grange, Marlow in Buckinghamshire. Not far, of course, from 'Old Father Thames'.

Having gained a musical scholarship to Balliol College at Oxford he became the Chairman of the University Music Club and a leading light in the weekly Sunday night music concerts. Deep and lasting friendships were struck up at Balliol and London with the likes of Patrick Shaw-Stewart, Rupert Brooke, Bernard Freyburg, Denis Browne and Arthur Asquith, the Prime Minister's son, all of whom would later serve together during the Great War. He attended university as the second Nettleship scholar, a music award first held by the pianist-composer and musicologist Sir Donald Tovey, Kelly's long-term mentor. Not that Kelly needed the financial assistance this scholarship provided as his father's money had supported him generously.

After arriving back in England, rowing had become a passion for Frederick and he was soon winning honours in both sweep rowing, (one oar per rower), and sculling, in which rowers have two oars each but his greater successes came in the sculls. He won the Diamond Sculls at Henley in 1902 and 1903 and also took part in the Oxford and Cambridge Boat Race. As a member of the Leander crew he won the Grand Challenge Cup at Henley in 1903, 1904 and 1905, winning various other amateur races during the same period. In 1905 he again won the Diamond Sculls; his time on that occasion –

8 minutes 10 seconds – stood as a record for over thirty years. One report on Kelly stated he had a, 'natural sense of poise and rhythm that made his boat a living thing under him.' The sheer strength, endurance and physical prowess of such a rower at his peak is arguably one of the highest states of physical conditioning of any athlete, attributes which would not have left Kelly for many years.

And yet music drew Kelly away from the river more and more. Two cars, a chauffeur, servants and good family connections opened a great many doors to an aristocratic social life in London where his increasing musical repertoire, good looks and witty nature stood him in good stead.

Having left Oxford, Frederick was still wrestling with what exactly he would do with himself. Worried about frittering away his inheritance, in 1906 he progressed to a music school in Frankfurt, perhaps with the thought of turning professional. What was certain was that club rowing and private music recitals for friends and acquaintances were not great sources of revenue. Two years in Frankfurt would, of course, give him a good insight into the life-style, language and temperament of the foe he would face only a few years later on the Western Front. Yet despite lengthy compositions and favourable piano recitals Frederick still appeared to be un-settled and when the call from his country came to row in the Olympics his heart leapt at the opportunity and he returned to Henley and the Leander club for training early in 1908. The Olympics that year were indeed the zenith of Kelly's rowing career and it also proved to be the last time Kelly appeared in a racing boat. His success at the highest level seems to have been a turning point and perhaps what he had been searching for. He left rowing and turned all his energies and attention to creative writing and pro-fessional performances in the music world.

Frederick was a keen diarist, his writings eventually ran to ten volumes, although they were more of a list of activities than an opening of the heart and few entries can be described as revealing or intimate. One glimpse into his feelings, however, is illustrated in the immediate aftermath of his switch from sport to music. Success in one arena does not necessarily carry over to another and the disciplines of athletic rowing and piano playing are as far apart as those arenas can be. The critics especially were not overly impressed with his 'crossover' and of course comparisons were inevitably drawn between his rowing ability and his musical prowess. His diary reveals that he wondered whether one of his performances was, 'perhaps a little too muscular for an interpretation of Chopin'. This comment had been in the morning papers after a performance the night before in Newcastle in October 1910. 'I foresee this will be repeated wherever it is known that I was a sculler', wrote Kelly. Professional debuts are important and in order to gain maximum positive coverage with sympathetic reviews he decided to return to his native Sydney for his 'real' first night.

It proved to be a masterstroke, not only musically but also spiritually, as Kelly found himself replanted back into his Australian roots, visiting the playgrounds of his childhood and body surfing, swimming and sailing on Bondi Beach with his brother Bertie. He writes, in his usual straightforward style, about walking many miles in the Blue Mountains and along the Snowy River and, thus rejuvenated, worked on refining his piano pieces. He was even invited to play for Lord Chelmsford, the Governor of New South Wales, on what he later wrote was 'a wretched piano'.

On 17 June 1911, Kelly made his professional debut as a pianist at the Sydney Town Hall in what was billed, somewhat misleadingly, as the 'First Musical Festival of the Empire'. He played the Beethoven Piano Concerto No. 4 in G, with the Sydney Symphony Orchestra under the baton of Joseph Bradley as part of a concert featuring the visiting 220-voice Sheffield Choir. Although something of an aside to the main event, Kelly nonetheless received favourable press from the Sydney critics and Kelly felt that a substantial platform had been established to enable him to return to London.

Once in London, however, his musical appearances in the years 1912–13 began to dwindle with Kelly acting more as patron to groups such as the London Classical Concert Society, whilst also being instrumental in bringing Australian written opera to London. A far larger stage was also being set, however, as the possibility of a war loomed large. Such subjects laced the Sunday debating societies which Kelly relished and he made plans to join and serve with his friends if possible in the event of war breaking out. Why he wished to serve in the British Forces as opposed to Australian is not entirely clear, and such inner thoughts were certainly not to be revealed in his diaries but perhaps he saw himself as a 'British Australian' and part of a new generation bridging the divide whilst at the same time taking their culture with them. His diary entry of 4 August 1914 reads, 'I am wondering whether I ought to join the Territorials?' The next day he travelled to London and together with a friend they went to see an acquaintance who worked at the Treasury.

Hugh Godley met them at No. 10 Downing Street. Their objective was to seek advice as to which Corps to join. In what now reads like a Who's Who of Britain at war, Kelly found himself having the ear of and receiving advice from none other than Lord Haldane, Lord Kitchener and Prime Minister Asquith. Heeding their advice the two friends headed first for the Inns of Court training office in Lincolns Inn, London but were turned away due to lack of experience. The next attempt at signing up was with the Grenadier Guards, where they were told the list was closed; too many names, not enough places. He was then told to report to No. 72 Victoria Street for work with the National Service League, sorting postal applications for service with Kitchener's New Army. Anxious to gain a commission but without his call-up papers he and three friends took to the water once more at Henley and sculled down river. Kelly records in his diary that upon reaching Marlow Lock, 'a fisherman shouted in a bitter tone that we would make four good recruits.'

On 3 September official papers arrived at his home at No. 29 Queen Anne Street. The Public Schools Corps had called for Kelly to undergo medicals at Wellington Barracks and a day later he and 160 other recruits were marching through Whitehall and undergoing drill instruction. During those tense days, he frequently lunched with friends at the Union Club when not undergoing drill, went to the national portrait gallery or composed further music, inspired by the war. On 16 September a telegram addressed to Sub Lieutenant F.S. Kelly arrived and Frederick said his goodbyes and headed for HMS *Victory* for further training.

Kelly joined the Royal Naval Volunteer Reserve as a Sub Lieutenant and became part of what was probably the most gifted, diverse, well educated and talented group of friends in His Majesty's Forces. Gathering in the Naval Infantry were Rupert Brooke (Poet), Charles Lister (Diplomat), Patrick Shaw-Stewart (Financier), Arthur Asquith (Prime Minister's son) Bernard Freyburg (later to win the Victoria Cross and become Governor General of New Zealand) and Denis Browne (fellow musician). These men were to all play a pivotal role in the formation, training and fighting of a unique Division, they also became known as 'The Latin Table'.

Whilst at the Admiralty, Winston Churchill had ordered the formation of an 'Advanced Base Force' for the seizure, fortification or protection of any temporary naval bases necessary for the employment of the Fleet. The original size was of one Royal Marine Brigade but this was soon enlarged by the addition of two additional brigades of four battalions of naval reservists. Each of the eight battalions so formed were given names of famous ships or admirals. Thus, were born the Drake, Benbow, Hawke, Collingwood, Hood, Anson, Nelson and Howe battalions. Eventually they were to wear British Army uniforms but with the badges of rank, insignia and traditions of the Royal Navy. With events moving apace in Belgium, Lord Kitchener approved of the formation which became known as the Royal Naval Division (RND) in early September 1914. This fledgling organization was to go on to become one of the finest fighting formations with the British Expeditionary Force.

The Royal Marine contingent saw some brief actions at Ostende before the remainder of the largely untrained RND arrived at Antwerp for some blocking and rearguard actions against the Germans advancing in Belgium and France. Kelly, meanwhile, was still undergoing training at Walmer Barracks on the south coast. Rifle practice, drill and physical training were the order of the day and in the evening, when not on duty, Kelly wrote letters and entertained the other officers by playing the piano. Whilst the First Battle of Ypres raged in Belgium, Kelly recounted an almost comical day at the rifle training butts where, in the driving sleet, just about everything that could go wrong went wrong. Someone forgot the key for the target shed, only five rounds of ammunition had been provided per man and there was no cleaning equipment available. Lastly the chimney in the troop shelter building was full of birds' nests which were discovered only when a fire was lit and the men seeking shelter got smoked out.

The fighting element of the division (less nearly three battalions which were interned after an incident crossing the Dutch border) returned to England amid great praise from the First Sea Lord, Winston Churchill. 'The officers and men acquitted themselves admirably and have thoroughly justified the confidence reposed in them', he remarked. This first overseas expedition was not to be their last of course and over the winter training continued and Kelly, hearing that he may be left behind on the next posting, arranged his transfer to command 5 Platoon, B Company the Hood Battalion, in which, coincidentally many of his Balliol chums also served. They also finally received their khaki uniforms and standard Army issue field webbing as opposed to their Blue Navy uniforms they had startled the Belgians with at Antwerp!

Hood Battalion was destined for far sunnier yet even more inhospitable and dangerous climes – in the Dardenelles. A finger of land pointing west from Constantinople (Istanbul), the Gallipoli peninsular was the next port of call for the RND and it was to play a part in a well conceived but poorly executed plan to knock Turkey out of the war and open the sea lanes to the beleaguered Black Sea ports of Russia.

Gathering from Crystal Palace and Blandford camps the division was marshalled to Avonmouth in late February 1915 and embarked on 28 February for what was, to the men, an unknown Eastern destination aboard a number of ships. They were soon cruising up the brilliant jewel of the Mediterranean aboard the *Grantully Castle*. With Africa behind them and the Greek islands and Constantinople ahead the men of Hood Battalion were filled with confidence and hope but settling down to the monotony on board. Sub Lieutenant Kelly gave every spare moment to his music but who knows what he would have made of the divisional band playing the Marseillaise, God Save the King and other impromptu numbers when at harbour in Malta and Mudros (Lemnos). Mudros lies only fifty miles from the Dardanelles and Turkish waters but anchored reassuringly alongside the troop ships were some of the finest ships in the Royal Navy, the *Queen Elizabeth, Ocean, Implacable, Cornwallis, Inflexible* and the cruisers *Triumph* and *Swiftsure*. The last two were originally destined to be sold to the Turkish Navy but were wisely held back for British use. The other Allies were also present, the Russian cruiser *Askold*, promptly nicknamed 'woodbine' on account of its five slender, smoke stack funnels and the French battleships *Charlemagne* and *Henri IV* (which looked ancient enough to have been built during his reign).

Despite the gathering of such nautical strength the assembled fleet failed to 'force the narrows' with naval power alone and the fleet of the Mediterranean Expeditionary Force (MEF) now readied itself for an amphibious landing on the Gallipoli peninsular. Further training on dry land followed in the soft sand dunes near the Egyptian city of Port Said. Able Seaman Joe Murray in his memoir *Gallipoli 1915* describes a humorous moment when the men were ordered to

82

cut down their trousers into knee length shorts. Having not been issued with tailors' scissors they resorted to using their jack knives, 'these knives were better use at opening jam tins and were far from ideal for tailoring. However, the order was cut, so cut we did.' He describes the sailors laying the trousers on the sand in an effort to make the cuts on each leg equal: 'the owner now on his knees, with nakedness exposed to the sun, endeavouring to make the legs equal before hacking off the unwanted part, we must have looked like ardent pilgrims ... The hacking often continued until some chaps had neither much left of either trouser leg.'

A diary entry for Monday 5 April 1915 reads, 'One of the most uncomfortable days I have ever spent, the strong wind made the air thick with the eddying sand and everything in the tent got covered with it.' It is apparent that during these confined times on ships and in tents Frederick became very close to Rupert Brooke:

> I had a delightful talk about literature with Rupert after dinner. He strikes me as being made of really fine stuff, both physically and mentally ... I asked him to read me his five sonnets – Peace, Safety, The Dead 1&2 and The Soldier. I enjoyed the sound of his voice ... I don't understand Safety but enjoyed the others.

Surprising news for Frederick arrived on 9 April 1915 when his sister Maisie wrote to him, 'My dear Koochface, I daresay you will be as speechless as the dogs ....' She then went on to say that she had married a family friend, John Kelly (no relation but whom, as Sir John Kelly, went on to become Admiral of the Fleet), whilst he was on leave from the Navy in the Mediterranean, 'The only regret about the hurried wedding is that you were not there. Goodbye and good luck.'

Final preparations were nearly complete and the landings only three days away, when tragedy struck the battalion. Rupert Brooke had been bitten on the lip by a Mosquito. The pneumacoccus germ had poisoned his blood and his face became swollen with infection. 'I looked into his cabin and found him very dazed and dangerously ill. The Doctors made me realize it was far worse than the night before and it is now likely that he will not live, and I felt very depressed.' Kelly goes on to record, 'I have a foreboding that he is one of those like Keats, Shelly and Schubert, who are suffered not to deliver their full message', in his diary entry of 22 April. Brooke was transferred to a French Hospital ship at anchor in Skyros harbour but died at 1645 hrs on 23 April. In view of the fleet's order to sail next morning arrangements were at once made to bury him on the island he had come to love.

Brooke's coffin was lowered into a small boat with the burial party from the French ship and rowed ashore. General Paris, Colonel Quilter (Hood Battalion), Kelly and Browne were joined by Asquith, Lister, Freyburg and a dozen French officers as the pall bearers struggled slowly over the rocky ground to the prepared grave a mile inland. At the head of a small valley in an olive grove, under a half moon on a cloudy night, the service was read by a chaplain and concluded with a volley from a firing party. Kelly later wrote that, 'the scent of wild sage and olives gave a strong classical tone which was so in harmony with the poet that to some of us the Christian ceremony seemed out of keeping.'

The small group of intimate friends hung back as the mourners drifted away, then collected stones to pile on the grave and erected crosses at each end of the grave. The inscription read, 'Here lies the servant of God / Sub Lieutenant in the English Navy / Who died for deliverance of Constantinople from the Turks'. 'Oppressed with the sense of loss ... we took one last look in silence, then the sense of tragedy gave place to a sense of passionless beauty, of both the poet and the place.' Perhaps the last words should be from the Poet himself:

If I should die think only this of me:
That there is a corner of a foreign field
That is forever England.

Thirty-six hours later the ANZAC and British troops poured ashore in the landings on Gallipoli. The RND played a part in acting as a diversion to the north at Bulair and it was during this action that Freyburg showed outstanding qualities of courage, initiative and leadership for which he was awarded the Distinguished Service Order. Adding to the diversionary tactic Freyburg – smeared with camouflage paint and grease – swam ashore alone, towing a small raft. Armed only with a revolver and sheath knife he reconnoitered Turkish emplacements then lit flares from his raft to show enemy positions. This invoked the Turks to open fire with machine guns and thus give away their positions. Royal Navy gunfire then retaliated, raining heavy shells down upon the enemy. After two hours swimming on a compass bearing Freyburg finally got back to the ships, relieved but nearly dead with cold. In contrast, Kelly, after tea, played Chopin's F minor Ballade.

Two days later Hood Battalion landed on the Helles Peninsular, facing the Turks on the foothills of Achi Baba. Their positions were to remain largely the same until January of the next year. 'Johnnie' Turk was a tough and resourceful opponent and mutual respect was soon evident at the front.

For a good deal of time on Gallipoli Kelly's Hood Battalion and most of the RND were used piecemeal, often supporting attacks by other units, reinforcing the line and generally propping up which-ever part of the line seemed about to crumble. The constant threat of shellfire, 'bombs' (hand grenades), being thrown from nearby trenches and sniper fire meant that movement above ground during daylight was impossible and ration parties, patrols and repair teams had to operate at night. At least at night the heat of the day sub-sided. Conditions in the heat of the day were awful, flies were every-where, disease and dysentery were rife and sanitary conditions impossible, yet the fighting continued.

Hood Battalion attacked in what is now known as the Battle of Krithia on 6 May alongside French Colonial troops. At eleven in the morning, having advanced up Achi Baba Nullah (ravine) the battalion advanced in waves, dashing forward in the scrub towards Krithia village. Fewer and fewer men rose after each rush but still they charged forward, more being cut down each time by superbly sited, hidden machine guns. By 1230 hrs both Hood and Anson Battalions were well forward yet were still short of the main Turkish lines but the French had hardly moved at all. Men were forced to ground in the open, taking cover in the scrub which often caught fire. Rifle fire came from all around as many Turks had lain hidden and well camouflaged and were now shooting at the men from all sides. The urgent desire to dig down for safety yet not wishing to draw attention by movement was an agonizing choice. Many of the injured were picked off or died of shock and exposure as the heat of the sun or rifle fire consumed them.

Despite the French being so well held on the right flank Kelly and his men of Hood had gained nearly 600 yards, a distance captured that was never to be repeated at Gallipoli again. The cost had been high and for some time afterwards the battalion was not used in the forefront of an advance again, needing time to be reinforced with replacements, one of which was to take command as Colonel Quilter had been amongst those killed on 6 May. The division as a whole was badly depleted and down to only 5,000 having arrived with 10,000 men on 25 April.

Kelly was involved in the next great assault on the dusty village of Krithia when the British launched a three division attack, again alongside the French, on 4 June. Following a desultory bombardment where artillery was only one third of that supplied on the Western Front and the ammunition allowance even more paltry, the men advanced once more. The bombardment which was to have disorganized defences and driven the Turks below ground had achieved nothing. Immediately upon climbing the parapet, man after man was hit by accurate rifle and machine gun fire as it swept along the sand bags. Only half the officers and men of the lead battalions (Hood, Anson and Howe) reached the first Turkish line which by then was largely deserted. Others pushed on further still but were slowly forced back to the forward Turkish trench. Described in the Divisional History as 'an orderly and dashing advance' events are described somewhat differently by Joe Murray of Hood as he got to the trench:

> The trench was three or four deep with bodies. They were slumped over the parapet, some head-first, riddled with bullets as they tried to escape ... We could have pulled their bodies in but there was simply no room, in death they were serving the living providing more cover. The trench had become a mere narrow passage between human flesh, bones and blood.

After these two devastating battles across the stony scrubland of Krithia events on the Helles peninsular ground down further still into trench warfare similar to that raging in France and Flanders. It was on 7 June that the inevitable finally happened and Kelly was slightly wounded, most probably by shellfire. He was promoted to Lieutenant the same day.

F.S. Kelly gains mention in the divisional records as having, 'credit for bringing the reorganized Hood Battalion to that brilliant standard of efficiency which was to later assist the Division to gain Historic success.'

As summer faded to autumn and finally turned to winter, a daily routine dominated with 'stand to', patrols, raids, sniping and endless working parties. Rotation out of the line did, however, mean a glorious dip in the Aegean or snatched periods of sleep above the very same landing beaches – by then stuffed full of the huge plethora of Army impedimenta – where months before the gallant Lancashire Fusiliers had won 'six VC's before breakfast'. These breaks were often interrupted albeit briefly, by 'Asiatic Annie' a giant Turkish railway gun positioned across the Dardanelles which sent over huge shells to interrupt the bathers at Helles Beach.

When the hardships of the summer campaign turned into the equally harsh conditions during the winter months of November and December, the reality of the precarious position held by the Allies on Gallipoli set in. The Australians and New Zealanders, so deeply dug in on the slope of ANZAC Cove, were literally washed away. Equipment, stores men and corpses were swept away in trenches turned into raging torrents whilst down on the exposed Helles plain biting snow and sleet blew across the battlefield, freezing men and animals alike.

A great plan of evacuation was hatched and put into action during late December, deceiving the enemy by withdrawing slowly and evacuating the peninsular of surplus equipment and men. By 6 January 1916 nearly every spare man – in muffled boots – was away and, leaving guns behind to fire on ingenious timers and booby trapped stores, the last few men filed down to the beach in darkness to the waiting ships. It was this last operation – the evacuation – which showed a true brilliance by the staff, a brilliance which had, up to that point, seldom shown itself in the campaign. It was during these final weeks on Gallipoli that Kelly was awarded the Distinguished Service Cross (DSC). His *London Gazette* entry of September 1916 simply states, 'In recognition of services with the Royal Naval Division in the Gallipoli peninsular'. He was also mentioned in despatches by General Sir Ian Hamilton several weeks later, 'for distinguished service in 1915.'

Promoted once more Kelly arrived in France with the rank of Acting Lieutenant-Commander in the summer of 1916. His role as commander of B Company in Hood had seen him with a pivotal role in the re-equipping and reorganization of the battalion, for the army fighting on the Western Front in mid-1916 was vastly different to that which had fought on Gallipoli in late 1915. An Army brigade had now been added to the division, which now became known as the 63rd (Royal Naval) Division. This was seen as a further step by the Army to 'take over' the division but the Navy managed to keep a grip. Later in the autumn their beloved divisional commander Major

General Archibald Paris KBE, who had been with them from the start, was injured and replaced by an Army officer by the name of Shute. An unpopular man, on arrival his first suggestion, though quashed, was to replace all the Naval officers with those from the Army!

Hood Battalion, now rested and replenished, was being drawn ever closer to the meat grinder of the Somme. Several 'quiet' months had been passed near Arras but orders came through in November to move down next to the Ancre River at the heart of the British Somme sector. Six divisions were to attack roughly eastwards towards villages that had first been assaulted almost five months previously on 1 July but had yet to fall. Serre, Beaumont Hamel and Beaucourt were the objectives north of the Ancre along with the hamlet of St Pierre Divion on the south bank of the small river. The 63rd Division was to capture Beaucourt in the Ancre valley. Advancing north-east with their right flank against the river and railway line in the valley bottom, they had a series of colour coded objective lines to reach; Green, Yellow and finally Red.

The German front lines here, as in most sectors, actually consisted of three lines of trenches and the rearmost of these, as it met the valley bottom at ninety degrees was the 'Green Line' – the objective for the spearhead, right flanking Hood Battalion. Once the first line had been taken, the plan dictated that Drake Battalion would pass through and drive on to the next phase. The area to be crossed was already a repugnant wasteland of shell holes, mud, tree stumps and twisted metal. The onset of winter and torrential downpours had added to the de-humanizing and demoralizing effects on the men who were to face the enemy once more.

At 0545 hrs on Monday 13 November 1916, shrouded both by darkness and thick mist, the men of Hood Battalion attacked. Across the centuries mist and fog have aided both the attacker and the defiant defender in battle. Advantages can be gained by both sides. The defenders cannot see their opponents coming, perhaps until it is too late, but equally, attackers lose their way and are often dis-orientated. Both scenarios were played out in the Ancre valley wasteland on 13 November 1916. Some German positions were rapidly overrun whilst others in concrete bunkers were missed and laid down deadly fire into the flanks of the disorientated Hood sailors. Approaching the Green Line around 0730 hrs the attack slowed; men had been trained not to advance too quickly and to ensure that all dugouts and tunnels were cleared behind them before going past. The steep embankments along the railway provided ideal dugouts and bunker entrances for the Germans, some of which lead to the infamous Schwaben Redoubt and other positions across the Ancre valley. One stout position in 'Station Trench' (Green Line) was yet to fall. A German machine gun was providing covering fire from a sandbagged redoubt, while bombers threw grenades at anyone trying to approach. Acting Lieutenant Commander Kelly realised that the position must be eliminated before the objective was fully secured and led an attack on the redoubt. He was killed in the process. The attack was, however, pushed home and units following up marked his body for burial.

The Ancre battle was the final offensive of 1916 and concluded the Battle of the Somme. Kelly was buried just behind the front lines at Martinsart with others from the RND. Visitors to the battlefields today will see that the Imperial (now Commonwealth) War Graves Commission were experimenting with different materials as they buried the dead of the Somme post-war and at Martinsart Military Cemetery the architect used an unusual red sandstone.

Housed at the National Library in Australia are the two works which remain as a legacy of this talented, brave man. His diaries and his musical compositions are referred to there for musical studies and some of his work has been recorded by various groups. Kelly composed his *Elegy for Stringed Orchestra* whilst at Gallipoli, in memory of his poet friend Rupert Brooke and at a memorial concert held in London in May 1919, some of his pianoforte compositions were played and some of his songs were sung. However it was his *Elegy for Stringed Orchestra*, a work of profound feeling, which was so well received. Kelly was perhaps past his prime in the sporting arena but, like Rupert Brooke, his life was not long enough to tell its full tale.

Chapter 8

Alex Sandy Turnbull

'Much more to sacrifice than many men I know'

Now they say that a good sporting regiment is also a good fighting regiment and we want all of you who know anything about the noble art to come forward and give us your names. The same if any of you are good at running, jumping etc, come forward now, don't be afraid.

So ran the welcome speech of Lieutenant Quartermaster G. Baines of the 8th (Service) Battalion of The East Surrey Regiment. He was addressing a ninety-three strong reinforcement draft of men from the Middlesex Regiment who had swapped their cap badges piece-meal and had been sent up the line.

The location was Grovetown Camp, Meaulte, today the site of a perfectly tended Commonwealth War Graves Commission cemetery of the same name. On 15 July 1916, however, the area was a throng of men and materiel making their way up to the newly gained ground as the Battle of the Somme reached a crescendo in this sector.

The 8/East Surreys had earned their place in the annals of British military history two weeks earlier by capturing the important Dantzig Alley position and playing their part in the capture of Montauban. The sector fought over by 30th and 18th Divisions of the New Army proved a costly, yet rare, success on the first day of the battle.

Partly down to the assistance of neighbouring French heavy artillery and the tactics employed at divisional level by Ivor Maxse, the inspirational 18th Divisional commander, the East Surreys' success on the day was memorable due to the kicking of footballs over the top into no man's land as the attack started. Principally the idea of Captain Billy Nevill, an officer of the East Yorkshire Regiment attached to the battalion, he had purchased four footballs to be kicked over by his platoon when the whistles blew. One of them was inscribed, 'The Great European Cup, the Final, East Surreys v Bavarians, Kick Off at Zero'. Nevill himself was killed in the attack and today lies in Carnoy military cemetery although his platoon's objectives were carried. The story became an instant legend and two of the balls were already safe – firmly held in the hands of the regimental museum – by the time the quartermaster briefed the newly arrived draft.

Sitting amongst the draft was Private Alex 'Sandy' Turnbull, the blistering goal scoring hero of both Manchester United and Manchester City. With two FA Cup winner's medals and two League Championship medals to his credit he was quite a catch for the battalion and one that Captain Nevill himself would doubtless have approved of.

Life for Alex had begun in the colliery town of Hurlford, East Ayreshire on 13 April 1884. His father James was a local miner and the family lived at No. 152 Cadger Street. Alex was the second eldest in a family of seven; four girls and three boys. Tragedy struck in 1900 when his father passed away aged just forty-one, by which time the family had moved to No. 12 Galston Road, and by the age of sixteen Alex had followed his late father down the mines.

Famous for its coal mines and iron works the town also boasted Hurlford Thistle Football Club. Formed in 1895 it had both junior and senior sides playing in the local amateur league. As the English game continued to flourish financially, club scouts began to turn their attentions on Scotland as a pool of emerging talent. Promises of large appearance fees and, in some cases professional contracts, would lure many a Scot away from the land of lochs and heather.

As early as 1901 scouts representing the mighty Bolton Wanderers were attracted to Hurlford to have a look at Alex. Perhaps feeling the responsibility as head of the family he declined an offer but a year later Tom Maley, the new Manchester City manager, made a second approach to the young striker. In July 1902 he signed for City and headed south to Manchester. Maley, an ex-amateur player, had left his job as a school governor north of the border to take up the post with City. Within his first season he would lead them to the Second Division Championship, building a side around the goal scoring talent of Alex 'Sandy' Turnbull, Billie Gillespie the rock of the side and captain Billy Meredith an accomplished Welsh international.

In their first season following promotion Maley's side shocked the footballing world by challenging for the title; Turnbull establishing himself in the first team by scoring twelve goals. Although they eventually finished runners-up to Sheffield Wednesday, their league campaign was matched by their cup exploits. City defeated Sunderland, Arsenal, Middlesbrough and title rivals Wednesday en route to the final.

Before a crowd of 62,000 at Crystal Palace on St Georges Day 1903, the first all Lancashire cup final was played out against Bolton Wanderers. Often referred to as the 'Lancashire Invasion of London' the travelling support was captured in the following report by the *Manchester Evening Chronicle*:

> The true character of the London invasion could not be gleaned until midnight and during the early hours of Saturday morning. At Euston, St Pancras, King's Cross and Marylebone, the trains, heavy laden, steamed in continuously. 'What a cheer!' I heard a jovial porter say, shortly after midnight. 'This is great, ain't it? Blimey! Did you ever see so many pubs in bottles? What, oh! Don't they grub?' And truly, the trippers upheld the tradition of the North. Each little party seemed to have brought their own stack of provisions for the weekend. Nine gallon barrels of beer, stone jars of whisky and big baskets filled with 'baggins' were almost as plentiful as blackberries in autumn, while there could never have been as many toastmasters on Euston station before; 'Good Health!' rang perpetually in one's ears. 'Hooray!', 'Play up, City!'

And play up they did, with Billy Meredith scoring a disputed but winning goal in the twentieth minute. It was his only real contribution to the game according to match reports but it was enough and allowed City to lay claim to their first piece of major silverware and place a winner's medal around the neck of twenty year old Alex.

The sharp rise in success for the Hyde Road men aroused suspicion within the Football Association who carried out a formal investigation into the running of the club. Little out of the ordinary was found and the club was cleared in time for the start of the 1904–05 season.

The season proved another success for Alex and his team mates. Alex finished as top scorer with twenty goals in the league, although a second round cup exit dashed their hopes of retaining the trophy.

As the final day of the season approached City were still in with a chance of clinching the championship, needing a win over newly crowned cup winners Aston Villa who stood between them and the title. Alec Leake, the Villa captain, marked Turnbull throughout the game but Alex turned him inside out in the initial stages of the game. The game turned when a frustrated Leake threw mud at Turnbull who reacted by showing him two fingers. Leake then threw a punch at Alex and some contemporary reports claim he was also dragged into the Aston Villa dressing room and given a thorough roughing up at the final whistle. The match ended in a 3-1 defeat for Turnbull and his side but their troubles were, however, only just beginning. Unbeknown to many of the spectators it would be the last time Alex 'Sandy' Turnbull would play in the blue shirt of Manchester City.

In a post match interview Alec Leake announced that he had been offered a £10 bribe to throw the game by City captain Meredith, the subsequent investigation by West Midlands Police and the FA found this to be true and as a result Meredith was fined and suspended for a year. Manchester City refused to assist the disgraced former star financially during this period so it was now Meredith's turn to go public on events. He approached certain members of the press with his version of what had been going on behind closed doors at Hyde Road:

> What was the secret of the success of the Manchester City team? In my opinion, the fact that the club put aside the rule that no player should receive more than four pounds a week, the club delivered the goods, the club paid for the goods delivered and both sides were satisfied.

Given the severity of the claim by one of the games leading players the FA launched a further investigation into the clubs' financial activities. This time they returned a damning verdict. Evidence was found that the club routinely paid its players additional payments above their wages. The resulting punishments included a lifetime suspension from football for manager Tom Maley whilst seventeen senior players received fines and suspensions until January 1907, Turnbull and Meredith being among them. To be fair to Manchester City they had simply been found guilty of what had become a fairly widespread activity within the English game at the time.

The short lived dynasty created at the club was effectively ended by the punishments imposed by the FA. The majority of the players then had to be sold in the close season to raise the money to meet the fine handed out and City's close neighbours Manchester United were following the events closely.

During his brief spell in Manchester City colours Alex 'Sandy' Turnbull had played 110 games, scored 53 goals, lifted the FA Cup, claimed a Second Division title and challenged for a league championship in consecutive seasons.

In May 1906 a unique player auction was held at the Queen's Hotel, Manchester. In the audience sat Ernest Mangnall the Manchester United manager. A month earlier Mangnall's club chairman had provided the financial backing for the disgraced Billy Meredith in the establishment of a sports shop. Now Meredith would strengthen his ties with United as he was bought for a cut price £500. Mangnall also added the trio of Alex Turnbull, Herbert Burgess and Jimmy Bannister to his squad that afternoon in a bid to bring the heart of the successful City team together in the red shirts of United.

When the new players became eligible to play, United were in a mid-table position. Alex made an immediate impression on his debut; scoring the winning goal against a Villa side that had opposed him in his last City appearance. It was the first of fifteen appearances in the 1906–7 season, during which time he scored six goals including further winners against Bolton and Liverpool as United climbed to eighth in the league.

In April Alex's team mate Thomas Blackstock collapsed after a reserve game and died shortly afterwards, when the verdict of 'natural causes' was passed at the inquest the responsibility for his death was lifted from the club and no compensation was offered to the player's family. Outraged, Turnbull, Meredith, Burgess and Charlie Sagar vowed to set up a new players' union.

Players from United, City, Sheffield United, Bradford, Tottenham Hotspur, Newcastle, West Bromwich Albion and Notts County packed into the Imperial Hotel in Manchester on 2 December for the inaugural meeting of the newly formed Association Football Players

Union (AFPU). Further meetings, held in Nottingham and London, were a great success and by the New Year most players had paid the five shillings joining fee supplemented by a weekly subscription of sixpence.

The 1907–08 season was perhaps Turnbull's most productive for United. He scored twenty-five goals in thirty appearances as his club claimed its first League Championship in its history. Notable performances by Alex included a hat trick against Liverpool in a 4-0 win in September; the same month also brought braces against Middlesbrough and Sheffield United. Later that year both sides of Alex's sporting character were on display when he grabbed all four goals in a victory over Arsenal. He scored two more against his old club City a few weeks later before becoming the first player ever to be sent off in a Manchester derby.

A bizarre episode occurred in the close season when the new champions embarked on a continental tour of Austria and Hungary. In Vienna a straightforward 4-0 victory was followed by a visit to Budapest to play their emerging side. In the first match the United team were applauded from the field by the Hungarian crowd after a dazzling 6-2 display but the second game was played in front of a more hostile crowd and when the referee decided to send off three United players a riot erupted among the home supporters. The game ended in a 7-1 victory for Alex and his side despite finishing the game with only eight players. Order on the terraces was only restored by a mounted police charge with swords drawn! The hosts then provided an open top bus to convey the English champions back to their hotel which was confronted by an angry mob outside the ground and under a barrage of rocks seven team members received head injuries. Although an apology from the Hungarian authorities was accepted by the club and reassurances were given that no harm was done on their safe arrival back in Manchester, Mangnall vowed never to return to Hungary again.

The 1908–9 season kicked off with the first ever Charity Shield fixture being played between league champions Manchester United and cup winners Queen's Park Rangers. A large crowd saw United win the replay 4-0 at Stamford Bridge with Alex Turnbull scoring a hat trick. The defence of the league crown was far less successful as United finished a disappointing thirteenth. Turnbull scored just five times in the league, including twice in a 2-2 draw against Nottingham Forest and in grabbing the consolation goal in a horror show, 6-1 defeat at Sunderland on Hallowe'en night. United's fortunes in the cup were decidedly better, however, as victories over Brighton, Everton and a 6-1 thumping of Blackburn courtesy of a Turnbull hat-trick saw them reach the quarter final stage. Leading Burnley 1-0 away, the game was abandoned due to snow and when the teams tried again a few days later on the 10 March 1909, a 3-2 victory for United set up an appetising semi-final against eventual champions Newcastle United at Sheffield's Bramall Lane. The game was played in torrential rain before a packed stadium with Harold Halse scoring the winning goal for United as they progressed to the cup final amid jubilant scenes.

The final was played at Crystal Palace on 24 April and a crowd of 71,401 turned out to see Manchester United take on Bristol City. Both sides traditionally played in red shirts so it was agreed to play in away strips. Both clubs sported badges on their shirts; United the red rose of Lancashire and City the crest of Bristol. This event marked the first appearance of commemorative kit in football history and resplendent in a white shirt with a large red 'V' on his chest, Alex scored the winning goal in the twenty-second minute. The game had proved to be an ill-tempered affair but ended with a second cup winner's medal for the miner from Hurlford. The victors were then entertained at the Alhambra Theatre by the legendary comedian George Robey before a gala dinner. On waking next morning, the team – many with sore heads – found that the lid of the FA Cup was missing. It was discovered only after a lengthy search in the pocket of Alex Turnbull's jacket!

On the team's return to Manchester 300,000 fans packed the central station and surrounding area to welcome home their heroes. Behind the scenes, however, the political storm clouds over Alex's career were gathering once more.

A long running dispute over wages and players' bonuses between the AFPU and the football authorities came to a head the same month and by June the FA ordered all its professional players to leave the union or risk the termination of their registration. As a result the AFPU joined forces with the General Federation of Trade Unions. Whilst most players followed the FA guidelines and left the union, Alex and his hard line United colleagues refused to back down. As a result, and for the second time in his career, Alex Turnbull found himself suspended; this time by his club as opposed to the sport's governing body.

After a national debate the FA agreed in late August, to support the reinstatement of the players concerned although it would take almost a year for the back pay of wages to take effect. None of the players involved would ever represent their country.

When the season opened, the side took to the field wearing AFPU armbands and posed for an infamous team photograph declaring themselves 'The Outcasts'. The campaign ended with United finishing a respectable fifth in the title race and although they suffered a disappointing early cup exit at Burnley, Alex Turnbull scored thirteen goals. A major event of the 1909–10 season for Alex's club was the move from Bank Street to Old Trafford; the old main stand at Bank Street collapsed shortly after its closure damaging a number of local buildings. In contrast the new stadium was intended to hold up to 100,000 supporters in state of the art surroundings, although with the project estimated to run overtime and over budget, this capacity was later reduced to 60,000. The opening game at Old Trafford on 19 February 1910 saw Liverpool beat United 4-3 even though Alex scored on his club's debut at its new home – a home that would later become one of the most well known venues in the world and earn the soubriquet the Theatre of Dreams.

A great partnership developed a year later when Enoch West joined United from Nottingham Forest. He immediately hit it off with Alex Turnbull on the field and the 1910–11 season saw the pair appear regularly on the score sheet. With eighteen goals for Alex and a further nineteen for West the final day of the season saw them vying with Aston Villa to win the championship. Manchester United saw off Sunderland with an emphatic 5-1 victory, Alex scoring one of them and all attention turned to the Liverpool versus Villa game. Charlie Roberts described the scene in the *Manchester Saturday Post*:

> At the end of the game our supporters rushed across the ground in front of the stand to wait for the final news from Liverpool. Suddenly a tremendous cheer rent the air and was renewed again and again and we knew we were the champions once again.

With Aston Villa losing 3-1 the crown went to Old Trafford and Alex had a fourth major honour to his name.

The following three seasons passed relatively quietly for Alex Turnbull as his side finished thirteenth, fourth and fourteenth respectively with Alex claiming twenty-one goals in total. His manager Ernest Mangnall departed in a shock move across Manchester to City and John Bentley took over.

In 1914 the Manchester derby was declared a benefit game for Alex who had by that time served the football clubs of the city for twelve years. The game ended in a 0-0 draw and £1,216 was taken in gate receipts; a sizable sum for the day.

The 1914-15 season saw a period of great upheaval within the game as attention turned to events in France and Flanders. Alex Turnbull had his career cut short not by the coming of war but by a further suspension when he was implicated in the match fixing scandal of 1915. United, facing a relegation battle, played Liverpool on 2 April at Old Trafford. With the game at 2-0 to United the referee and numerous onlookers made note of Liverpool's lack of effort, even appearing to miss a penalty deliberately. At the final whistle it was discovered that a number of bets at odds of 7-1 had been taken for the score to end up 2-0; some from the players themselves. Jackie Sheldon, the ex-United player then on Liverpool's books, was found to be the ring leader and a total seven players received life bans, one of them being Alex 'Sandy' Turnbull. During his time for Manchester United he had played 245 games, scored 101 goals, claimed two league titles and an FA Cup winner's medal.

With the Great War now in its second year Alex journeyed south to enlist and remove himself from the controversy. He had heard of the Footballer's Battalion of the Middlesex Regiment so joined the regiment along with fellow suspects Jack Sheldon and Arthur Whalley. Team mate Oscar Linkson who had played fifty-nine times for United was also in the ranks of the 17th Battalion, The Middlesex Regiment and would be killed on the Somme in August 1916. Whilst in training, Turnbull and Whalley turned out for Clapton Orient and Rochdale in exhibition games as their suspensions only related to the league matches.

Notification of Turnbull joining the army appeared in the Manchester United club secretary's notes in November 1915:

I understand that 'Sandy' Turnbull has decided to join the Footballer's Battalion, and that Davies, who has figured at outside right, and Knighton have also decided to don khaki. This will bring the club record to sixteen, not bad figures everything considered. I was pleased to hear that Turnbull was setting such a fine example to the younger generation of footballers, for he has much more to sacrifice than many men I know. Turnbull, like Meredith, has done much to raise the standard of football in this district and I hope he will be able to assist Rochdale again next weekend, when the Spotland team are due to appear at Old Trafford.

Unlike Whalley and Sheldon, Alex Turnbull did not serve overseas with 17/Middlesex. Instead, when his time to embark for France arrived he formed part of a draft of ninety-three men whom, as we have seen, joined 8/East Surreys on 15 July 1916.

His first experience of trench life came on the Franco-Belgian border near Erquinghem Lys. The division relieved the New Zealanders in the sector which at that time was enduring heavy bombardments daily. The 18th (Eastern) Division decided to employ a new tactic to minimize the daily casualty rates, they withdrew the trench garrison from the front line to the support lines and left 'fighting patrols' of one NCO and six men every 300 yards to fire rifles and very lights into the night sky. The majority of the battalions then slept on standby to reinforce the old front line if attacked. Alex settled into the routine of military life fairly quickly and was soon promoted to Lance Corporal. Throughout August the East Surreys attended bombing and gas schools in the area when out of the line. On 7 August they were raided whilst in the trenches, fifteen men were killed, thirty-one wounded and two were missing as a result of the action.

On 21 August a formal letter was written by the adjutant of the battalion with regard to the drafts from other regiments now in the ranks of the East Surreys:

A large number of letters continued to be received by officers and men of the Battalion who had been slightly wounded in late June and early July and on recovering were posted to other battalions in the brigade. These men feel a great injustice has been done to them and from a battalion point of view it would be worth any trouble to get them back. It is hoped that even now any steps may be taken to rectify the appalling muddle resulting from the actions of those responsible for reinforcements sent to battalions in July. There could be no military value for sending drafts for the East Surreys to the King's

Liverpool Regiment at the same time as Middlesex Regiment men were sent to us as the 8 East Surreys and the 18 King's Liverpool Regiment were billeted in neighbouring villages.

A copy of the above letter appears in the battalion war diary and clearly there was a strong feeling regarding this new approach to sending drafts where they were needed as opposed to where they were supposed to go. For Alex it was just a case of mixing in, perhaps letting his football do the talking when out of the line.

As September approached the East Surreys prepared to return to the Somme and throughout the month they underwent training in the area of Puchevillers. Their daily routine out of the line was punctuated with parades, medal award ceremonies and kit inspections, one of which concentrated specifically on identity discs and iron rations.

On 13 September Alex made his debut for the battalion football team which beat the 7th Battalion, The Queens Royal West Surrey Regiment 5-0. They were soon to make their way up the line to Blighty Valley in preparation for an assault on the fearsome Schwaben Redoubt position.

Though in divisional reserve for the initial attack on 26 September, four days later they were occupying the newly won east face of the redoubt, their next objective being to push further into the massive defensive complex. C Company suffered 5 per cent losses including all their officers though Lance Corporal Smith made good use of the Lewis Gun, accounting for fifty Germans and taking the surrender of a further seventy in the process. Enfilade fire then tore into A Company and whilst a couple of men managed to crawl back to the support lines by dark the majority of the company were posted as missing. The overall failure to break through was blamed on a number of platoons being kept out of the attack to undertake labour tasks in reserve; it was felt that these men, if available, could have made the difference and turned the tide at a critical moment in the action.

October saw the battalion at Candas where they undertook further training on lessons learnt during the Somme fighting and took part in an active sports programme. Before long they were back at the front alongside the Canadian troops near Regina Trench and there some good examples of patrol work were undertaken prior to an assault on Desire Trench on 19 November 1916.

After advancing behind a creeping barrage Alex and his men emerged from a heavy mist to see their objective but just after 0600 hrs a disorientated Canadian unit stumbled across their frontage causing a delay to the advance. Within the hour the battalions were consolidating their position 150 yards forward of the objective, during which time Alex had to keep his head down as sniping activity intensified. At 0805 a bombing party was sent out to deal with the snipers and shortly afterwards contact was made with a battalion of the Royal West Kents on the left and Canadians on their right. An excellent trench was then dug, wired and reinforced by machine gun positions so that by midday Turnbull and his comrades were overlooking the impressive Boom Ravine. The day was not without cost to the battalion, they had suffered thirteen men killed, ninety-seven wounded and eleven missing.

December brought a break from offensive operations for the men of 8/East Surreys and after their recent battles Alex and the men of his draft were now well embedded as part of the unit. The spell also brought an opportunity for him to display his sporting prowess as the 18th (Eastern) Divisional Cup got underway. The first round saw his side stroll past the 8th Battalion, The Suffolk Regiment by 8 goals to nil in front of an enthusiastic crowd at Hautville on 5 December.

A week later the second round tie against 55 Brigade Headquarters Staff was scratched half an hour before kick off as they were unable to raise a team. This meant a bye for Alex and his team. As the month progressed battalion training in the morning was supplemented by football training in the afternoon as the battalion took their place in the competition seriously and not simply as a diversion for the men away from the trials of trench life.

The next round saw them secure a comfortable 5-2 victory over the 10th Battalion, The Essex Regiment setting up a Christmas Eve clash in the semi-final against No. 3 Divisional Supply Column. Once again a large crowd at Hautville saw Alex and his team mates run out narrow 2-1 victors but alas the goal scorers are not recorded in the war diary to provide a more thorough report of the games.

A day later, on Christmas Day 1916, the final was played at Buigny St Macloux against the Divisional Royal Army Medical Corps (RAMC). A closely fought game ended in a 1-1 draw after extra time so a replay was arranged for News Year's Day to be followed by a concert party for all those in attendance.

As the year ended the men of 8/East Surreys underwent intense battle training in the Forest l'Abbeye, special attention being paid to bayonet practice. Ivor Maxse, the divisional commander was especially keen to instill the spirit of 'lead in the belly' to his troops, a tactic that had proved itself so well during the fighting on the Somme.

On the morning of 1 January 1917, the entire battalion was present to witness the Divisional Cup Final and in a thrilling game the East Surreys came out on top 3-2. The spirited celebrations that followed were only tainted when news was received that Private Ernest Shelley had seriously injured himself in an accident with a grenade, he died a few days later and today lies buried alone in the Forest l'Abbeye Churchyard cemetery.

A final game was played on 8 January against 55 Brigade Machine Gun Company and Turnbull's side lost, uncharacteristically, 1-0. It would be the last chance for many of the team to play for a while as the battalion then moved back into the line near Grandcourt.

14 February saw a very costly attack by 18 Division on Boom Ravine. Communications broke down early on and although the battalion achieved a limited advance by the day's end, they had suffered sixty-five casualties. It was later discovered that prisoners from a neighbouring unit captured a few days earlier may have alerted the Germans to the forthcoming attack; this would certainly account for their readiness on the day.

Just ten days later the Germans withdrew over a wide frontage and moved back to their newly constructed Hindenburg Line. Due to the continuing British offensive in the sector, this impressive construction project made the best use of a partially completed canal and tunnel system some way to the east of the Somme. The Germans left a trail of destruction behind them with time delay explosives, suicide machine gun teams, poisoned water holes and booby trapped dugouts adding to the dangers.

It was a very cautious British Army that pursued them across this ground, inheriting destroyed villages and blocked roads as they went. Alex spent the month of March billeted in the shelter of Thiepval Wood, itself the front line only six months earlier during his time at the Schwaben Redoubt.

April 1917 brought a change in sector as the division moved north to play their part in the Arras offensive. On 2 April the entire battalion, including transport, paraded on the road from Wittes to

Aire for the benefit of the Corps Commander in order to display 'a Battalion on a mobile war footing in readiness for the instant pursuit of a retreating army.' This optimistic exercise showed the confidence enjoyed by the British Army during this time; alas the Germans held a different view as the battle progressed.

At Steenbecque on 7 April 1917, Alex Turnbull's football team began their defence of the Divisional Cup, when they beat the 18th Division Headquarters team 2-1 in their opening game. Two days later they were held to a 1-1 draw by the Divisional Royal Engineers in a game that would have been played in unusually snowy conditions to the background roar of heavy artillery heralding the start of the great battle for Arras. It was a day which would go down in history as the day the Canadians successfully stormed Vimy Ridge.

A day later the battalion team won the replay 2-1 setting themselves up for a semi-final place on 12 April against the 7th Battalion, The East Kent Regiment (The Buffs). The Buffs were swept aside 4-1 as Turnbull's team eased into the final once more. A few days later, however, all football was cancelled as 8/East Surreys were placed on immediate notice to move up to the front line. Alex Turnbull had played his last competitive football match.

On 3 May 1917 the 18th Division was given the task of capturing the village of Cherisy but the occasion was to be the first time in its history that an attempted advance was well and truly checked by the enemy. The attack was part of a general advance by the British from Lens in the north to Bullecourt in the south. General Allenby had intended to exploit the gains of early April whilst taking German pressure away from the French to the south. The battalion had had only three days to plan for their part in the advance; not nearly enough time for the artillery to make gaps in the massive barbed wire belts that faced them.

The start time of 0345 hrs meant the attack was conducted in complete darkness leading initially to extreme difficulties. Tanks from neighbouring divisions added to the confusion by trundling across the battalion's frontage and the counter barrage from the defenders was heavier than expected. As they struggled to get a footing in Fontaine Trench, a message to retire – still disputed – was passed along the divisional front. By nightfall pockets of the East Surreys still remained on the outskirts of the village, some clung to their original objective and were in touch with the Rifle Brigade on their left. On their right, however, a dangerous gap had formed and large numbers of Germans were seen massing in the village preparing to counter attack.

Eventually, and with no chance of reinforcement, the remnants of the battalion were withdrawn under heavy fire. During the nineteen hours of battle numerous accounts of individual bravery were recorded. One of particular note appears in the *History of the 18th Division in the Great War*:

> There is the story of 'Sandy' Turnbull, the Scottish International professional footballer who played inside left for the Manchester United team when they became champions of the Football League. Turnbull had become a sergeant in the 8th East Surreys. He was a good soldier, earnest, extremely wide awake, and a man of good influence. He had gone through towards Cherisy with Captain Lonergan and his company; he was wounded, but went on. Early in the advance he spotted some enemy machine guns and turned a Lewis gun on them. He got hit again when trying to rush an enemy gun; then a third bullet smashed his knee and brought him down. But he waved his companions forward, shouting instructions from the map which he carried. He directed other men who came up, and refused to be taken back. Afterwards he was missed and it was hoped that he had been taken prisoner, with a chance of recovery of his wounds. But nothing has ever been heard of him. He was a gallant man, and met a soldier's end with calm fearlessness.

Sergeant Alex 'Sandy' Turnbull was placed on the list of missing after the attack, eventually to become one of the 1,100 men killed with the 8/East Surreys in the Great War. News of his fate was broken to the public in the *Manchester Evening News* on 22 May 1917:

> Sergeant A. Turnbull (Sandy) is known to have received four wounds, and is missing. Whether slain or picked up by the Germans is not known. Turnbull was a great inside left, and, considering his size, even more dangerous with his head than Sandy McMahon. We hope for better news.

A later notice appeared in the *Athletic News* on 26 May:

> From a letter sent by his officer, Mrs. F.A. Turnbull believes that her husband, 'Sandy' Turnbull is wounded and a prisoner in

Germany. Sergeant A. Turnbull of the East Surreys has been missing since May 3. He bore himself most gallantly after being thrice wounded.

As it turned out this proved to be a false hope and Alex is today listed amongst the names on the Arras Memorial to the Missing; his body remaining undiscovered or identified. Though he flirted with controversy throughout his amazing playing career he is without doubt one of those incredible sporting greats who lived and died in extraordinary times.

Chapter 9

Jack Harrison VC, MC

An 'Airlie Birds' Legend

Standing on the south-eastern fringes of the French coastal town of Dunkirk, sheltered by mature trees and flanked by serene canals, is the town cemetery. Within the ranks of the civilian tomb stones and memorials stand several plots of the familiar Commonwealth war graves with their trademark headstones of Portland stone. In plot two, close to the fabulous Dunkirk memorial by Philip Hepworth and the glass engraving depicting the famous Dunkirk evacuation of 1940 is a headstone engraved, 'Captain John Harrison, Duke of Wellington's Regiment, 1st June 1940.' Whilst not the end of a story it is tangible evidence of another sad twist in the tale of an extraordinary family from Hull.

John Harrison was killed in the defence of the shrinking Dunkirk perimeter whilst an armada of vessels – including the famous 'little ships' – rescued the BEF in 1940. He was fighting against the invading Germans, just as his father had done twenty-three years before him. In 1917 Harrison's father, also named John, paid the ultimate price in the defence of France and the freedom of Europe. The honour of a soldier's burial in a named grave was, however, denied John senior in 1917 and he is now simply commemorated on a memorial to the missing.

Surviving both father and son as bereft widow and grieving mother was John Harrison senior's wife Lillian. Not only had she lost her husband in 1917, she had then seen her only son go to war in 1940, never to return home. On her death in 1977 Lillian left her husband's Great War medals to the Regimental Museum in York for safe keeping, knowing that they would attract much interest, for amongst the medals was a Victoria Cross.

106

The shipyards of Hull around the turn of the last century might have been as unlikely a place as any to forge a sporting icon and Victoria Cross recipient, but it did both in the form of John 'Jack' Harrison. 'Jack's' parents recognised that he had academic skills and intelligence that would allow him to break out from following his father as a ship's boiler maker and with their help and encouragement he left school to be trained as a teacher, first in St John's College, York, then at Lime Street School, back in his native Hull. Whilst at York, Harrison pursued his interests in cricket and rugby football. His sprinter's speed and strong build helped mould him into a valuable winger or centre in the college line up. Finding himself a permanent starter on the First XV exposed him to scouts for the York Northern Union Rugby League Club, which desperately needed new and vibrant talent. Turning out for them five times in the 1911–12 season he scored three tries and further enhanced his standing by doing so. Rather like modern Premiership football management, however, Jack's relationship with York was destined to be short lived and having completed his teacher training he returned to his home town of Hull in the summer of 1912 and married his sweetheart Lillian.

Living at No. 75 Wharncliffe Street in Hull, and now an assistant school master, Hull, the local Rugby League team, invited him to join them for the 1912–13 season. Running out in the famous 'Black and White' of Hull for his first game in September 1912 he made an immediate impact on both the game and the fans. At five feet eight inches he was reasonably tall for the era and so he was able to command space physically. Allied with his ability to read passes and to 'make the plays' he was a good team player who also, to the joy of fans, regularly scored tries with his speed and panache. Playing alongside Harrison in the Hull side was record signing Billy Batten – brought in for a not inconsiderable £600. Hull FC is one of the oldest clubs in the League and was formed by a group of ex-public schoolboys from York in 1865. Following games at a succession of grounds, the club eventually moved into the Hull Athletic Club's ground at the Boulevard and played their first game there in September 1895, when a record crowd of 8,000 witnessed the 'Airlie Birds' defeat Liversedge in the very first season of Northern Union Football. Hull FC was one of the original clubs to break free from the RFU. Hull prospered and their black and white irregular hooped jerseys became one of the most famous and feared strips in the league. Having played at the Boulevard for over 100 years Hull FC moved to its new ground at the KC Stadium in 2003.

In the 1913–14 season, Harrison scored a remarkable fifty-two tries, a record that still stands today. He went on to score a total of 106 tries in 116 matches for Hull up to 1916. He scored one of two tries scored by Hull in the Challenge Cup victory over Wakefield Trinity at Halifax in 1913 and was selected to tour Australia in 1914, a tour that was cancelled due to the start of the First World War. Jack, along with others from the rugby club, later undertook a very different and far more deadly kind of tour.

Lillian gave birth to their son John in 1915 and it appears that having seen the pregnancy through, Jack volunteered for duty in the army and enlisted in the Inns of Court Officer Training Corps (OTC) on 4 November 1915. Stationed for this period of training in Hertfordshire he had temporary digs at 55 Kitsbury Road, Berkhamsted. It is possible that he carried on playing the occasional game for Hull even while under training. When he resigned from the OTC in August 1916 to take up a commission, however, there was no longer any time for playing at Hull. He was posted initially to the 14th Battalion, East Yorkshire Regiment; a reserve unit based at Whittington Barracks in Lichfield.

The East Yorkshire Regiment, like many other regionally recruited regiments answered the call of Lord Kitchener in 1914 to form locally recruited and raised units that would train, serve and fight together. Initially 100,000 volunteers were required to form the New Army and this was achieved so quickly that second and subsequent batches soon followed. It was not all plain sailing for the 'Pals' recruiting idea however; a letter in the 1914 *Hull Daily Mail* from 'Middle Class of Newland' records, 'many men were not enlisting because they did not like the idea of having to herd with all types of men now being enlisted. It is keeping young athletes and men of good birth and training from joining the colours.' Middle Class continued, 'Larger employers in Hull should use their influence to organize a corps of middle class young men, Clerks, Tailors, Drapers, Grocers, Warehousemen and Artisans.' This was clearly not a lone voice and soon with the blessing of Lord Kitchener, Lord Nunburnholme, the Lord Lieutenant of the East Riding, was authorized to raise a service battalion with the name 'The Commercial Battalion'. Recruiting was brisk and in one day over 600 Hull men signed on. By 12 September 1914 the 'Commercials' was full and a second battalion started, this time of 'Tradesmen'. In three days that too was full. Wishing to encourage still more the *Hull Daily Mail* urged, 'If you mean to play the Game, join at once.' This third battalion of Hull men was to be called 'Sportsmen' and its ranks were swelled though not full, of men from football, rugby, cricket and other sporting backgrounds. During December 1914 the battalions were renumbered to bring them into line with a more standardized Army system. Thus the 'Commercials' became the 10th Battalion, The East Yorkshire Regiment, 'Tradesmen' became the 11th and 'Sportsmen' the 12th. One final Pals unit was raised, and, short of a new name and bearing in mind by now it was a rare mix of all sorts, the 13th Battalion gained the humourous title of Hull 'T'Others'!

As Jack Harrison was joining 11/East Yorks late in 1916, the Hull Pals were still reeling from the effects of the blackest day faced by the British Army until that point. The four Pals battalions had been put together in the same brigade in the 31st Division which had attacked the fortified village of Serre on the Somme on 1 July. Thick, uncut barbed wire entanglements held up the waves of pals as well-sited, murderous machine gun fire scythed through their ranks. The exact date of Jack's arrival date as a reinforcement with the 11th Battalion is uncertain but we do know that he joined B Company as a Second Lieutenant just before Christmas 1916. The battalion was back in the Hebuterne sector, near Serre and involved in typical actions of a battalion holding the line. On 23 December 1916, for instance, the battalion mounted a night trench raid for two hours but failed to penetrate the enemy line, finding only dense, newly erected barbed wire resting on heavy wooden 'knife rests'. Proving once again that the Christmas Truce was but a one off on a narrow sector, far back in 1914, the War Diary records another failed attempt at a night time raid on 25 December.

The New Year of 1917 took Jack and the battalion out of the line for some rest at the village of Couin. A delayed Christmas dinner was had, the officers serving the men as was traditional in the Army. There followed a concert at the village hall hosted by the new commanding officer and led by the Divisional Concert Party known as 'The Stunts'. It was common for each division to gather together a group of talented singers, musicians, card tricksters, jokers, entertainers and drag artistes to form the Concert Party. One of the best known such groups was that of 12th Eastern Division which was known as 'The Spades' (after the Divisional flash – the Ace of Spades). They were granted permission to use the theatre in Arras in 1917 and, complete with full electric stage lighting, scenery, make up and band, they played to packed houses night after night. Such entertainment may today sound trivial, camp and amateur but it provided a welcome relief from the dangers and reality of the front, hence so much effort and time being expended on it.

In February 1917 the Hull brigade entered the line once again to take its place at the front and Jack was soon in the thick of the action. On 25 February Jack led a patrol into no man's land and in this action his bravery earned him the Military Cross. The citation appeared in the *London Gazette* dated 17 April 1917: 'For conspicuous gallantry and devotion to duty. He handled his platoon with great courage and skill, reached his objective under the most trying conditions and captured a prisoner. He set a splendid example throughout.' The War Diary again allows us to gather more details of the incident. Jack was leading a platoon from B Company which was to raid the enemy lines for intelligence at 0600 hrs. Just to the north, leading a platoon from A Company, was Second Lieutenant Thackray. As the members of the raiding party slithered out of their own trenches it was still dark near Gommecourt (another village that witnessed so many casualties in July 1916). By 0750 hrs Jack had sent word back to battalion that he had captured the front line trench with little sign of the enemy. By 0900 hrs the third line was captured with one prisoner taken but stiffening resistance and increasing amounts of fire were being directed at them by the now fully awake Germans. By 1000 hrs Thackray's patrol had also reached the third line. Around this time it became clear to Harrison that a patrol to his south had not penetrated alongside him and that enfilade fire was now catching his men in the flank. Monitoring progress the Brigadier General, ordered a withdrawal but many enemy artillery shells were by now crashing down around the little patrol in a 'box barrage' and a square of bursting shells was isolating Harrison and threatening to wipe him out. Unable to pull back, the British artillery was ordered to fire a counter battery mission on the German guns. This was so effective it caused most of the German guns to stutter to a stop in disarray, just long enough for Thackray and Harrison to get their patrols home without further casualties. In fact all the casualties were taken by the northernmost patrol under Thackray which listed two men killed, three wounded and one missing. Immediate awards for gallantry in the field were made by the Field Marshal, Sir Douglas Haig. Second Lieutenant Thackray also received the MC.

Plans were already afoot which involved the Hull volunteers taking part in further action to the east of Arras. Under General Horne's First Army the 31st Division was to further the advances made since 9 April when the battle of Arras began on the slopes of Vimy Ridge. The 31st Division under Major General O'Gowan, was to attack the village of Oppy with the 2nd Division on its left flank. Opposing them were men from the German 1st Guards Reserve Division and 15th Reserve Division. Harrison's own division was termed as 'rested' and in order to spread the share of work they took over a wider stretch of the line and had extra artillery and machine gun units seconded to them for the task. Oppy village was protected for the Germans by the natural barrier provided by the wood of the same name on its west side. An earlier attempt to take the village at the end of April had led to the destruction of much of the village and also the wood. Trees had been blown down and the undergrowth churned over and over again:

> The key to Oppy was a wood beside the village, and this wood the enemy had fortified in an amazing manner. It was a grand rookery of machine guns. The guns were mostly placed in the boughs twenty to thirty feet above ground, and the gunners took shelter during a bombardment on ladders running down the east side of the trunks. On the ground, the deep dugouts placed behind barricades were concealed and strengthened by felled trees. And even after a heavy bombardment the manor house survived with its broken roof and empty windows clearly visible through fringes of dead trees.

As 6 Platoon Commander, Jack was to lead one wave of B Company in the attack scheduled for 3 May. Two days before the attack he found himself in dugouts in the railway cutting at Bailleul, two miles west of Oppy. Practice was under way for the attack before some enforced rest during the day on 2 May. His brigade (92nd) was to attack directly towards the wood, push through and get beyond the village to a line drawn on a German trench called 'Oppy Support Trench' some 350 yards to the east of the village.

Just after 2100 hrs on 2 May the battalion moved out from the railway cutting and, following the line of a light railway running due east, they headed toward Oppy. Guides from 13/East Yorks came to meet the troops and lead them forward to their jumping off positions. A clear spell of bright weather during the day brought a bright moon which helped light their way but this also aided keen-eyed German sentries. The British had to go over a low, exposed crest with the moon behind them. German artillery fire soon started to fall amongst the men from Hull and numerous German Very lights went up, illuminating the whole battlefield. By the time the men got into position 100–200 yards from the German lines west of the wood, it was 0145 hrs, two hours before Zero. The brigade lined up with 12/EastYorks to the north, 11/EastYorks in the centre and 10/East Yorks on the right flank, next to 93 Brigade.

At 0345 hrs the infantry rose and went forward. The British artillery bombardment then started to creep forward at a rate of 100 yards every four minutes, with the infantry, in theory at least, staying only fifty yards behind the curtain of fire in front of them. What with the darkness, smoke and dust thrown up by the barrage, however, men became disorientated and had great difficulty seeing exactly how far they had come and how far ahead the barrage was. Consequently the leading waves of infantry started to fall behind as the barrage moved too far ahead. The enemy guardsmen manned their guns and began taking a heavy toll on the advancing British, first with rifle fire from outposts, then with machine gun fire from dugouts and on high from the tree houses. The first wave was repulsed. Officers and NCOs galvanized their men in no man's land, reorganised and began the attack again. One or two small parties then got through to the village and this was reported by an air patrol at 0600 hrs. They were later cut off and surrounded. With night-marish similarity to its ill-fated attack a year before on the Somme, the battalion was again held up by uncut wire. Pinned by fire from a dug in machine gun on the southern tip of the wood 6 Platoon were floundering and taking more casualties for every minute that passed. Rifle fire, streams of machine gun tracer, high explosives and bursting shrapnel shells turned the front of the wood into an inferno. It is at moments such as this that great men of valour step forward.

Second Lieutenant Harrison realized the machine gun was the main obstacle and told the men close by to keep the machine gun under constant fire. Armed with his revolver and a Mills bomb he charged towards the enemy post. Dodging and weaving he moved

112

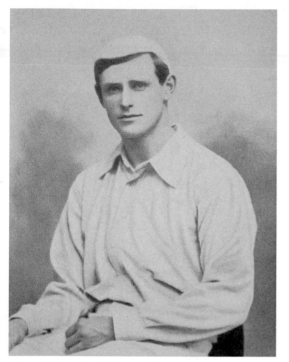

Ronald Poulton Palmer, the sportsman.

Ronald Poulton Palmer, the soldier.

Poulton Palmer slicing through the French defence, early 1914.

Ronald Poulton Palmer's original field grave near Anton's Farm, Belgium.

Anthony Wilding in pre-war civilian attire.

Wilding (second left) takes a break in a doubles match.

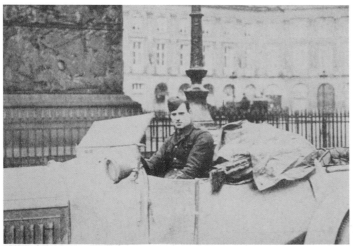

Anthony Wilding in an early Royal Naval Air Service armoured car.

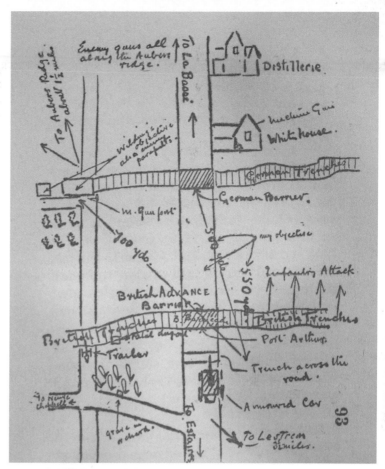

An original hand drawn sketch map of Wilding's last movements and his field burial location.

A wartime photograph of Wilding's original grave near the orchard off 'Edgeware Road', Neuve Chapelle.

The 1910 England side that faced Ireland, Henry Berry is standing third from left; Edgar Mobbs is on the extreme right of the centre row. The game ended in a 0-0 draw.

The 1910 England side that beat Wales 11-6. England won the inaugural Five Nations Championship and Henry Berry, ever present, played alongside Ronnie Poulton Palmer in the game.

R. W. POULTON

L. HAIGH

D. R. GENT

W. A. JOHNS

B. SOLOMON

F. E. CHAPMAN

H. BERRY

A. D. STOOP (Capt.)

E. L. CHAMBERS

J. G. G. BIRKETT

H. J. S. MORTON

D. F. SMITH

W. R. JOHNSTON

L. E. BARRINGTON-WARD

C. H. PILLMAN

Arthur Jones in the Lefroy 1912 State Premiers side, seated centre row, second from right.

Poppies adorn the Canberra memorial in Australia where Arthur Jones is commemorated.

One of many 'Deeds that Thrilled the Empire'. An artist's impression of Donald Bell's VC action, 1916.

Punch lends its humour to the fight against Germany.

The authors at 'Bell's Redoubt', Contalmaison, Somme.

Frank McGee (standing far right) with the dominant, pre-war Ottawa Silver Seven side.

Frank McGee the soldier. Wounded in Ypres, he fell at Courcelette, September 1916.

Contemporary sketch of Frederick Kelly rowing on the Thames.

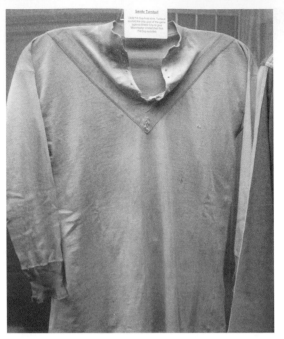

Original 1909 FA Cup Final match shirt worn by Alex Turnbull, now housed in the Manchester United museum.

Jack Harrison VC, MC memorial at the modern KC Stadium, Hull.

Faubourg d'Amiens memorial to the missing, Arras. Jack Harrison, Walter Tull and Sandy Turnbull are amongst those listed here.

"This is not the time to play Games" *(Lord Roberts)*

RUGBY · UNION · FOOTBALLERS
are
DOING · THEIR · DUTY
over 90% have enlisted

"Every player who represented England in Rugby international matches last year has joined the colours."—Extract from *The Times*, November 30, 1914.

BRITISH ATHLETES!
Will you follow this
GLORIOUS EXAMPLE ?

Lord Roberts and the rugby community unite in the cause with this recruiting poster.

The RFU War Memorial displayed at Twickenham today, one omission would appear to be Major Blair Inskip Swannell. Swannell served with the 1st Battalion AIF and is buried in Baby 700 cemetery, Gallipoli.

1914 — 1918

RUGBY · FOOTBALL · UNION
IN MEMORIAM

H.ALEXANDER.	R.E.INGLIS.	A.F.MAYNARD.	J.E.RAPHAEL.
H.BERRY.	P.D.KENDALL.	E.R.MOBBS.	R.O.SCHWARTZ.
A.J.DINGLE.	J.KING.	W.NANSON.	L.A.N.SLOCOCK.
L.HAIGH.	R.O.LAGDEN.	F.E.OAKELEY.	F.N.TARR.
R.H.M.HANDS.	D.LAMBERT.	R.L.PILLMAN.	A.F.TODD.
A.L.HARRISON.	G.E.B.DOBBS.	R.W.POULTON PALMER.	J.H.D.WATSON.
H.A.HODGES.			C.E.WILSON.
			A.J.WILSON.

The magnificent Menin Gate Memorial, Ypres where Edgar Mobbs is commemorated.

England and Northampton Rugby hero, Mobbs – killed at Ypres, 1917.

Colin Blythe the cricketer 'as innocent looking as a babe.'

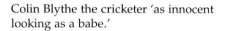

Blythe standing second from left in the Kent County Championship side. Standing, far right, is Kenneth Hutchings, fellow England international, killed on the Somme in 1916.

Tour de France winner François Faber freewheels to victory.

Memorial plaque to cyclist Francois Faber at Notre Dame de Lorette.

Boxer Arthur Ireland (No. 2) in uniform alongside fellow boxers in khaki.

French *Outdoor Life* magazine makes the connection between sport and war.

Typical small unit Army football team, 'somewhere in France'.

French football team of POWs at Minden prisoner of war camp, Germany.

Fore! Golfing soldier Lieutenant Hemmant of the Rifle Brigade; killed in 1917.

Stone cairn memorial at Contalmaison commemorating 16/Royal Scots; raised by the Heart of Midlothian Football Club.

THE LATE
LORD ROBERTS'
STIRRING WORDS
TO LONDON'S SPECIAL SERVICE BATTALION:

"I respect and honour you more than I can say. My feeling towards you is one of intense "admiration.

"HOW VERY DIFFERENT IS YOUR "ACTION TO THAT OF THE MEN "WHO CAN STILL GO ON WITH "THEIR CRICKET AND FOOTBALL

"as if the very existence of the country were not "at stake!

"THIS IS NOT THE TIME TO PLAY GAMES

"We are engaged in a life and death struggle, "and you are showing your determination to do "your duty as soldiers, and, by all means in your "power, to bring this War to a successful result. "GOD BLESS AND WATCH OVER YOU ALL."

CAN YOU READ THIS UNMOVED?

Propaganda poster with stirring words from Lord Roberts.

Men of 17/Middlesex, including the Orient star William Jonas, standing fourth from right.

Postcard photograph of the 'Sportsman's Battalion' at billets in Hornchurch, Essex.

20/London (Woolwich and Blackheath) Battalion gymnastics squad.

Bayonet fighting class, Army Gymnastic School, Aldershot 1915.

Army gymnastic staff on the Somme. CSM Coleman, seated right, was a champion wrestler.

'The Spirit of the Bayonet' 1918

Punch magazine of October 1914 exerting pressure on footballers not answering the call to fight for their country.

from shell hole to shell hole until he got close to the machine gun nest. He then leaped forward hurling the bomb at its occupants. By the light of a star shell and flare he was seen to fall as he threw the bomb. The machine gun was silenced but Harrison was not seen to get back up. Despite this the attack failed to gain further momentum and troops later fell back to their start line. Isolated groups who had got into the wood or village either fell back or were captured. By nightfall the remnants of the battalion were back in dugouts at the railway cutting near Bailleul. The 11/East Yorks War Diary records that eight officers, including Harrison, went missing that day, four more officers were wounded, nine men were killed with 150 wounded and a further ninety-eight went missing (mostly killed).

News was soon passed to Lillian of Jack being listed as missing and one can only imagine what agonising news that was to receive. Investigations began to find out what had happened to Jack after the attack. Red Cross officials were asked to see if he was listed as captured by the German guardsmen, while enlisted men were asked if they had seen him or his body.

In a different turn of fate another Rugby League player was meanwhile being applauded and cheered by 40,000 supporters at St James's Park, Newcastle. Another Yorkshireman and a former Castleford player, Thomas Bryan, then of the Northumberland Fusiliers, was awarded the VC by the King for actions at Arras in April 1917. He too had assaulted a machine gun team but had survived. Broughton and Healy Street Rugby League professional Thomas Steel also earned the VC in the Great War in Iraq. Wounded no less than eleven times in all he survived the war and continued to play post-war.

Before any confirmation of death was received by Lillian she was told of the award of the Victoria Cross to Jack. The *London Gazette* of 14 June 1917 carried the following citation for his Victoria Cross:

T/2nd Lieutenant John Harrison, MC, 11th (S) Battalion, The East Yorkshire Regiment, Oppy, France. For the most conspicuous bravery and self sacrifice in an attack. Owing to darkness and to smoke from the enemy barrage and from our own, and to the fact that our objective was in a dark wood, it was impossible to see when our barrage had lifted off the enemy front line. Nevertheless, 2nd Lieutenant John Harrison led his company against the enemy trench and under heavy rifle and machine gun fire, but was repulsed. Reorganising his command as best he could in no man's land, he again attacked in darkness under terrific fire, but with no success. Then turning round, this gallant officer single-handed made a dash at the machine gun, hoping to knock out the gun and so save the lives of many of his company. His self-sacrifice and absolute disregard of danger was an inspiring example to all (He is reported missing presumed dead).

Months passed with no news of Jack. The testimony of Private Blake, today held at the National Archives within Harrison's Service record says, 'He was our Platoon Officer. I saw him hit by a shell at Ypres (sic) on May 3rd, in the open. He was killed outright, I saw him brought in but do not know where they buried him. Blake Private 1534. 31/8/1917 Etaples.' A stretcher-bearer who later wrote of the period in his diary, tells proudly of scouring the area and not leaving any bodies uncovered, but stacking the bodies up like logs for later burial.

A communiqué from the War Council to Lillian Harrison dated 13 December finally announced that sufficient time had elapsed to inform her that Second Lieutenant Harrison's death must be accepted. It is highly likely that Jack was buried somewhere near Oppy and today lies beneath a headstone of an 'Unknown Soldier' but he is listed on the Arras memorial to the missing. Lillian was invited to Buckingham Palace in 1918 to receive the VC on behalf of Jack. Lillian's plight as a war widow with a young son was recognized by the local community who raised a fund to pay for his education in 1923. St Johns College and Lime Street School both erected memorial plaques for Jack Harrison VC MC and a development of flats was named Jack Harrison Court in the 1980s. The latest evidence that Jack is not forgotten by the rugby world is the Jack Harrison VC MC Memorial at the KC Stadium in Hull.

Finally, in honour of this extraordinary soldier and player, the Army Rugby League presented the Jack Harrison VC Memorial Trophy to the Combined Services Rugby League in the year 2000, to be contested for annually in the Inter-Services fixture between the Army and the Royal Navy. The Royal Navy is the current holder.

Chapter 10

Edgar Mobbs

'For God's sake, Sir, get down'

Every year since 1921 the Barbarians have paid a visit to Franklin Gardens in Northampton to play the East Midlands in the 'Mobbs Memorial Match'. In south-west Northampton a new one mile link road which joins the A45 and a redeveloped part of the town was opened in 2006; the road is named 'Edgar Mobbs Way'. Who is the man behind the memorial match and street signs?

Born in 1882, Edgar Mobbs was the third son of a middle class business family. Educated at Bedford Modern School (BMS) his strength and physique soon shone through on both the athletics track and field. There was no sign of his rugby prowess in his early days, he could not even make the school's First XV. It was not until his family moved to Olney that Edgar first took the oval ball game seriously, preferring hockey in his formative years.

He first played for Olney as winger aged twenty-one and then moved on to the Weston Turks, formed at the nearby village of Weston Underwood. By 1905 his skill and ability to move and handle the ball quickly was attracting attention from higher levels and he was approached by Northampton Saints. Northampton Football Club, as it was then known, was founded in 1880 by the Reverend Samuel Wigg. The Reverend was a local clergyman and curate of St James, which is how the club came to obtain its nickname of 'The Saints'. It was from these humble origins of a 'church club' which kept boys off the streets through healthy sporting activity that the 'Saints' grew into the hugely successful and popular Rugby Premiership club it is today. As the club progressed into the early 1900s one player's arrival soon began to dominate this new era. That player was Edgar Mobbs.

115

Making his debut against Bedford he had a short spell at fly-half before he moved out to the wing and two years later was appointed Club Captain. After his first eventful season he was chosen to captain the Midlands in their match against the visiting Australians. The Mobbs led Midlanders were the only side to beat the Wallabies on tour and Edgar had come to the notice of the English selectors.

He made his debut against the same Australian touring side at Blackheath – Twickenham was still a cabbage patch then – and scored England's only try in a 9-3 defeat. The next season he was chosen by his country to captain the national side in Paris. It was, however, to be his last game for England as then, just as now, politics played its part in the English rugby regime.

He played with the Saints until his retirement in 1913 but the threat of war was already darkening the horizons of Europe. Initially denied an officer's commission because, at the age of thirty-two, he was considered too old, Edgar joined as a private soldier and set about using his position to encourage others to join with him. At the next game at Franklin Gardens it was agreed that after the final whistle, Mobbs would address the crowd. A larger than average gate turned out, many to hear the advertised speech. Dressed in his straw boater he gave a short, simple address regarding his attendance at the recruiting office and asked others to join him there the following Monday. He must have been a persuasive man; over 400 men answered Mobbs' call. Of these 264 were fit enough for active service and 'Mobbs' Own' was born. Although often called Mobbs' battalion, 264 men was only enough for a company not a battalion and they subsequently became D Company of the 7th Battalion, The Northamptonshire Regiment. Following national RFU guidelines and with many members of the club departing, the Saints drew their season to a close pending the war's conclusion.

The battalion mustered and went to camp in Shoreham for training. Mobbs was soon promoted – elevated straight to Sergeant Major – but this was no easy promotion, for to hold such a rank one must have had experience of army life, procedures, discipline and protocol; none of which was held by Mobbs. He was more comfortable when 'demoted' to Sergeant. Whilst training for the best part of a year Mobbs and his D Company XV played numerous games around the country and only lost one; at the hands of the Barbarians. With training over and now posted as part of the 24th

Division with men from Bedfordshire, London, Kent, Middlesex and Sussex, the battalion embarked for France. Mobbs was promoted again and this time was commissioned as a captain.

Soon after arrival in France the division was thrown into battle at Loos on 25 September 1915. Arriving after an exhausting route march of over fifty miles in full kit in two days, 7/Northamptons were moved into trenches vacated by Scottish battalions which had attacked earlier. The survivors were drifting back and being pursued by Prussian Guards counter attacking with the bayonet. Mobbs was seen to rally his men under fire and lead charges at the burly Prussians who began to surround them. Mobbs' uniform was in shreds; torn and tattered by shell splinters and barbed wire. The battalion was withdrawn days later having suffered close to 50 per cent casualties. In the New Year of 1916, Mobbs went on leave and was asked by many anguished families about the fate of their loved ones still shown as 'missing' at Loos. He was able to offer little news or comfort. On return to the front he was promoted, first to major and then to full command of the battalion as lieutenant colonel; a promotion in fifteen months that in peace time would have taken fifteen years.

Determined to improve upon their performance at Loos 7/Northamptons were to take part in the Battle of the Somme. In fact fifty-three out of fifty-six British divisions in France that year took part in the momentous battle.

The 24th Division escaped the horrors of 1 July 1916 but was committed to battle on 18 August at Guillemont. Mobbs' battalion's progress to the battlefront was entirely typical of a battalion moving up the line; gradually moving from hutted camps, to tents, then bivouacs and finally into the trenches. At every step of the way the men were involved in working parties, digging trenches and carrying supplies at night.

Attacking from positions just east of Trones Wood, at 1445 hrs, the battalion was in the centre of an advance aiming for the heart of Guillemont. Fierce enemy resistance was based around a small quarry in front of the Northamptons and from it came streams of machine gun fire. Artillery from both sides dropped shells close to the advancing troops so it is impossible to say whose shell it was that eventually struck Edgar Mobbs. When artillery shells burst, the jagged pieces of white hot iron shell splinters whizz through the air with deadly velocity. The size of such splinters can vary from those as small as a pea to those the size of a half brick with the severity of injuries from such missiles varying accordingly. If the jagged sides of the splinter strike the body they can produce horrific injuries, whereas if the blunt outer casing hits the body the recipient might be slightly more fortunate. It was such blunt force trauma that Mobbs experienced only an hour into the attack. Hit in the ribs, with deep bruising, he was winded and doubled up with the pain. Despite his attempts to carry on it was necessary for him to get to an aid post, and, to his displeasure, he left the battalion. Only small gains were achieved by the battalion that day and a heavy price was paid, with over fifty killed, fifty missing and over 250 wounded.

To mark Edgar Mobbs' return to the battalion, a football match was arranged in October. The 'Steel Backs' as the Northamptons were known, beat the Sherwood Foresters 2-1. As winter set in Mobbs' earlier chest wound symptoms returned and he was hospitalized for a short period with bronchitis and mild trench foot. The strapping healthy rugby player of 1914 was beginning to succumb to life in the trenches, however, his sterling work both on the Somme and afterwards, was recognized and he was awarded the DSO in the New Year Honours of 1917.

The battalion still held a nucleus of sporting excellence despite the casualties and new drafts, and did very well in the brigade football competition of February 1917, winning 7-0 and 11-0 against the Trench Mortar team and Machine Gunners. Through to the final against the HQ team a very creditable 4-1 win earned them the prize of a silver cup presented by General Capper CB. Such sporting interludes punctuated the monotony of rear area 'rest' and provided distractions from the next operation on the front line. To be hit by blunt shrapnel once was a fluke but to be hit a second time in the same manner is miraculous. This second, more minor, wound received on 7 June 1917, did not, however, mean that Mobbs had to leave the battalion and there were those, including Mobbs, who were beginning to think that he had a charmed life. This did not last too long, however, for Mobbs 'copped a Blighty' on 10 June, meaning he received a further wound, serious enough to necessitate his evacuation from Ypres to England. Mobbs had been giving a briefing near the front line prior to an attack when a shell landed close by blasting all the men to their feet and showering them with debris and mud. Upon dusting themselves down and congratulating themselves on how lucky they had been it was noticed by the other officers that Mobbs had a laceration in the side of the neck and was by now bleeding profusely. He was patched up but became weak with blood loss and was evacuated.

Mobbs was by now a changed man. Injured three times and worn out with fatigue he was considerably less robust in physique but it was his psychological condition that was equally worrying for friends and family alike. Whilst at home convalescing it was noticed he seemed to have lost his energy and zeal for the fight. Perhaps weighing on his mind too were how many deaths the battalion had suffered and how many of those were men he had personally encouraged to join up, therefore perhaps sending them to their deaths? He talked also of the feeling that this was his last journey and that he would not survive the war. Such dark thoughts were far from being in print and a letter to the editor of *The Independent* of Northampton joyously talked of Colonel Mobbs being, 'back in our midst and among the lucky ones ... he says our gifts of smokes reached them in places at the front where it was impossible to buy them and they were a great boon.'

After two weeks Mobbs returned to the Ypres Salient in time for the launch of the Third Battle of Ypres, commonly called Passchendaele. In-depth rehearsals, mock attacks and briefings were held in the run up to 31 July 1917 and every man knew what was required of him and the nature of the ground and defences ahead. It is an old military dictum that no plan survives first contact with the enemy and so it was to be on 31 July at Zero hour – 0350 hrs. Mobbs soon found that his right flank, just south of the Menin Road at Shrewsbury Forest, was held up with increasing numbers of casualties being inflicted by machine guns firing from a spot known as Lower Star Post. He ordered a young subaltern and a detachment of men to join him and gather up grenades in preparation for an assault on the obstinate machine gun nest. Fellow officers begged Mobbs not to lead the attack in person in case he was killed and the battalion was left without its commander. Perhaps Mobbs' mind was made up long before that and that he had resigned himself to his appointment with fate or perhaps he thought that the mission needed leadership and momentum for which he was best suited. Perhaps his judgment was clouded and drove him on into an irresponsible mission which he should have delegated to a more junior rank.

Whatever the motives, Mobbs' small party moved out across the open ground to the attack and such was the intensity of the incoming fire that Second Lieutenant Berridge shouted, 'for God's sake, Sir, get down' but it seems that Mobbs was truly 'playing his own game' and stormed ahead trying to get within grenade throwing range. It was in vain; the enemy gunners picked him out and fired on him. He was seen to fall, injured, into a shell hole and out of sight forever. The attack did continue and despite the shellfire, machine guns and boggy, shell blasted ground, it succeeded in driving the Germans back from their positions. Unfortunately, due to the intense nature of the warfare, the darkness and the confusion, searches for the body of Lieutenant Colonel Mobbs failed to locate him and he was listed as killed at the end of the day. Mobbs' body was never found and his name is engraved, with 54,000 others on the Menin Gate at Ypres. News soon reached Northampton of the grievous losses further suffered by the 7th Battalion that day and the death of their hero, Edgar Mobbs added a particular note of sadness for the townsfolk. A flurry of letters regarding Mobbs and his death were published in the papers at local and national level. Second Lieutenant Spencer had been a student at BMS under Mobbs and wrote, 'I was perhaps one of the last to speak to Mobbs ... and we talked about Bedford', and he went on:

> ... in the tornado of shelling he got ahead and seeing a number of his men cut down charged it to bomb it – and he went down. For a man of his standing and rank it was magnificent ... I saw the old three-quarter in his own 25 yards get the ball from a crumpled scrum and get clean through and on ... One of England's finest Rugby players, in the greatest game man can play.

The battalion continued to serve on the Western Front until the war's end, suffering twice more in 1918 – once by the hand of the huge German attacks in March and later with the fatal 'flu epidemic.

On its return and demobilization in 1919 it was decided that a Mobbs Memorial Fund should raise money for some form of memorial to the man in the town. Over £2,000 was raised – £500 being donated to the East Midlands Rugby Union, a silver cup to BMS and the remainder put aside for the memorial itself. Unveiled in 1921 in the Market Square the resulting memorial was eighteen feet high topped with a bronze statue of the female goddess of fame holding a flaming torch and laurel wreath. On the base pedestal was a bronze bust of Mobbs surrounded by a wreath on either side of which were depictions of him as both sportsman and soldier. It now stands in the memorial gardens at Abington Square. The next time you see or hear of the Mobbs Memorial Match, think of him – the 'one who played the game, faithful unto death.'

Chapter 11

Colin Blythe

'A thing of beauty'

Born on 30 May 1879, Colin Blythe's life started in the family home at No. 78 Evelyn Street, Deptford. Originally hailing from Kent, his family had settled in south London in the 1840s where it ran a warehouse in Gresham Street.

His father Walter, born in 1854, was one of nine children who had found work as an engineer on leaving school before marrying Elizabeth Dready on Christmas day 1878 at St Clement's Church. At the time Elizabeth was four months pregnant with Colin.

Life in Deptford was not easy. The development of new iron ships led to the shipyard closure and the collapse of the local economy in 1867 and so, with an unemployment rate of over 30 per cent throughout the 1880s, Colin spent his formative childhood years in one of the most deprived areas of London. It would be unfair, however, to suggest that Colin's parents were unable to provide for him despite his humble surroundings. With twelve siblings, only one of which died in infancy, the family eventually sought a larger home in the more upmarket location of No. 38 Wooton Road.

After his education at Alverton Street School he entered into an apprenticeship as an engineer fitter at the Woolwich Arsenal. Determined to succeed, a combination of hard work and studying triggered a deterioration in his health and he was advised by his doctor to take as much open air exercise as possible. With hindsight this illness may have been the first bout of epilepsy that would later blight his cricket test career.

The emergence of Colin's sporting prowess remains shrouded in mystery as various sources claim that he played cricket for St

Luke's, Blackheath Boys' Club and the Royal Arsenal, although documented evidence in local press reports confirms this. Given the close proximity of the vast Blackheath where dozens of hastily arranged games played out by local youngsters could be witnessed daily, it is highly likely that he learned the art and 'grooved' his own personal style of spin bowling on its worn, uneven surface.

It was on a balmy Saturday, way off in July 1897, that Colin made his way to Rectory Field, Blackheath where the result of a Kent versus Somerset match was very much in the balance on the final day. An opening innings of 282 by Kent was followed by a knock of 253 for the visitors. Kent further extended their lead by the end of the second day to 246 runs thanks mainly to Jack Mason closing on 105 not out. Although the crowd barely outnumbered the players (the far larger draw of Middlesex versus Surrey was being played out at Lord's), Colin watched on as the Kent all-rounder Walter Wright warmed up in the nets. Though hard to believe when compared to the distance between superstar player and fan in today's modern game, Wright turned to his onlooker and asked him to 'bowl him a few.'

An additional witness to this unlikely spectacle was William McCanlis, one time captain and underhand lob bowler. With over thirty years service to Kent under his belt, his coaching days enabled him to appreciate the somewhat raw talent on display and after a handful of deliveries he arranged for Blythe to come and bowl at him one evening. The rest of the day's play left Somerset requiring 365 to win, by tea time with the last innings standing at 94 for 3 it seemed almost certain to everyone that the game would be drawn. Not so for Jack Mason whom, already having scored a century the previous day, set about dismantling the visitors taking 5 wickets for 23 runs as they were eventually dispatched by the tidy margin of 213 runs. This display was to have a profound effect on Colin Blythe as it was on the English game in general, given the chance discovery of his bowling ability earlier in the day.

Following a successful meeting and trial deliveries as arranged between Colin and McCanlis on Charlton Park, Colin was recommended for a trial at Tonbridge. He sailed through, still having received only rudimentary bowling coaching and was therefore selected for further training with Kent with a view to joining the playing staff for the opening of the 1898 season.

The Tonbridge Nursery was perhaps the country's most famous cricketing academy of its day, born out of the economic need for success – a more successful side meant increased revenue through the turnstiles. Its inception was to lead to Kent's emergence as a dominant force in the Edwardian game. Colin was one of forty-eight young players to trial in 1898 and a punishing schedule of net practice, often from 10.00 am to 5.00 pm each day, meant that Colin had to leave Deptford and seek lodgings in Tonbridge. Listening intently to his coaching staff he showed a quiet determination to succeed and was rewarded with a second season at Tonbridge for his efforts.

That year saw him in demand as a guest player for local clubs; an arrangement encouraged by his coaches as it enabled him to gain vital match practice. Bowling in excess of 600 overs with an impressive haul of 105 wickets averaging around 13, his concentration during batting practice was also reaping its rewards with a respectful average over 16 and a top score of 44 not out.

Colin made his county debut on 21 August 1899 against Yorkshire. His captain that day was none other than Jack Mason, hero of the match witnessed two years earlier on Blackheath and still idolised by the twenty year old Blythe. With fourteen straight wins behind them, Yorkshire were widely regarded as the country's top side and after losing three wickets for just a single run Frank Mitchell steadied the ship for them effortlessly racing to 55 and a more respectable score of 86 for 4. Jack Mason turned to the young Blythe to open his county career and a local reporter described the scene:

> Towards the bowling crease stepped Blythe, as innocent looking as a babe. The ball pitched just off the wicket, the burly Yorkshireman played forward, but the leg bail fell, and Blythe had phenomenally taken a wicket – and a good wicket too – from the first ball he ever bowled for his county.

He was to make a further three appearances for Kent as the season drew to a close and his eventual haul of fourteen wickets led to an entry in *Wisden* describing him as a 'new and promising' bowler. Colin Blythe had arrived on the sporting stage.

1900 saw Blythe take the cricketing world by storm, taking 114 wickets, bowling 232 maiden overs for an average of under 19. His finest moment came during the Canterbury cricket week in front of a packed house against a star-studded Lancashire side where he took 11 wickets for just 72 runs. Despite Lancashire just eclipsing their underdog hosts the crowd passed a hat around for Blythe in recognition of his efforts that day, raising a tidy sum of £7-1s-6d.

The arrival of Blythe on the stage of the national game was yet to bring financial returns. The 1901 census has him listed at his parents address in Wooton Road, Deptford and his occupation then was still recorded as 'engineer fitter'. A winter payment of twenty shillings a week topped up his earnings from working at the Woolwich Arsenal but the winter was blighted by a return of his previous illness. This did not go unnoticed by the Kent cricket authorities who arranged for a two week coastal break before he began his summer training at Tonbridge. The long summer took its toll on pitches but despite this he returned figures of 93 wickets taken, including taking the scalps of nine of the touring South African side in a single innings and this at a time when the Boer War raged on in their homeland.

His first overseas tour came on the 1901–2 Maclaren tour of Australia. Thriving on the social side of these adventures he even received a gold medal for playing for an England soccer XI against Freemantle. On the cricketing front, despite a defeat in the opening game against South Australia (although Colin took 5 wickets) his test debut was a remarkable victory. His return of 7 wickets for 56 runs off 29 overs earned him the honour of 'man of the match', resulting in the presentation of a gold pocket watch, suitably engraved. As had been the case on his county debut Blythe had made an immediate impact on the international stage.

Followers of English cricket will not be surprised to learn that the remaining four tests were lost and an injury to a finger of his bowling hand during the Adelaide test put paid to any influence he was able to have over subsequent matches.

Enjoying a sustained period of good health and now no longer required to attend the Tonbridge Nursery, the following seasons saw Blythe continue to bedazzle spectators back home. Space does not permit a detailed list of his performances but a wonderful description of his bowling style can be gleaned from the following extract from a piece by G.D. Martineau:

> As he trod his measure to the wicket, it was as though he stepped to a tune played on his own violin. Then the left arm

whipped round behind his back and came up and over in a curve as beautiful as the swoop of a gull. The ball seemed to float for an instant, then struck down and upwards – a thing of beauty.

The reference to his violin was not just poetic licence. A more than capable violinist, Colin could play a range of musical styles if required and found the instrument a perfect way to relax and distance himself from the pressures of first class cricket.

Colin was blessed with a calmness and genteel personality that rendered him likeable to all he met. His south London roots came across in a happy-go-lucky attitude and dialect that appealed to his team mates and opponents alike. Nicknamed 'Charlie' he famously once applauded Reggie Spooner for hitting a six off one of his balls announcing, 'Oh, Mr Spooner, I'd give all my bowling to bat like that.'

In every season bar one between 1902 and 1914 Colin Blythe took in excess of 100 wickets per season; the exception being 1906, which was nevertheless notable in that his Kent side won the county championship, thus breaking the monopoly held by Surrey and Yorkshire for the previous twenty years.

By 1907 he had taken part in winter tours to Australia, South Africa and America earning a further eleven test caps in the process and, whilst still working as an engineer when at home, he worked for amongst others the Maxim Gun Company. This was also the year that he met and married Janet Brown in Tonbridge (although they married in Greenwich Registry Office). The newlyweds settled in St Mary's Road, Tonbridge, much to the delight of their neighbours, privileged to have such a sporting icon in their street.

Janet, the daughter of a painter who had passed away some years earlier, was ten years younger than Colin. Extremely attractive with brown hair and big, soft eyes she was known to the Blythe family by her middle name of Gertrude. Blythe celebrated his new lease of life as a married man by taking his 1,000th wicket, continuing his good form despite a disappointing season overall for Kent which finished a disappointing eighth the season after their championship winning year. Ill health continued to take its toll on Colin with numerous cases of nervous exhaustion after important matches.

1907 also saw his most remarkable performance against county cricket new boys Northamptonshire who were destroyed by

Blythe's figures of 17 wickets for just 48 runs; an amazing feat and a record for the most wickets taken for the least number runs in first class cricket that remains to the present day. A further championship was won by Kent in 1909 with Blythe being a key element in their success again, although at various stages in the season ill-health dogged his game. That season was also a benefit year for Colin and by the end of it a sum of over £1,500 had been raised and invested in trust funds for the future and his eventual retirement.

But storm clouds were beginning to gather and 1913 saw the last great Kent victory in the county championship. Within a year Blythe, like so many of his contemporaries, would be in khaki and all thoughts of the quintessential English sounds of willow on leather and white clad players on the greensward had to be suspended.

Colin Blyth's last first class match ended in defeat against Middlesex. He took 5 for 77 in the first innings and 2 for 48 in the second and whilst there is no doubt that Colin's spiritual home was Canterbury, fittingly this display took place at the home of English cricket, Lord's.

His latter performances were punctuated with updates from the press boxes of news from France and by late August, keen to enlist, he had joined No. 1 Reserve Company of the Kent Fortress Royal Engineers along with fellow cricketer and good friend Claude Wooley. Whilst stationed on home service in the Tonbridge area Colin was able to keep tabs on the domestic game although it is widely reported that he had made the decision to retire from first class cricket irrespective of war being declared.

The Kent Fortress Companies of the Royal Engineers were a pre-war territorial unit split into six companies across the county with No. 1 at Tonbridge, No. 2 at Ashford and No. 3 at Gillingham. These were designated 'works companies' and specialised in bridge and light railway construction. Their primary role was to reinforce the defences and military infrastructure around the south coast; no simple task given the expansion of the army at the time. The first three companies were supported by Nos 4–6 based in Gillingham which carried the title 'electric light companies'. These were an early form of searchlight batteries and came into their own during the Zeppelin and later bomber raids over England. A few of the units proceeded overseas; notably No. 3 Kent Fortress Company which was involved in a tragic incident aboard HMS *Hythe* on 28 October

1915. Only weeks before the evacuation from the Gallipoli peninsular this vessel collided with another ship off the coast of Mudros which led to the loss of 127 lives.

As part of No. 1 Company, Colin had enlisted in his local territorial unit and initially remained in the Tonbridge area but as the war progressed drafts of men from his unit were eventually sent overseas.

His post-war career was in place as it is believed that, Colin, along with his wife, visited Eton College on Eton's invitation to be offered the post of chief coach when the war ended. This incident suggests that whilst he had been fairly clear about retiring from playing the game his heart was still very much in it. Sadly it was a position he never got to take up as his newly acquired military engineering skills made him a valuable commodity up the line and in mid-1917 he was attached to the 12th Battalion of the King's Own Yorkshire Light Infantry (KOYLI).

This unit had been raised in September 1914 by the West Yorkshire Coal Owners Association in Leeds. Known as a 'miner's battalion' and affectionately dubbed 'T'owd Twelfth', it formed part of the 31st Division in its role as divisional pioneers. Their first overseas posting came in December 1915 when they manned the Suez Canal defences in Egypt. The division's arrival in France the following March would culminate in it seeing action on the Somme at Serre on 1 July; the fateful first day witnessing the destruction of many of the Pals units in the division and 12/KOYLI certainly played its part in the tragic events.

The next few months were spent recovering from the Somme experience and the unit was next to see action in the Battle of Arras in the spring of 1917, most notably around Oppy Wood in May of that year.

By August 1917, 12/KOYLI were serving in the Ypres Salient engaged on light railway construction and on 2 August received a draft of 1 officer and 108 men. Sergeant 49296 Colin Blythe joined as part of that draft. A mixed bunch of Kentish men and Durham miners, they set about their dangerous work in the line at night then returned to rest in a hutted encampment just east of the ruined town of Ypres by day. As a well known sporting icon of his day, Blythe would undoubtedly have been recognised by his new colleagues. Some of the keener followers of Yorkshire cricket amongst them may even have remembered his first ball in county cricket bowled to

128

their own hero Frank Mitchell in 1899. The war diary for the unit however makes no reference to cricket being played during this period, instead listing the laborious routine of construction work followed by references to the camp being subjected to air raids when in rest. This problem continued to blight them with five men injured on 16 September, three on the 18th and two men killed the following night as the German Imperial Air Service located their camp.

It was during this time that the battalion began work on the Cambridge Spur line; this task brought Colin under the command of The ANZAC Corps during their fight for Polygon Wood. When at the front his job was skilled and dangerous; supervising night patrols laying temporary railway tracks between the trenches and ammunition stores.

A number of notable Australian cricketers were serving within the ranks of the ANZAC Corps, the most notable to lose his life was fast bowler Albert 'Tibby' Cotter. Cotter had taken 89 wickets in 21 test matches before the war and he once made an ageing W.G. Grace leave the field in disgust after continually bowling into his body; this incident taking place decades before the infamous 'body line' series. Cotter was to lose his life just days before Colin Blythe, serving in Palestine with the 12/Light Horse. It has been said that prior to the Battle of Beersheba he turned to a chum after bowling a cricket ball of compressed mud and stated, 'that's my last bowl blue, something's going to happen.' on 31 October 1917 he was shot dead by a Turkish sniper.

Blythe and Cotter had been on opposing sides in the 1907 Ashes series and at the time of Albert Cotter's death Colin Blythe was supervising work on the Wild Wood Spur; this construction and grading task would enable ammunition to reach the forward gun positions for the forthcoming operations around the Broodseinde Ridge and the village of Passchendaele.

By early November work continued on the Forest Hall, Bedlington, Gravenstafel and Pommern Castle lines, the latter running just south of the Ypres-Wieltje road. On the night of 8 November a random shrapnel shell exploded above the heads of Colin Blythe's working party and a shard of jagged shrapnel pierced his tunic passing through the leather wallet in his breast pocket and completely obliterating the photograph of his wife Janet. Colin was fatally wounded along with his colleagues Edward Bennett aged twenty-one from Chatham, Harry Dye aged twenty-seven from

Leeds and Osmond Salt a nineteen year old from Tonbridge Wells. All four were buried in the nearby Oxford Road Military Cemetery. Up until the mid 1980s it had been suggested that an Edwardian cricket ball, left by a battlefield pilgrim, lay at the foot of Colin Blythe's grave. If that had been the case it has long since disappeared. Colin is also commemorated on a memorial in the St Lawrence Cricket Ground at Canterbury, although at the time of writing there was some worrying speculation over property development to this part of the old ground. Perhaps the most memorable memorial to him, however, was captured in one of cricket's most famous paintings, 'Kent v Lancashire at Canterbury, 1906', by Albert Chevallier Tayler. This splendid work, currently on display at Lord's, captures Colin's graceful bowling action perfectly and ensures that the memory of this great sportsman lives on for cricket fans today.

Chapter 12

Sporting France in the Great War

'Les Bleus'

The nations have poured the cream of their race into the arena for the final victory.

Decoin, 1916

Like many aspects of life, sport had developed very rapidly since the turn of the twentieth century and nowhere more so than in France. Gymnastics, which had been the most practised discipline, gradually became supplanted by cycling and the so called 'English sports' of football, athletics and rugby. Spurring this transition along were events such as the restructured Olympic Games and the first Cycling Tour de France in 1903. Rugby had become popular, largely in south-west France and there were 200 Football clubs with 200,000 licensed players by 1914. Motor racing, aviation, winter sports, tennis and horse racing were also rising in popularity but largely amongst the well-to-do. The appeal of sport to the masses, however, grew due to the increasing quantity and quality of sports news coverage elevating sportsmen into household names; names which inevitably were to become even more well known during the coming war.

The sporting press regularly draws parallels between sport and war. Matches become 'battles', games become 'wars of attrition'; losing teams mount 'fight backs' and there are many more such examples in the tabloids each week. Such parallels in the newspapers of France in 1916 were entirely typical. An editorial in *L'Auto* by Parisian Henri Desgranges, entitled 'The Great Match' reminded the French people that, 'we have a long distance race to run.'

Desgranges was an award winning cyclist and key figure in the founding of the Tour de France who submitted himself to a harsh regime of fitness training and urged others to do likewise. He saw the poor state of fitness as a reason why France had performed so poorly in the Franco-Prussian War of 1870 and, to set an example, joined the French Army in 1916 despite being over fifty years old.

To feed the front with the seemingly endless lines of 'poilus' (the accepted nickname for a French Infantryman, which, taken literally, means 'the hairy ones'), meant a concerted effort to recruit, and again the sporting press, sports associations and clubs were fully involved. The French cycling union Union vélocipédique de France (UVF) urged its members to join the Forces and then provided a training package to train military cyclists. Such moves were complemented by the French National Football Federation committee proposing foreign football tours to neutral countries during 1917, in order to display French vitality and to gain support. Henry Delauney, Secretary of the Federation said, 'Sports and games should no longer be merely a fashion or an entertainment, but should be an essential part of national education and the future of our race may depend on it.'

The French nation united in total war and sport and sportsmen became another weapon in the arsenal of France and also, to a degree, its propaganda machine. In April 1916 the well known French swimmer Henri Decoin was quoted in *L'Auto* as saying:

> Who said the Olympic games of 1916 would not take place? ... Let us look at what is happening: the Olympic Games, the real games, the great games are taking place at this moment with intense fury. The nations have poured the cream of their race into the arena for the final victory.

Remember that this was being said in 1916 when the horror of the Battle of Verdun was still burning itself into the nation's psyche. This, the longest single battle of the war, lasted from February until December and claimed nearly 1,000,000 lives.

Sport was recognised in France, as in Britain, as being indispensable in preparing soldiers for combat. Parallels are frequently drawn. Throwing the cricket ball or javelin is likened to throwing grenades; running over hurdles is compared to jumping barbed wire. The French magazine *Vie au Grand Air* (Outdoor Life) declared, in June 1916: 'It is noticeable that it is among sportsmen that the best soldiers are to be found: they do not suffer from fatigue or weakness, they posses energy, coolness and presence of mind.'

Jean Bouin was possibly France's first great sportsman to fall. Mobilised into the 163rd Infantry Regiment Bouin went into battle in September 1914 with the war only a month old. As silver medallist in the 5,000 metres in the 1912 Stockholm Olympics, Bouin received media attention and gained popular support, for he displayed energy, courage and the desire to win. His death on the field of battle at Montsec, defending the Meuse region on 29 September 1914, meant that he became a national symbol. Later the Stade Jean Bouin in Paris – the ground where Stade Français now play their Rugby Union matches – was named after him. The International Rugby Board sevens tournament is also played at Stade Jean Bouin.

High in the skies above the Meuse border town of Verdun many duels in the sky were fought, as the slog of battle continued beneath the wings of the pioneering aviators. Amongst them was another sporting icon from the pioneering class; Georges Boillot. Emerging from the ranks of mechanics, as was often the case in the early days of motor racing, Boillot first raced in 1908 and in 1909 joined the Peugeot team. In 1910 he took part in the Targa Florio, the world's oldest motor racing endurance test. Always one of the toughest competitions in Europe, the first Targa Florio covered 277 miles in Sicily, through multiple hairpin curves on treacherous mountain roads, at heights where severe changes in climate frequently occurred. Two years later at the wheel of a Peugeot L76 Boillot won the French Grand Prix at Dieppe on the west coast. He became the darling of French racing fans a year later when he won the Grand Prix for a second time, at Amiens, in 1913. He then raced at Indiana in the Indianapolis 500 where he led the race for some time and, clocking 99.8 mph, came closest to reaching motor racing's Holy Grail of 100 mph. He was all set to win the coveted title when he was beset with tyre problems and fell back to fourteenth place. By then he had, in fact, already won his last race, for when the French Grand Prix of 1914 at Lyon was under way his Peugeot let him down again. Despite all manner of mechanical problems Boillot raced on just behind the leaders but finally broke down and stopped on his last lap. It was his last Grand Prix but his daring nature, mechanical skills and mastery of fast machines naturally led him to join the French Air Force when war began later that year. He had already done National Service in the Army but when mobilized in 1914 joined the Air Force, first in Escadrille (Squadron) 49 then Escadrille 65. Rising to Squadron Leader he was credited with three kills and awarded the Legion d'Honneur before his last aerial combat. Pounced on by five German Fokkers on 20 May 1916 he was shot out of the sky after first claiming one of his adversaries for himself and crashed near the Voie Sacre close to the town of Bar Le Duc.

Boillot died in the crash, but his younger brother Andre, also a racer, survived the war and went on to win the Targa Florio and dedicate the victory to his brother. In yet another amazing twist – and there are so many where sport and the Great War intertwine – George's son, Jean became the Director of Peugeot and took them into rallying in the 1980s. In another turn, the Peugeot car company named a limited edition of its late 1980s classic the Peugeot 205, the 'Roland Garros'. Garros was a noted pre-war aviator and had flown the first ever aircraft across the Mediterranean from France to Tunisia. Having then joined the French Air Force he shot down four enemy planes. He found that flying with one hand and reaching up to shoot with another weapon was troublesome and so mounted a machine gun on the nose of his aircraft. He also added armour to the propellers in order not to damage his own aircraft. This tactic was, of course, the forerunner of modern mounted forward firing machine guns.

On 18 April 1915, whilst on patrol far over the enemy lines near Langemark, Belgium with Escadrille 26 his plane developed a fuel line blockage after a dog fight in which he shot down a German Albatross aircraft – his fourth confirmed kill – and he was forced to make a landing on German held ground just after 1000 hrs. He was captured and the plane was taken away and examined. This may have contributed to what the British press later termed 'The Fokker scourge'. New planes equipped with interrupter or synchronisation gear swept our aircraft from the skies and tipped the balance of the air war in Germany's favour from late 1915 to mid 1916. Garros meanwhile was held as a POW but escaped from his German camp in February 1918. He managed to get back to French lines and rejoined his squadron. Sadly he was later shot down over the Ardennes in October 1918 and died. Not perhaps an 'Ace' but certainly a superb aviator and considered by many as possibly the world's first true fighter pilot, Garros was to leave a legacy which forever linked sport and war. The Stade Roland Garros was opened in 1920 as a venue for tennis tournaments such as the French Open at which venue the same event is held to this day.

The heavy cost to French sportsmen is also evident amongst the men who took part in that most famous of French sports – cycling – and its magnificent Tour de France event. In the 1919 race only sixty-eight cyclists took part, seventy-seven less than in 1914. Many great names had disappeared including the three winners of the 1908, 1909 and 1910 races. First competed for in 1903, the cycling Tour de France was a throw away suggestion of a promotional race to boost circulation of the aforementioned *L'Auto* sporting newspaper. The publicity stunt worked and the race proved so popular that the rival sports paper *Le Velo* was shut down. The race grew in popularity. Surrounded by controversy today, the stories behind the headlines were little different in the early 1900s. Poor behaviour, skullduggery, and downright cheating were commonplace, yet the crowds flocked to see their favourites wheel through the streets of Paris, flash through the sleepy villages of the Dordogne and haul themselves up steep mountain passes in the Alps.

The first ever double winner of the great race was a man named Lucien Mazan, who also went by the pseudonym of Lucien Petit-Breton. A native of the Loire region, he had been taken to Argentina by his father as a small boy, where he had won a bicycle in a lottery and started riding accidentally. French conscription led to him being called back to the colours on his twentieth birthday to serve with the French Army. As his service came to an end his cycling took off. In 1905 he broke the record in the one-hour race, cycling a distance of 41.1 km. The event was held on the 300 metre oval track at the Buffalo Velodrome in Paris; a stadium which took its name from the Buffalo Bill Cody circus that had used the grounds, but which was later demolished in 1915 to make way for an aircraft production factory. In his next season Mazan came second in the Tour de France. The winner that year, Rene Pottier, clearly took little satisfaction from holding the yellow jersey as he then hanged himself from the hook he used to hang his bike on. 1907 and 1908 were both victorious years for Mazan and he won the Yellow Jersey twice. Recalled to the Army in 1914, Mazan was killed in a car crash just behind the front line in 1915.

Competing against Mazan in the races of 1907 and 1908 was the next winner, Francois Faber. Born in France in 1887, with a French mother and Luxembourgian father, he had dual nationality.

135

Standing six feet two inches tall and weighing over fourteen stones. He was a very powerful athlete with great endurance and became known as 'The Colombes Giant'. He won two stages in 1908 but dominated and won in 1909, winning five consecutive stages, a record which went unbroken for nearly a century.

The race of 1909 was a pitched battle between Mother Nature and Francois Faber. The cold temperatures, rain, wind and even snow were unwelcome additions to the already demanding race schedule serving to make that Tour the most difficult since its inception in 1903, and arguably the most difficult of all time. It seems, however, that as the weather got worse, Faber got better.

After losing the sprint on stage one to Belgian Cyrille Van Hauwaert (Belgium's first ever stage winner), Faber rode the next five stages in grand style. During substantial rain storms the paved roads, with poor drainage, would flood. This caused the riders to navigate through deep flows of water and on the rural dirt roads the rain turned the route into muddy ruts.

In freezing rain on stage two he pulled away for an incredible solo 200 km through the mud and secured the stage ahead of the pack. He seemed to be thriving on the conditions whilst others faded. Further, legendary drama was to follow in stage three. Starting in temperatures only just above freezing the pack started towards Belfort. Faber attacked the front and soon pulled away in an amazing lead. Disaster struck, however, and Faber's chain snapped. Bound by rules which deny any outside help whatsoever, Faber was forced to run the last mile, pushing his bike at his side. He won the stage and astonishingly achieved it with an incredible ten minute margin! His Alcyon team manager called him, 'the God who came down to ride a bicycle.'

Lining up at 0200 hrs for the start of stage five, 3,000 loyal fans braved yet more foul weather to see the now legendary Faber. The day was to be yet another of notable incidents in this most memorable race. Faber was in the lead when a strong gust of wind sent him plunging off the road into a ditch. Brushing himself down Faber pushed on and later regained the lead only to be involved in a freak, almost comical, accident. An errant horse strayed onto the road and kicked out at Faber sending him and his bike crashing across the road. The master of adversity remounted and cycled on towards Grenoble, winning the stage.

136

His record setting fifth stage win saw him roll into Nice having dominated on the cruel and punishing climbs of Col Bayard and Col de Laffrey. With crowds swelling daily, 20,000 fans, cheering wildly, lined the route as their superstar hero crossed the line. Consistency and domination of the first half of the race enabled him to become the first 'foreigner' to win the Tour de France of 1909 which saw 150 cyclists start but only 55 finish. The determined Faber won stages in later races including two stages in the 1914 Tour, which incidentally commenced the day that Archduke Franz Ferdinand was assassinated in Sarajevo.

Faber joined the French Armed Forces as soon as war broke out, as did the 1910 winner Octave Lapize. An Olympic Bronze medallist in 1908, Lapize was best known in cycling as a 'climber' where Faber was a sprinter. For the 1910 race they were equally matched for it was the year that a new stage up into the Pyrenees was included, much to the disgust and horror of many riders and fans who thought it was too gruelling and was courting disaster. Famously Lapize is recorded to have shouted, 'Murderers, yes you, murderers!' at the organiser Henri Desgrange of *L'Auto*, as he topped out one of the vast climbs. Despite this, Lapize went on to win and Faber was second. Both winners were to die in the Great War. Faber joined the 1st Regiment of the French Foreign Legion and Lapize was another flyer whom, as a Sergeant, was shot down over Verdun in 1917. The Foreign Legion were in action across many of France's foreign battlefields but were also involved at home defending the mother country.

In what is known as the Second Battle of Artois, British and French forces attacked on a wide front with the French attempting to dislodge the Germans from their commanding positions on Vimy Ridge just north of Arras. On the morning of 9 May 1915, in a two pronged assault, the French Tenth Army attacked both from the north-west and the south-west. In order to get to the Vimy Ridge they had to first clear the Notre Dame de Lorette spur and the villages of Ablain, Souchez and Carency. All were heavily fortified and connected by deep tunnels and trenches. Days of heavy bombardment seemed to have achieved little and most of the enemy – well dug in – were waiting. At 1000 hrs the infantry of General Petain's XXXIII Corps went forward, and during the attack 'The legendary Colombes Giant', Legionnaire Francois Faber was hit and fell, fatally wounded, near Carency. The fighting along the entire front of the French attack degenerated into one long, hard slog as the Germans disputed every trench, shell hole, house and cellar. Carency remained in German hands until 12 May by which time nothing remained other than piles of rubble, burned timbers and the decomposing dead of both sides. French casualties amounted to nearly 100,000.

The French dead were cleared later and were mostly concentrated in the vast cemetery and National Memorial of Notre Dame de Lorette where now lay buried around 45,000 men; 20,000 lay in identified graves, the remainder in mass burial plots. The body of Faber was never identified. Lost in the furious fighting at Carency, this French sporting icon and cycling legend is now listed amongst the many '*disparu*' but inside the chapel, by the font, is a plaque commemorating Faber as '*Vainqueur du Tour de France Cycliste 1909, Mort pour La France*'.

Chapter 13

Boxers of the Great War

Seconds Out!

Whereas a native of southern Europe in excitement or dispute
flies to his knife and the wild westerner grips his six-shooter ...
the Britisher is handy with his fists in an emergency.

Professor A.J. Newton, 1910.

Problems of definition and controversy plague the sport of boxing
and this has led to a lack of study and exposure at the wider levels
enjoyed by, say, football or cricket through the years. It is relatively
easy, for instance, to identify a distinct body of professional footballers or cricketers who represented their league club, county, or
country at first class level, but to attempt the same for boxers is
impossible. Numerous weight divisions, regions, styles and associations all led to fragmentation of the sport and even the amateur/
professional distinction is not clear because in the early 1900s it
was not unknown for winners of 'amateur' fights to get a cash prize.
The other problem of controversy remains; boxing still evokes
passionate debate in many quarters as it involves competitors
deliberately 'fighting' and trying to inflict physical damage on each
other. This results in patchy coverage in newspapers when compared with other sports.

Boxing gloves only became mandatory in 1892, twenty-five years
after the Marquis of Queensbury's rules attempted to regulate the
boxing world (until that time eye gouging and head butting were
permitted), but the Amateur Boxing Association (ABA) was in place
by 1880 and public schools and universities encouraged boxing,
seeing it as both character building and good exercise. Social

139

commentators believed that the self-discipline of boxing may well have been the answer to post-Victorian problems of crime and hooliganism which resulted in boxing clubs being established in many of Britain's most deprived inner city areas. At the other end of the social spectrum, however, King George V and the Prince of Wales were often seen alongside the rich and famous at boxing bouts held at the National Sporting Club in Covent Garden. Boxing promotions provided mass entertainment for the working class, often attracting attendances of several thousand, and travelling fairs with boxing booths reached every corner of the country. Clearly boxing had become a major source of recreation for both spectators and participants alike in the period running up to the outbreak of war, its popularity far exceeding that of the present day. Thanks to newspapers and early cinema the most famous boxers were household names. No wonder, then, that the British Tommies soon nicknamed a powerful German artillery shell which left a smoky black trail and delivered a knockout 'punch,' a 'Jack Johnson,' after the famous African-American world heavyweight champion.

Boxing and its associated news coverage was to prove a great vehicle in the recruitment drive for the army of 1914 just as it did with football and rugby. By 12 September 1914, *Boxing* magazine featured a special patriotic cover; a soldier beckoning others to join him against a backdrop of the Union flag. *Mirror of Life and Boxing World* launched an offer of one guinea to the first fifty boxers to enlist and made rather rash claims that proportionally more boxers had joined up than any other sportsmen. There is evidence of large numbers joining up of course. Thirty-three well known Welsh boxers are known to have joined by 1915 and twenty-three members of the London Adelphi club are listed as in service in March 1915, seven of whom were already dead by that time.

With the two armed services already running boxing contests and the great recruitment drive in full swing, it is easy to see why boxers were given continuing encouragement to fight when conditions permitted. Pre-war north of England bantamweight champion, Joe Durham, joined the 7th Battalion, The Rifle Brigade and was given leave to appear at Belfast Opera House in February 1915. The blessing of the Army Gymnastic Staff (AGS) must have helped in these cases as they were keen on boxing as a tool for improving general fitness within the ranks of the New Army troops. Not all answered the call so keenly and draft dodgers seemed drawn to the dark inner city halls. Lightweight title holder Robert Spencer tried to pay an American boxer 'Dixie Kid' to lie on his behalf to avoid conscription. Duly 'rumbled', Spencer was taken to court and fined £100. Dixie, a drug user, was deported as an undesirable alien. He is reported to have also been involved in low level spying whilst in Spain and was deported again, back to the USA. Deserters were to find no refuge at the boxing halls in London. A combined Military and Metropolitan Police operation raided The Ring in Blackfriars in September 1916. As the front door was forced open at midnight many criminals, villains and deserters alike scrambled for the back doors only to have their escapes blocked by a wall of 'Red Caps' with fixed bayonets! – thirty were arrested, including seven who had avoided the call-up and seven who were absent without leave.

Another boxer who did join up and who was later embroiled in controversy was Arthur Ireland. Ironically, his picture had been used in a montage of recruited boxers by *Boxing* magazine, but a year later he was court-martialled for inciting others to 'mutiny'. Whilst at Aldershot he encouraged his comrades not to turn out for parade after their meat ration was poorly cooked and substituted with bully beef. His encouragement was seen to amount to threats and bullying and the 'mutiny' collapsed. On a far more serious note, one of those responsible for discharging shots during the infamous mutiny at Etaples in France in 1917 was British light heavyweight champion Harry Reeve.

Others who achieved more deserving attention would be the ten VC winners who are listed as boxers. These included Lance Corporal Michael O'Leary of the Irish Guards. A former mounted policeman in Canada, he stormed two barricades, knocked out a machine gun, killed eight and captured two Germans at Cuinchy in 1915. A popular song of the time, written by Jack Judge (who also wrote *It's a long way to Tipperary*) was *Have you heard of Michael O'Leary?* which was recorded and became a big hit. O'Leary survived the war, worked part-time packing poppies and later became a Mayfair doorman. In the same year, at the battle of Loos, Captain Anketell Read of the 1st Battalion, The Northamptonshire Regiment, also earned the VC but died in the action. Eight times heavyweight and twice middleweight champion in the officers' class of the Army Championships he rallied his men in an attack under extremely trying conditions, despite being smothered in gas and hit by a sniper. His remarkable powers of endurance were a testimony to his superb physical condition. He is buried at Dud Corner near Loos.

Named on the Thiepval Memorial to the Missing of the Somme is Sergeant Tom McCormick of the 12th Battalion, The Manchester Regiment. Aged twenty-five his boxing career was cut short by the war but by 1914 he had already become British, European and World welterweight champion. His battalion formed part of the 17th Northern Division and was tasked with pushing forward at Fricourt on 6 July 1916. It was reported that during the attack his last words to his sparring partner were, 'careful where you tread.'

Raising money for wounded boxers and their families helped to continue the war efforts of the boxing fraternity. A charity football match was held at Goodison Park in April 1915 between an all-star boxers' team and an Everton eleven containing eight of the 1906 FA Cup winning team. The 'Toffees' won by 3-1 in front of a crowd of 10,000. A 'pretend' engagement of fisticuffs was followed by the crowd 'counting out' a player knocked down in the box.

Soldiers tried to carry on their chosen sports wherever they happened to be whilst not actually in the front line. Providing a useful diversion and therapeutic interlude to life in the trenches were key motivating factors in addition to that of maintaining fitness levels. Brigade and divisional competitions were held to foster these elements. The winner of an open heavyweight bout in 1916 for the 21st Division was Sergeant Harry Littlewood of the 9th Battalion, KOYLI. Deserving of special mention, Littlewood was a fine boxer of considerable standing. He packed a hefty punch for a nine stone fighter and won twenty-three of his first twenty-seven fights. Going on to nearly 100 victories he won the prestigious twenty round Pitman title in 1913 for boxers employed in the mines. Born in Wakefield, Yorkshire, *The Sporting Chronicle* of August 1916 carried an obituary for him stating that, 'he was one of the most gentlemanly young fellows who ever entered the ring; a clever boxer who never exceeded the bounds of good sportsmanship.'

Littlewood was also killed near Fricourt on the Somme on the opening day of the Somme offensive on 1 July 1916 and is buried at Gordon Dump cemetery.

There were few fairy tale comebacks and a great number of returning boxers after the war were compelled to give up their careers as a result of their serious wounds. Some, driven by their plight, even resorted to what amounted to little more than taking part in 'freak shows' in which one-legged boxers would challenge similarly affected all-comers. Whether many of these potentially degrading spectacles took place we cannot say, but whether aristocrat or miner, champion or journeyman, these boxing men had good reason to say they had gone the distance for their country in its greatest fight. As General Sir Charles Harrington remarked in 1919, 'Few have realised what we owe to the boxing glove and the football; the two greatest factors in restoring and upholding morale.'

Chapter 14

Association Football
Goes to War

Football was already at war in the summer of 1914; at war with itself. Growing into a sport played by the masses, for the masses, control was being wrenched from the ruling classes which had for so long yearned to retain the game's amateur status. They were fighting a losing battle for thousands of fans, the professional players, club staffs and even some board members were overwhelmingly from working class backgrounds. The actual outbreak of the war in 1914 and the massive recruiting drives that followed provided an opportunity for some to try and restore the romantic idea that players should be amateurs. The press, Parliament and the Church all conspired to bring an end to the professional game in 1914, an abolition that would have meant the end of clubs then still in their infancy and an end to those clubs that most of us love and cheer for today. Fortunately most of our clubs laboured long and hard throughout the war to hold on until the final whistle, keeping their status, maintaining their grounds and even retaining some players.

How this feat was achieved can be told through the story of two great clubs, the authors' favourite clubs, Charlton Athletic and West Ham United. Whilst these are only a few miles apart in east and south-east London, they are separated by differing social demographics, the Thames and the clubs' wartime paths.

Tough 'Hammer men' of the Victorian era forged and beat the iron in the foundries along the north bank of the River Thames helping make some of the greatest ships ever launched from the docklands of east London. From the Thames iron works and its spirited Corinthian workforce sprung a football team known first, in 1895, as The Thames Iron Works and later simply West Ham United (The Hammers).

Playing in the Southern League, at the Boleyn Ground, they averaged crowds of 12,000 to 15,000 in the season 1913–1914. Pitted against other clubs such as, Swindon, Bristol Rovers, Watford, Reading, Crystal Palace, Brighton and local rivals Milwall they finished sixth in the league. The players and staff had enjoyed the summer recess of 1914 and the new Southern League season was just getting underway when war broke out.

The boss at West Ham was Sydney King; an outsize, larger-than-life character with close-cropped grey hair and a flowing moustache. He was a 'personality plus' man, a man with flair who liked a drink and led the club for nearly thirty years. King and the board decided to try and complete the 1914–15 season thinking, as was the case for most, that the war would be 'over by Christmas.' Many suggested it unsavoury to carry on playing games whilst others fought abroad, yet some saw the continuance of the games as an effort not only to help with recruiting drives at matches but as a method of showing a semblance of normality and a diversion away from the tensions of war.

Just across the Thames a promising amateur side, Charlton Athletic, had evolved in the shadow of Woolwich Arsenal. Playing on a pitch near to today's Millennium Dome, opposing sides were treated to post match haddock and chips giving rise to the nickname 'The Addicks', which survives to this day. Charlton's rise through the local leagues was steady and when the Arsenal moved north in 1913 it took up the mantle as the senior club in the area. Situated in a heavily populated area of dock workers and heavy industry, it also attracted extensive support from suburban Kent; a tradition that remains.

In March 1915 a meeting was held to discuss the immediate future of Charlton Athletic as attendances since the outbreak of war had steadily diminished. Players were equally hard to come by and as the 1927–8 handbook so succinctly put it: 'The majority of the boys left to take part in the greater game overseas.' Faced with such severe financial and playing restrictions the brave but unanimous decision was taken to close down operations for the duration of the Great War.

145

Across the river at Upton Park, however, the decision was taken to carry on playing in the Southern League for the 1914–15 season. A representative from the club was present at the passing of a resolution from London Clubs:

> While strongly of the opinion that the present agitation section of the London Daily Press is unscrupulous, unwarrantable and undignified and wholly opposed to English traditions and is an abuse of the liberty of the press, [we are] nevertheless prepared to discontinue and close the grounds simultaneously with the closing of racecourses, golf links, theatres, music halls, picture palaces and kindred entertainments.

Few present could have foreseen that it would take over four years and 713,000 British lives before peace would return to Europe and thoughts could once again turn to the beautiful game.

Of course many supporters and some players from both clubs went immediately to join the armed forces or to work in nearby munitions factories; some as pre-existing Territorials, others to join Kitchener's New Armies.

For Charlton lads both the Royal Artillery (in 1914 this arm was split into three branches-the Royal Horse Artillery, The Royal Field Artillery and The Royal Garrison Artillery) and the rapidly expanding Army Veterinary Corps (from 900 to 28,000 men by 1917) were based in nearby Woolwich and drew many of the 'Addicks'. In addition a number of war raised infantry battalions recruited from south-east London, amongst them the 11th (Lewisham) Battalion, The Royal West Kent Regiment and the 12th (Bermondsey) Battalion, The East Surrey Regiment. The region also supplied many men to the London Regiment, a territorial formation that had been formed in 1908 from old local militias. The 15th (Civil Service Rifles) Battalion included a company made up of employees of the Woolwich Ferry and the Blackwall Tunnel, the 21st (First Surrey Rifles) Battalion were based in Camberwell and the 20th (Woolwich and Blackheath) Battalion were housed in the impressive Holly Hedge House in Blackheath, a building subsequently destroyed in the Blitz.

The 20/London was full when war was declared with many Charlton supporters already in its ranks. Like other London Regiment units, membership proved so popular that a second battalion (2/20th) was raised from local stock and also served overseas for the duration of the war. As well as its Blackheath Headquarters,

20/London had a number of satellite recruiting depots including Trafalgar Road, Greenwich just a five minute walk from the football ground. How many of the remaining officials and supporters marched in following the meeting to wind the club up in March 1915 is a matter for conjecture but what we do know is that the original building survives today as a body piercing studio! These battalions of the London Regiment battalions would go on to fight with distinction at Loos, High Wood, Ypres, Salonika and Beersheba.

Upton Park is now well and truly within the London Borough of Newham but in the 1900s it was still part of Essex. This county affiliation was a factor which influenced recruiting for the Essex Regiment. As early as December 1914 the Mayor of West Ham was authorised to raise a further local unit. The ranks of the 13th (Service) Battalion, The Essex Regiment, informally known as 'The Hammers' or 'West Ham Pals' were thus swelled with West Ham supporters and workers from the ironworks. Their path to war was initially to be with 33rd Division but around the time of the battalion's arrival in France in November 1915 they were transferred to 6 Brigade of the regular 2nd Division. One may be forgiven for thinking that the existence of these pals' units was a purely northern phenomenon, due to a heavy slant in the literature of the Great War, but many such units sprang up in London and the south. Like the rest of the country, locals were not restricted to joining one unit and around Upton Park other supporters joined the 1st/17th Battalion, The London Regiment (Poplar and Stepney Rifles). Later Mayor Crow also pushed to recruit a local Field Artillery Brigade and ultimately raised a Howitzer Brigade (179). The gunners from West Ham along with others raised at the ironworks formed the bulk of the Artillery for the 39th Division.

Whilst Charlton Athletic effectively wound up, records show that thirty members of the club's playing and administration staff joined the forces during the Great War and that four lost their lives whilst another seven were severely wounded. Amongst the casualties was the former club secretary John Mackenzie of No. 5 York Street, Charlton. John a founding member of the club in 1905 was a lifelong seaman, he returned to sea as a ship's cook in November 1908 and was killed on 30 September 1917 aboard the SS *Heron* aged twenty-eight. Today he is commemorated on the Tower Hill Memorial.

Another club casualty was Fred Chick. He appears in the 1913–14 team photograph in the attire of one of the training staff and is listed in the casualty return for the 13th Battalion, The Middlesex Regiment, a unit formed in Mill Hill some distance from Charlton and partially an overspill for those joining the 17th (Footballer's) Battalion of the Middlesex Regiment. As Private 245365 Frederick Chick, Royal West Kent Hussars attached 13/Middlesex, he was killed on the Somme on 31 August 1916, and is buried in Caterpillar Valley Cemetery, Longueval. Also serving King and Country from Charlton was Private 656981 Albert Purdy of the 21/London (First Surrey Rifles), Albert was a survivor of the fighting at High Wood on the Somme. Signed from Tottenham Hotspur he played at right half but owing to lasting wounds received he was never the same defender post-war and doubled as a groundsman. Here he put his unique 'rat catching' skills, developed on the Western Front, to good use and was often seen beneath the main stand at The Valley catching rodents.

Another post-war player for the Addicks, Arthur Whalley was a centre back known as 'the Black Prince'. Whalley had been charged with match fixing alongside Sandy Turnbull – featured elsewhere in this book – whilst in the colours of Manchester United. Though he did not take part in the infamous game against Liverpool on Good Friday 1915, he was found guilty of taking part in the scandal and permanently suspended from football. To his credit he headed south to enlist in the newly formed 17/Middlesex (Footballer's). Sergeant F/1930 A. Whalley was wounded at the battle of Passchendaele in 1917 and in the light of his war service his ban was lifted by the authorities in 1919 and after a brief spell at Southend United he went onto play ninety-eight times for Charlton scoring nine goals.

Finishing fourth in the Southern League for the 1915 season was the last vestige of normality for the war Hammers. A new, highly rated centre forward – Hackney born Arthur Stallard – had made his name at West Ham, helping them to their high league position and scoring seven goals in the last eleven games. Playing sporadically in claret and blue for the following two years, he is best remembered for putting five past the hapless Millwall keeper in a friendly in 1916. Alas, his goal scoring potential was cut short as he enlisted in the 14/London (London Scottish) and was killed at the Battle of Cambrai on 30 November 1917. Only eight months earlier he had been playing for the first XI. On that momentous day near the village of Moeuvres the London Jocks, as part of 56th (London)

Division held on valiantly to a stretch of the recently captured Hindenburg line, against overwhelming odds:

> The 30th November will be a proud day in the lives of all those splendid British soldiers who by their single hearted devotion to duty, prevented what would have been a serious situation had they given way. [It was] a glorious achievement in which the enemy had come against them at full strength and had been defeated with losses at which even the victors stood aghast.

Stallard is today commemorated on the Louverval memorial to the missing of the Cambrai battle. By contrast his team mate, Hammers goalkeeper Joe Webster, joined up early on the creation of the 17/ Middlesex (Footballer's Battalion). Surviving the war, he returned to keep goal in 1919.

The FA took the decision to suspend the footballing leagues for the duration at the close of the 1914–15 season. They banned any professional signings, banned professionals being paid and restricted games to being played only on Saturday afternoons so as not to clash with essential war efforts. They did, however, agree that 'combinations' of regional teams could continue to play, as long as no cups or medals were awarded. This essentially meant that players could continue performing but without remuneration. Regionalisation was urged to reduce unnecessary travel costs and this resulted in three wartime leagues emerging which would become known as the Lancashire, Midlands and London Combinations. West Ham found themselves pitted against the likes of Chelsea, Millwall, Arsenal, Fulham, Tottenham, Queens Park Rangers and Watford in local derbys for the next three seasons. One player whom we must not fail to mention during the 'combination' years was Danny Shea. Prior to the war he had been West Ham's highest scorer for four consecutive years and was then signed for a record breaking £2,000 by Blackburn Rovers. Dan's share was £550, a massive sum at that time. Starting for Blackburn in 1913 he made a great start scoring twenty-eight goals in thirty-six games. Danny returned south when war broke out and made a further seventy-five appearances in claret and blue as what was termed a 'guest player'. These players, like Danny, were by that time nearly all employed as munitions workers and so could play for clubs as and when they chose in their free time. Danny Shea's ability to strike a ball like a thunderbolt from his position at inside right, coupled with an eye for tactics way ahead of his time made him a most valuable player before and during the war years.

Outside of the league action the FA Cup final of May 1915 was played between Chelsea and Sheffield United. Old Trafford hosted the game on what has been described as a 'grey and austere day', in front of a sombre crowd. The crowd was dominated by men home on leave or in training and largely wearing army uniforms. It therefore became known as 'The Khaki Cup Final'. The mood of the crowd seemed reflected in the play on the field, especially from the London club, which failed to shine without showing a glimmer of the magic they had displayed for the previous twelve months. An early mistake by Chelsea keeper Jim Molyneux was pounced on by Jim Simmons (who signed for Hammers in 1920) and the Blades of Sheffield went one up. Two more goals compounded the misery and it finished 3-0 to the Blades. Mention must be made here of one Chelsea player – their centre forward Bobby 'Winker' Thompson – who surely must be the only ever player to appear in an FA Cup Final with only one eye! The victorious players lined up for their winners' medals and the presentation of the last cup of the war era. Lord Derby presented the cup to their captain, George Utley with the rousing speech, 'You have played with one another and against one another for the cup, play with one another for England now!'

Lord Derby (Edward Stanley, 17th Earl of Derby) KG, GCB, GCVO, TD, had served in the Grenadier Guards and went on to become Secretary of State for War 1916–18, but he is remembered most for his role as Director General of Recruiting, a position he took up in the autumn of 1915. His words at Old Trafford reflected both his and the Government's need to rejuvenate dwindling volunteer numbers at army depots. In what became known as the 'Derby Scheme' men between the ages of eighteen to forty were urged to register and volunteer before conscription called them up. Lord Derby's words at Old Trafford effectively ended conventional, organised football until 1919.

Players continued to hang up their boots and serve King and Country, although some were actually found not fit for service, usually with ear and eye problems. Ironically, by 1917, the anti-football lobby was becoming slightly less vocal but by then it was too late in any case as it proved increasingly hard for clubs to carry on. Another who had gone overseas was Frank 'Bronco' Burton, standing at over six feet the Mexican born full back played for both

150

West Ham and Charlton. His war service saw him sign on as Sergeant GS/47737 F. Burton of the Royal Fusiliers; he originally joined the 23rd (Sportsman's) Battalion but was later transferred to the 1st Battalion. Whilst overseas he saw action at Ypres, the Somme and Cambrai, was wounded no less than six times and was awarded the Croix-de-Guerre for bravery. He went on to play 107 times for the Addicks between 1921 and 1925.

The soldier sportsman to have the biggest impact on Charlton Athletic was a young coal miner from Tyneside who had signed professional terms for his boyhood heroes Sunderland in April 1914. Just three months into his new career and with the season yet to start, war was declared. Originally joining the Army Cyclist Corps in Sunderland with his team mates, he was drafted overseas as Private 22934 Jimmy Seed, 1/8th Battalion, The West Yorkshire Regiment (The Leeds Rifles). Whilst his brother Alex, also a professional footballer, would go on to win the Military Medal with the 17/(Footballer's) Middlesex, Jimmy would be gassed in early November 1918 just days before the end of the war. The effects of this gas wound prematurely ended his Sunderland dream, for on his return from the war he was found to be not fully fit and they released him.

Seed resurrected his playing career with Spurs – picking up a 1921 FA Cup winner's medal – and Sheffield Wednesday, where he captained the side to the league title twice. On turning to management he joined Charlton in 1933 and both parties never looked back. Successive promotions took them from the Third to First Divisions in which they were placed runners-up in their first season; four Cup Final appearances between 1943 and 1947 drew regular crowds of 70,000 plus to The Valley, a stadium whose south stand today proudly bears Seed's name.

The Combination League really had kept West Ham United alive during the war years and many suggest that that experience helped elevate the club into the Second Division in 1919 followed by further promotion to the First Division four seasons later. This rise may have been deserved; after all during the war they won more matches and scored more goals in London than any other team despite being outside the old 'top league'. Perhaps in a way the tale of West Ham at war tells the story of English football in general; whilst many clubs prospered others simply faded away.

151

If it had not been for the Great War the top teams of the modern day Premier League, the so called 'big four', may now read Clapton Orient, Merthyr Tydfil, Rotherham County and South Shields, not Arsenal, Manchester United, Chelsea and Liverpool.

Whilst the Hammers could perhaps be said to have profited from the war, the West Ham Pals of the 13/Essex had served with distinction throughout and suffered heavily. During their time on the Somme in late July 1916 they spent time around Delville Wood and Guillemont and later, in November 1916, they served near the Redan sector and assaulted old ground near 'The Quadrilateral', an area littered with the dead of the previous July. Service continued in 1917 during the Battles of Arras and the Scarpe and then Cambrai. Before the end of the war, army reorganization led to the disbandment of many battalions in the spring of 1918 and with their battle cry 'up the irons' still ringing out the 13/Essex passed from the British Army. The total losses of men killed for the West Ham Pals numbered some 585 enlisted men and eighteen officers, this equates to one officer for every thirty-two men becoming casualties, similar to the ratio of officers to men in an infantry platoon and further evidence towards debunking the myth that officers did not die in the same proportion as enlisted men. West Ham fans today are fiercely proud of such lineage and know that, 'All these fought most valiantly. Their names are inscribed in the annals of the nation.'

Whilst we, as authors, have concentrated on our own two favourite sides, players from teams the length and breadth of Britain played their role in the Great War. Glasgow Celtic player Willy Angus was awarded a VC at Givenchy in 1915 and wounded so severely he never played for 'The Hoops' again. The club lost a further seven players during the war including Leigh Roose, a Welsh international goalkeeper who was awarded the Military Medal before his death on the Somme with the 9th Battalion, The Royal Fusiliers in October 1916.

Perhaps their most famous loss was the club legend Peter Johnstone. Having made 223 appearances and starring in the side that claimed six Scottish titles in a row, he was killed at the Rouex Chemical Works in May 1917 with the 6th Battalion, The Seaforth Highlanders and is listed alongside so many great sportsman on the Arras Memorial to the Missing.

152

Aston Villa were a leading pre-war side and lost their talented wing half Tommy Barber at Passchendaele on 16 August 1917 whilst serving in the 2/4th Battalion, The Oxfordshire and Buckinghamshire Light Infantry. Local Midlands giants West Bromwich Albion supplied a company of the 5th Battalion, The South Staffordshire Regiment and fought on the Western Front in the 46th North Midland Division.

William 'Tommy' Fiske who kept goal 217 times for Blackpool was described in a post-match report as, 'dashing and daring in his defence of goal, and was nimble as a cat with shots at close quarters.' He was killed on the Aisne in May 1918 whilst a sergeant in the 8th Battalion, The Border Regiment, last seen 'going over the top in his shirt sleeves' his body was never found and is commemorated on the Soissons Memorial. Swansea City players and supporters joined together forming the core of the 14th Battalion, The Welsh Regiment. Raised in Swansea in October 1914 by the Mayor and the Swansea Football and Cricket Club they served at Mametz Wood as part of the 38th Welsh Division. Welsh rivals Cardiff City also supplied men and supporters to the division, their local MP Lord Ninian Crichton Stuart, an ex-soldier, had acted as guarantor for the club's new ground. When opened in 1910 it was named Ninian Park in his honour; alas today marked for closure it bore his name for almost a century. As commanding officer of the 6th Battalion, The Welsh Regiment he was killed near Loos in October 1915.

North-east giants Newcastle United had forty-two members of staff who served in the colours during the Great War; five were never to return including Dan Dunglinson and Thomas Goodwill who fell side by side at Thiepval with the 16th Battalion, The Northumberland Fusiliers on the first day of the Somme.

Smaller clubs also boast a Great War heritage. The story of Clapton Orient is linked to the raising of the Footballer's Battalion and is told elsewhere in this book but lesser known is the contribution of their neighbours Ilford FC. Among the founder members of the Southern League in 1889, as a top amateur side they regularly travelled Europe prior to the Great War, their final tour match being as late as April 1914 in Kiel, the home of the Imperial German Navy.

Of the thirty-seven men who swapped football kit for khaki, five had played as amateur internationals for England. Amongst them, club captain Joe Dines lost his life in September 1918 as a Captain in the 13th Battalion, The King's Liverpool Regiment. The former school teacher was joined in the Roll of Honour of the club by Richard Deal of the Royal Engineers and Henry Fleming of 23/London Regiment; neither of which have a known grave.

Ernest Edgar Ellis had started his career with home town club Norwich City, before transferring to the 1912 FA Cup winners Barnsley, he remained a member of the 'Tykes' first team before moving north once more to Heart of Midlothian in time for their 1914 pre-season tour of Denmark. Like so many Tynecastle men he joined the 16th Battalion, The Royal Scots and was killed on the outskirts of Contalmaison during their fateful attack on 1 July 1916.

Harry Hanger was a stylish wing half who had played for Northampton Town and Bradford City before joining Crystal Palace in 1909 a club for which he would make 178 appearances. One match report read: 'No player has shown greater ability to retain possession of the ball, and his passes are invariably accurate and reach a forward so that the latter can make rapid headway.'

One of the first to enlist, Hangar gained the 1914 Star entering the theatre of war in France on 6 October 1914, serving with the 5th Battalion, The Royal Irish Lancers. He was killed on 23 March 1918 and is commemorated on the Pozieres Memorial to the Missing.

Football managed to survive the war and emerge better supported and more powerful than in 1914 but it could so easily have been taken away from the fans. This lesson was remembered in 1939 when war broke out a second time, as there was no clamouring for its immediate cessation. Football attendances grew dramatically after the Armistice but as the 1918–19 Combination season was already underway, the FA were insisting that the state that had existed prior to 1914, in terms of which teams played against each other and gate receipts, had to return before the players could be paid again. Thus there was no immediate return to normality. Clubs were reminded of their duty to those that had played 'the greater game'. The closing of the season in spring 1919 saw the busiest ever 'transfer window' as frantic bidding, often accompanied by squabbling, went on up and down the country with each club attempting to secure the burgeoning ranks of 'free agent' players. After that particular transfer 'free for all', full service was resumed and before long the players would run out once more to take their place on the football pitches of Britain in playing the 'beautiful game'.

Chapter 15

Sporting Units Raised during the Great War

Fore! King and Country – 13th Battalion, The Rifle Brigade

Sharing the call to duty with fellow sportsmen across the Empire was top golfer Albert Tingey. He perhaps felt the coming of war more personally than fellow professionals in England. As a founding member of the Professional Golfers Association (PGA) he had started a golf school in Paris in 1913 and his successful venture into France extended to Fontainebleau early the following year until French fears of the spectre of a German Army marching down the Champs Elysees scuppered further plans for expansion.

Returning to 'Blighty' via Dunkirk Tingey contacted fellow PGA member Charles Mayo with regard to raising a 'pals' unit from the sport. Charles Mayo was equally committed to war with Germany. As the professional of Burhill Golf Club in Surrey, owned by the Guinness family, he had recently taken to designing a new course at nearby Bramley. That course was due for its official opening in the spring of 1914 with the guest of honour being Prince Albert of Schleswig-Holstein. But uncertainties in Europe had by then overtaken the plans for the new course and another golfing career was halted in its tracks.

Initially known as the 'Niblick Brigade', the PGA gave the idea its full support with members William Robertson Reith and Wilfred Reid offering assistance. George Duncan, a British Open winner in 1920 who had once been offered a contract to play football for

Aberdeen, was also in the fold and between them it was decided that potential recruits should be single with no children.

Initially twenty-six men were accepted, many bringing their caddies along with them. A number of married men were turned away including William Robertson Reith who eventually joined the Royal Sussex Regiment in 1916.

The 'Niblicks' met for the first time in September 1914 at a luncheon at Gatti's Italian Restaurant in London's White Cross Street. After attendance at the nearest recruiting office it was learnt that places could be secured in the newly formed service battalions of the Rifle Brigade. The men then met with reporters and photographers from the golfing world at the base of Nelson's Column in Trafalgar Square. Few could have anticipated the events which lay ahead before the same column in front of which they had gathered would be permanently damaged by fire during the Armistice celebrations over four years later.

With places in the army filling fast they set off for Winchester immediately, full of enthusiasm and with their King's shilling already spent, the battalion history notes:

> Day after day in the late summer of 1914, hundreds of men pressed up the High Street of Winchester to the arched west gate of the Rifle Depot. All sorts and conditions of men, navvies, stockbrokers, artisans, clerks, miners, golf professionals, artists and students, they besieged the barrack square and waited long hours until the harassed staff could enrol them. At last they were sorted out and some of them eventually became the 13th (Service) Battalion of the Rifle Brigade.

The golfing pals served with B Company and having enlisted together shared service numbers starting S/44. They were not alone in their sporting prowess within the battalion; a sizable contingent of Stockton lads played football together as semi-professionals and would go on to make the 13/Rifle Brigade first XI the envy of the division. One of their officers, Captain Arnold Strode Jackson, had snatched a gold medal from the fancied Americans in the 1,500 metres at the Stockholm Olympics in 1912. The race had ended in a dramatic close finish after a very slow start and only after the judges had examined the photographic finish could the result be confirmed. Equally skilful at hockey, rowing and football, at which sports he had won Blues at Oxford, Jackson ended the war with four DSOs, three wound stripes that ended his sporting career and in command of a brigade, all at the age of twenty-seven.

The early days of army life were very similar for the vast majority of Kitchener's Army; learning to salute, to march, to clean and polish and taking part in seemingly endless hours of military instruction. It was not without its lighter moments, however, and what the ex-regular army men lacked in teaching skills they made up for by their enthusiasm and experience. The men of 13/Rifle Brigade recalled one such instructor concluding his lecture with the words, 'fall out them men what ain't had their names took; and them what ain't here today fall in again tomorrow!'

French leave was one way of escaping the lessons to snatch a few holes of golf and this involved scrambling over the high barrack walls between passing sentries. Slowly but surely, training and the arrival of kit shaped the men into a fighting force and by late November they had been billeted in High Wycombe. As the first male soldiers into the town the battalion history notes that they were given, 'a cordial welcome and in time many hearts were conquered by the charm of the Wycombe lassies.'

On one afternoon the golfers of B Company were the guests of Lady Astor at Cliveden Grange. Whilst many were admiring the lawns suitable for an 18th Green, the offer of some refreshment was welcome news. The men, unaware of their hostesse's teetotal values, were perhaps a little ungrateful on the receipt of 'two woodbines and a glass of lemonade'. Throughout their training in England Albert Tingey kept readers updated with the progress of the battalion via a regular feature in *Golf Monthly*.

By the April of 1915 13/Rifle Brigade were undergoing their final phases of training at Ludgershall on Salisbury Plain. It was rumoured, via a storeman, that the battalion's destination was to be the Dardanelles but this proved incorrect as a few weeks later the battalion was formally warned for France. Setting sail on the *Mona's Queen*, they slipped out of the Solent for the front on 29 July 1915. Some of those on board would never play the links again.

Their first experience of trench life came on 18 August when A and B Companies entered the front line near Armentières to come under the instruction of the 6th Battalion, The Queen's Own Royal West Kent Regiment and the 6th Battalion, The East Kent Regiment

(The Buffs). By September they were deemed able to defend their own trench and as part of the 37th Division they took over the Gommecourt sector from French troops with the Niblicks Brigade taking up positions near Fonquevillers. Updates from Tingey continued including the worrying incident of the rum ration being lost down a sump hole, retrieved only by the use of improvised fishing tackle and a determined Sergeant Major. Alongside Albert Tingey's news from the front was published a 'ditty' from an officer serving in the battalion:

A   is for the army of golfers and pros, who in Greece and in Flanders are facing our foes.

B   is the bombs that we're using for balls, our opponent lies dead whenever one falls.

C   is our Corps – not a rubber core now, but the pride of the army as French will allow.

D   is the driver – who comes with his car, to keep up our stock of munitions of war.

E   is the expert, our line who determines, he lays out the course as we lay out the Germans.

F   is the flagstick that through thick and thin, we'll carry and plant on the walls of Berlin.

G   is the game that we know how to play, however our opponents may wander astray.

H   is the hazards, from snipers and shell, but as long as we're careful we'll do pretty well.

I   is the iron that entered our soul, when a shot through our frying pan drilled a neat hole.

J   is a joke that is capital fun, when we aim at the sniper and hole out in one.

K   is the Kultur that is held by the ghouls, as a perfect excuse to keep breaking the rules.

L   is the language we use in the trenches; through practice at golf we astonish the Frenchies.

M   is the Mashie approaches we play, for the Huns are not more than a chip away.

N   is the Niblick we carry about, to dig ourselves in, and dig our boots out.

O   is the odd we at first had to play, but the Huns playing three more the rest of the way.

P is the pitch that we chose for our tent, it is weak as to headroom but cheap as to rent.

Q is the quarry that shelters our band, and were all full of grit for there's plenty of sand.

R is a run up as we're told to advance, the rage of the foe through whose trenches we prance.

S is the stymie we laid for the Hun, who putted for Calais but found himself done.

T is the trench that we carried one day, out driving the Germans who stood in our way.

U is the U Boat we dodged coming over, for we putted first and was run down of Dover.

V is the victory we're going to score, we feel we can do it by five up and four.

X is the extra delight we shall know, whence once more to the links we are able to go.

Y is for Ypres we're billeted near there, and the town's best described as ground under repair.

Z is for Zeps if they fly over the town, we give them a lofted shot that brings them down.

The year ended with the men of 13/Rifle Brigade out of the line at Humbercourt; their first Christmas on foreign soil was one not to be forgotten. B Company had £50 in their kitty and forward planning with Messrs Fortnum and Mason resulted in a banquet of turkey pheasant and ham. The feast, lasting from lunchtime to late evening, concluded in a concert party at which most of the audience were unconscious from an excess of whisky, claret and champagne.

By early 1916 the battalion were occupying the line near Le Gastineau; it was here the 'Niblicks' suffered their first casualty when Riflemen S/4407 Herbert Line was wounded, an incident described here by colleague S/4406 William Eastwood, himself a later casualty of the war:

> Rifleman Herbert Line, formally assistant at le Touquet, has been struck in the face by a bullet which ricocheted off the ammunition pouch of another recruit. Another rifleman went to Line's assistance but was hit through the lung and died before reaching hospital but Line himself was able, with the help of stretcher bearers, to walk to the dressing station. We are happy to say that he is already on the fairway to recover.

It was whilst out of the line in the pleasant village of Auxi le Chateau that the Niblicks, which had by now acquired an eclectic selection of golf clubs, would arrange putting and driving competitions. Many officers in the battalion had an interest in the sport and the opportunity to play alongside professionals was too good to miss.

It was around this time that *Golfing* magazine made reference to a fellow professional and golf course designer Ramsey Ross, serving in the Honourable Artillery Company. He had 'gone one better' than the Niblicks and actually built a course in the Ypres Salient! He was not alone. By the end of 1916 a further course had been constructed in Flanders with the help of Scottish pro Tom Fernie, then a member of the 9th Battalion, The Highland Light Infantry. The popularity of these facilities proved too much for the General Staff, they were losing too many vital man hours when officers went to play. Rather than close down the two courses they took the decision to construct a separate nine-hole course for the use of their attached staff near St Omer and this time they utilised the services of Allan Gardiner, a sports journalist then serving in the 12th Battalion, The Royal Irish Rifles, to design the course. *Golfing* magazine set up an appeal for unwanted golf balls (these had trebled in value since the war had begun due to the inflated price of rubber), to be donated for the men in France. What with barbed wire marking out the fairways, shell holes forming bunkers and water hazards and accompanied by the sound of the distant guns it must have seemed a far cry from Lytham St Annes or St Andrews.

For the men of 13/Rifle Brigade the following summer would change their battalion forever. By the time they marched beneath the shattered remains of the Basilica in Albert, the Battle of the Somme was in full swing. Temporarily attached to the 34th Division they renewed the attack towards Contalmaison on 10 July 1916.

Largely overlooked, this aborted battalion attack was launched at 0845 hrs, the men, as if on Salisbury Plain attacked in perfect formation. Just as they had completed the crossing of no man's land under a murderous German barrage and had entered the enemy trenches, the message that the advance had been cancelled reached them. In the resulting retirement further losses were incurred and by the time what was left of battalion had scurried back to safety and the roll call had been completed, twenty officers and 380 men had become casualties.

Incredibly none of the Niblicks had been killed although a number had been wounded including S/4405 Sergeant Jimmy Scarth the Doncaster pro and S/36435 Sergeant Fred Jolly who had been wounded in the arm. Jolly, the Beckenham golf professional, returned to the battalion where he reached the rank of Company Quarter Master and was awarded the Meritorious Service Medal for gallantry in June 1918.

After a spell out of the line the battalion returned to the Somme in August and again suffered heavily just south of Mametz Wood and later in the quarry at Bazentin made so famous by Robert Graves in *Goodbye To All That*. By the time 13/Rifle Brigade had bid farewell to the Somme for good in late November they had again suffered almost 300 casualties during the Battle of the Ancre; on this occasion S/4567 Rifleman Harry Towlson from Thorpe Hall Golf Club had received a hand wound, S/4451 Corporal Alfred Seward, a colleague of Fred Jolly's at Beckenham Golf Club, had received a gunshot wound to the leg and S/3337 Claude Macey the Littlehampton pro had been wounded in the shoulder.

Sadly killed in this last action on the Somme was S/4406 William Eastland the former Surrey golfing pro, he is today buried in Contay Military Cemetery.

As 1917, the fourth year of the war progressed, 13/Rifle Brigade received drafts from home on a regular basis; green keepers, caddies and golf equipment manufacturers attempted to enlist in the Niblicks to keep the unit alive. The spring saw them involved in the fighting at Arras, notably around Monchy Le Preux – where the 37th Divisional memorial stands proudly to this day – and Gavrelle on 23 April. After advancing in artillery formation behind an impressive barrage – how things had changed from the Somme – the battalion saw fierce hand-to-hand fighting in the German front line. A resulting enemy counter attack was also seen off and the battalion settled down to consolidate their newly won position. When the battalion commander Colonel Pretor-Pinney was mortally wounded, temporary command was given to Major Strode Jackson, the Olympic athlete. His battalion listed just four officers and 120 fit men.

The battalion moved northwards to the Ypres Salient by June and a lighter moment was recorded at the curiously named Dead Dog Farm in the shadow of Mount Sorrel. The surviving Niblicks from 1914 were thrilled at the chance arrival of Charles Mayo, then an officer in the Tank Corps. The reunion lasted well into the night as the men swapped golfing stories and for the shortest spell the men were able to return to memories of the greens.

It was during this time that another golfing talent Maurice Hemmant was killed nearby whilst serving as a Lieutenant in 11/Rifle Brigade. Hemmant, from the Sevenoaks Club in Kent, had played for Cambridge prior to the outbreak of war. With no known grave he is commemorated on the Menin Gate.

13/Rifle Brigade soon returned to a routine of working parties in the Ypres Salient, often in atrocious conditions and an emotive account of such work is recorded in their battalion history:

> In recalling those dark winter nights in Ridge Wood one remembers with horror the working parties which left each evening in the dusk to face toil and possible death up there in the dreadful Spoil Bank defences. Four abreast they set out in skeleton equipment, with arms and ammunition. Presently, after trudging along in dogged silence over a shell pocked road, they form into single file and come to duckboards that tilt forward with a squelch as weary feet tread them down. 'Make way there!' they hear, as files of men pass down the trench on their right. Then 'Mind the wire!' as a fellow in front stumbles and rises with a suppliant oath. So on with broken step and heavy breathing, past the dim light coming up from a dug out where a man is warming up something tasty and whistling 'There's a long, long trail,' until another 50 yards or so ahead the R.E. Corporal appears. Then, some struggling with baulks of timber or coils of barbed wire, others hoisting shovels and picks, the party moves on to its very dangerous task. They reach the scene of the job, a Verey light goes up and everybody stands rigid and still in the ghostly glare, realising that movement means a swift and horrible death ... the night drags on ... stakes are driven noisily into the ground, and barbed wire is uncoiled with curses and mutterings. Only ten minutes to go, and time will be up ... only five minutes ... then a blinding crash and frenzied shout 'Stretcher bearer! Stretcher bearer' ... The working party limps back to Ridge Wood, worn out with exhaustion and nerves, some having gone to the Casualty Clearing Station for the wounded, and some left behind lying dead in the wreckage and filth of the Salient.

As the final year of the war began the battalion and the few remaining Niblicks were spared the awful Somme battle of March. They remained in the Salient until April when they headed south, returning to their original 1915 haunts of Hannescamps Ravine. Tragedy soon struck when, for the second time since landing in France, they lost their battalion commander. On 8 April Lieutenant Colonel W.R. Stewart DSO, MC was shot by an enemy sniper, all ranks regarded him as, 'an ideal battalion commander, a brilliant soldier, a kind, considerate man who never forgot the welfare of his troops, who overlooked their failings, who dispensed justice with a human touch, and who gave a forgiving smile instead of a rebuke.'

Just thirty years old at his death, he had keenly sought tips on putting and his short game when mixing with the Niblick men. His funeral presents a very moving scene as the battalion, led by the Divisional Band playing Chopin's funeral march, moved slowly up the village high street of Couin. Stewart's body, in a coffin draped with a Union flag, was carried on a limber escorted by decorated NCOs before silver bugles sounded the last post and a firing party sent their volleys over his grave.

After a spell alongside Australian troops at Hebuterne, the prelude to the Advance to Victory began at Bucquoy and during the assault the battalion suffered 60 per cent casualties. Early on in the battle a struggle developed in an ancient civilian cemetery; the Germans making good use of the cover offered by tombstones and vaults. A larger party of enemy then worked their way around the flanks forcing the survivors of 13 Rifle Brigade back. Sergeant Gregg pushed forward and in some Herculean hand-to-hand fighting restored the balance. On seeing this the battalion rushed forward again and broke their way through the German counter attack. The advance was continued in broad daylight and Sergeant Gregg and Rifleman Beesley were both awarded the Victoria Cross for their actions. 13/Rifle Brigade, with its Niblick contingent, continued to fight on in the highest traditions of the regiment most notably at Achiet in August, Trescault Spur in September and finally, in October 1918, at Vaucelles. It was here, during the endless round of patrol work, that S/4565 Sergeant Harry Shoesmith, one of the last surviving Niblicks, was moving through a damaged building when he passed a German patrol in the next room. Shoesmith survived the war and alongside Jim Scarth and Claude Macey were the only Niblick men able to return to the post-war professional game.

It had been four long years since the group had dined on Italian food at Gatti's. During that time they had swapped drivers for rifles and plus fours for khaki, their home golf clubs had given up alternate holes for vegetable patches, female green keepers had been employed, the price of golf balls had rocketed and some famous courses had altered forever with the digging of practice trenches at the hands of keen Kitchener recruits. Indeed, for those who did return from the Niblick Brigade, much had changed in the world of golf and with the imminent domination of the world game by up and coming American stars things would never be quite the same again.

Chapter 16

The Heart of Midlothian

16th Battalion, The Royal Scots

As founder members of the Scottish Football League in 1890, Heart of Midlothian quite rightly view themselves as Edinburgh's premier team and have a history to match dating back to 1874. Named after a Royal Mile dance hall, in 1914 the club found itself faced with its harshest challenge after its forty years of existence.

When war came to the Scottish club the 1914–15 season was just about to get under way and most players were signed and ready to begin another campaign. But, as was the case at most other clubs, gates were dropping and players and fans alike faced the conundrum of whether they should be seen playing or watching 'a game' whilst others were involved in far more serious and often deadly affairs.

Sir George McCrae, a Hearts fan and hatter by profession, was the former Member of Parliament for East Edinburgh and was working in local government when he decided to approach the War Office about raising a local Edinburgh battalion for war service. The papers of 20 November 1914 carried the news that he had sought permission to raise the unit and if this proved successful, to take it overseas on active service. The next day McCrae began recruiting and made the unlikely statement that he would raise the unit in seven days.

In what is now seen as an historic moment, no fewer than eleven footballers from Hearts joined up together, including Tom Gracie, Duncan Currie and Harry Wattie. Hearts, leaders of the Scottish League, were then the most attractive side in Scotland, so news of the players' action caused a nationwide sensation and drew others to the colours, not only from within the Hearts fan base but also from city rivals Hibernian. Fans and players alike joined up in the heady, frenetic round of rallying, both at the ground and the recruiting office on Haymarket – from football pitch via fever pitch! Over the next few days other players like Jimmy Boyd, another from the Hearts dressing room, also took the King's shilling, as did professionals from Raith Rovers and Falkirk. Within McCrae's self-imposed target of seven days he had recruited over 1,300 men to the battalion. The men became known, familiarly, as 'McCrae's Own' but were officially taken on strength as part of Kitchener's New Army and given the more formal title of the 16th (Service) Battalion (2nd Edinburgh) The Royal Scots. The Royal Scots are the senior regiment of the British Army and are often referred to as 'Pontius Pilate's Bodyguard'.

Training was completed, first in Edinburgh, then in Yorkshire and on Salisbury Plain. When the battalion embarked for France in January 1916 it was as part of the 34th Division. This Division was originally part of the Fifth New Army and had been numbered 41st but had been renumbered the 34th in mid-1915. It was formed of many units that had been raised by public subscription and private projects and had been taken over by the War Office on 15 August 1915. It served with distinction on the Western Front throughout the war.

Within its ranks were the 15th Battalion, The Royal Scots, the 10th Battalion, The Lincolnshire Regiment (Grimsby Chums), the 11th Battalion, The Suffolk Regiment and eight battalions of Tynesiders from the Northumberland Fusiliers. They were all united by their divisional symbol of the chequer board worn on badges and signs.

Like most units arriving fresh at the front line the battalion were rotated through some 'quiet' sectors near Armentières before being drawn down to the Somme in readiness for the 'big push' on 1 July 1916.

Assaulting astride the Albert-Bapaume road, the twelve battalions of 34th Division attacked in four columns, one to the north of the road, the other three on the southern side near the village of La Boisselle. The 16/Royal Scots were in the second wave in the extreme right hand column. Aiding the assault was a bombardment which lasted for seven days prior to Zero hour and also, just to its left, the detonation of a large mine known as Lochnagar at 0728 hrs. The explosion of this 70,000 pound monster threw mountains of mud, chalk, sandbags and vaporized Germans hundreds of feet into the air and the yawning crater remains today as evidence of the massive blast. It is estimated that the blast displaced over 300,000 tons and would have been witnessed by 'McCrae's Own' who went over the top two minutes after the eruption.

The ultimate objective was a line running through fields slightly to the north of the fortified village of Contalmaison but to reach it the advance would need to push up 'Sausage Valley' driving through belts of barbed wire and overcoming several deep trench systems in the teeth of terrific fire from machine guns and trench mortars.

Pressing forward from their start lines 16/Royal Scots were following hot on the heels of their fellow Edinburgh pals of the 15th Battalion who had started their attack from the middle of no man's land in the quest to avoid prolonged exposure to enemy fire. 'With great heart and in grand form' 15/Royal Scots pushed on but were soon driven to the right by machine guns higher up Sausage Valley and men began to fall. The line was penetrated and 16/Royal Scots passed through as planned having crossed no man's land with relatively light losses. Scots Redoubt and Peak Trench were taken by 0845 hrs but order was beginning to break down. Losses, particularly amongst officers and NCOs were high, and soldiers of several units were jumbled up and losing cohesion. Follow up units faced an equally grim task when advancing as the collective firepower of surviving German gunners seemed to increase as time wore on. Some troops trying to 'mop up' just behind 16/Royal Scots were even burned to death by Germans equipped with large flame-throwers. In spite of this, the 16th was credited with achieving one of the deepest penetrations of the enemy line anywhere on the battlefront that morning. A small party from C Company fought their way into the ruined village of Contalmaison, only to be over-whelmed by the opposition and forced back out again. Up to this point the survivors included Hearts striker Harry Wattie but he later died in the struggle around Scots Redoubt. The diminishing band withdrew to join their comrades in the shell holes between the German lines and those around the redoubt but the day ended with an awful toll for both Edinburgh battalions with over 1,000 men being listed as casualties. Over 600 of those came from 15/Royal Scots, a casualty total which virtually wiped out its links with Edinburgh, the city being unable to provide sufficient recruits to replace the lost pals. Amongst those swept up in the initial Hearts recruitment drive and who lost their lives on that fateful day were Sergeant Duncan Currie, Private Ernie Ellis and Harry Wattie. None were ever buried in a recorded grave and all are commemorated on the Thiepval Memorial.

By late November 1916 Lieutenant Colonel George McCrae DSO was suffering with ill-health and exhaustion. He was diagnosed unfit for further service and returned to Scotland. Four more first team players died on the Western Front, however, before the Armistice of 1918 allowed the men to drift home but it is the attack on Contalmaison on 1 July 1916 that is inextricably linked with Hearts. In 1922 a small memorial was erected in Haymarket, close to where the men of 1914 joined up but in recent years fundraising has allowed the erection of a very fine and fitting sandstone 'cairn' memorial near the crossroads in Contalmaison to mark the terrific achievements of the men of both the 15th and 16th Battalions of a proud Scottish Regiment.

Chapter 17

The 'Footballer's Battalions'

17th and 23rd Battalions, The Middlesex Regiment

The following article appeared in the *Sportsman* on Wednesday, 16 December 1914.

F.A. WAR RALLY
BIG MEETING AT FULHAM
THE BATTALION STARTED
FIRST BATCH OF ENLISTMENTS

Yesterday's meeting at Fulham Town Hall must be pronounced a success. It was arranged for the purpose of giving a send off to the Footballer's Battalion, officially known as the 17th Service Battalion Middlesex Regiment of Kitchener's Army, and was attended by four or five hundred officials and players and others interested in the Association game. It had been intended to use the small hall, but the players trooped in as one big party just before the start in such numbers a move was made to the bigger hall.

Mr W. Joynson-Hicks, M.P. occupied the chair, having on his right Mr H. Norris (Mayor of Fulham) and on his left the Right Hon W. Hayes-Fisher, M.P. Others on the platform included Lord Kinnaird (President of the Football Association), Colonel Grantham, Captain Whiffen and Captain Wells-Holland (Clapton Orient). In the body of the hall were directors and officials of most of the leading clubs in and around the metropolis, including Messrs Crisp, Hall and Morrell (Arsenal), Mr Palmer

(Chelsea), Mr Bourne (Crystal Palace), T. Descock (Tottenham), P. Kelso (Fulham), and others too numerous to mention.

The Chairman opened with a rousing speech which ended with his own answer to the 'ultimate problem', by the 'successful formation of a Footballer's battalion' (hear, hear).

Applause then followed with the announcement that the War Office had given their approval for such a footballer's unit to be raised. Lord Kitchener had also granted those men special permission to play football on a Saturday if they were under contract, until the end of the season. Lord Kinnaird had also given his blessing for FA Headquarters at 42 Russell Square to be given over to the unit as its headquarters and the main recruiting office. A second recruiting office later opened at 64 Kingsway, WC2 (now a public house), but the first men to enlist in 17/Middlesex did so whilst the meeting was in progress, simply by going onto the platform.

Fred Parker, the Clapton Orient (now Leyton Orient) right winger and captain, was the first to take the King's shilling followed by thirty more, mostly from Orient and Croydon Common.

The meeting finished with the hearty singing of the National Anthem. The singing and rousing speeches of passion and patriotism certainly had an effect on the gathered crowds, as was evidenced by the first to sign up, but numbers were rather slow in coming forward and the ranks of the battalion took a relatively long time to fill. Clapton Orient led the way in demonstrating their support for the Footballer's Battalion and over forty of their players and staff joined its ranks. Over 4,000 players were registered as professional in the country, with less than 2,000 playing full-time. 600 listed themselves as single and these were the men targeted by the FA and the battalion for enlistment. Early plans even hinted at companies being enlisted from particular clubs, thus forming entities such as 'Chelsea Company', 'Tottenham Company' or 'Millwall Company' but this idea proved impractical.

When realistic battalion numbers were reached, the men marched off to camp in Surrey in April 1915 and then north to Clipstone Camp in Nottinghamshire in July. Shortly after the Footballer's battalion left for training, the founders, urged on by their success, raised a second football battalion, the 23rd Battalion, The Middlesex Regiment (Second Footballer's).

Landing in France on 18 November 1915, 17/Middlesex were attached to the 33rd Division, but soon found themselves being transferred to bolster the ranks of the regulars of the 2nd Division and took their place within 6 Brigade on the front line.

Alongside the new arrivals at the front were experienced soldiers such as men of 1st Battalion, The King's Liverpool Regiment who took them under their wing and began training them 'on the job' in the areas of Béthune and La Bassée. Officers went on exchanges with the Liverpool battalion for instructional purposes while men practiced trench fighting and field skills. 1/King's war diary notes that during a rest period, a divisional boxing and football tournament was organised. No scores are recorded but the work done with their new Merseyside friends is sure to have stood them in good stead for their trials ahead.

Back home the controversy surrounding the match fixing allegations centred on Liverpool and Manchester United players lingered on, in the *Athletic News* of 10 April 1916 the following letter was received from F/1695 Private Jack Sheldon from the trenches:

Would you kindly grant me space in your valuable paper to explain my position re-suspension? Perhaps it is unfair for me to ask this favour after my case has been dealt with so long ago by the F.A. But you understand how difficult it is for me to explain while doing my bit somewhere in France. I am taking the first opportunity I have had and wish to let the numerous followers of football know how I stand. I emphatically state to you, as our best and fairest critics, that I am absolutely blameless in this scandal, and am still open as I have always been, to give to any Red Cross Fund or any other charitable institution the sum of £20 if the F.A. or anyone else can bring forward any bookmaker or any other person with whom I have had a bet. Assuming I return safely from this country, I intend taking action against my suspension, and in the meantime you would do me a great favour if you would kindly insert me this letter in your next week's issue, begging to remain, Yours Faithfully, Pte J. Sheldon 17/Middlesex Regiment.

Sheldon, the Liverpool player who had missed the infamous penalty in the Good Friday game that led to the scandal, did make it home and, as suggested by the authorities, those who had enlisted had their suspensions rescinded. Along with his fellow accused

Arthur Whalley, Tom Fairfoul, Tommy Miller and Bob Purcell, Sheldon played first class football post-war.

On 1 June 1916 17/Middlesex were to be involved in their first true operation. At 2030 hrs, three large mines were blown simultaneously opposite the village of Souchez in the shadow of Vimy Ridge. Coupled with a heavy artillery barrage these 'blows' were designed to obliterate the German lines thus allowing the men, formed into mobile 'bombing' parties from both the Footballer's Battalion and 1/King's, to move up, occupy and consolidate the ground. An inexplicable delay of over an hour between the mines exploding and the infantry going forward seems to have been planned but it only allowed the Germans to recover from the shock of the explosions. Far from finding the enemy lines blown to pieces and mere piles of mud, the mines went off short of their intended targets and did not wipe out the garrisons. The raiding parties came under heavy artillery and machine gun fire as they rushed to gain the lip on the far side of the craters. Several officers and the leading NCOs were soon killed and it became apparent to Lieutenant Engleburtt that the far lip was not attainable and they consolidated the near lip of the Broadbridge crater and helped with two small posts on either side. Lewis Gun teams placed in the posts helped hold off the counter attacking Germans as the small parties around the craters became embroiled in several hours of bomb throwing contests and hand-to-hand fighting, all the while coming under fire from German artillery. The General Officer in command of the 2nd Division stated in his report to IV Corps that, 'This is the first occasion on which the 17th Middlesex have been engaged in serious fighting, but I consider they carried out the operation with steadiness and gallantry under very trying circumstances.'

F/28 Lance Corporal Herbert Dersley from Upper Norwood was killed in this action. He had been a member of the pre-war Croydon Common Football Club and had enlisted onstage the night the battalion had been raised.

On the Somme just weeks later, 17/Middlesex took part in costly actions in Delville Wood in late July. F/32 Private William Jonas was killed on 27 July along with nine colleagues. Jonas a Northumberland lad had made his debut for Orient in 1912 after an impressive goal tally for Havanna Rovers. A skilful player known for the quality of his passing, he had a turn of speed that frequently frustrated opposing defenders who were happy to chop him down in full flight. Adaptable and fully committed to his team, he once played in goal at Nottingham Forest after regular keeper Jimmy Hugall – a comrade in 17/Middlesex who would survive the war to play again – was injured. Jonas was a pin up of Orient's female support, it has been suggested he received up to fifty letters a week from admirers which led him to announce his happy marriage in the club programme!

He was once sent off for fighting with the Millwall goalkeeper in an FA Cup tie at The Den. Incensed, the home crowd took to the field and only mounted police and an escort back to East London saved the Orient players and supporters.

The loss of Jonas was especially felt by his striking partner and comrade in arms Dick McFadden:

I Richard McFadden sadly report the death of my friend and O's colleague William Jonas on the morning of Thursday 27 July aged 26. Both Willie and I were trapped in a trench near the front on the Somme in France. Willie turned to me and said, 'Goodbye Mac, best of luck, special love to my sweetheart Mary Jane and best regards to the lads at Orient.' Before I could reply to him, he was up and over. No sooner had he jumped up out of the trench, my best friend of nearly twenty years was killed before my eyes. Words cannot express my feelings at this time.

Wounded in this action was Captain Vivian Woodward who, as a Spurs, Chelsea and England striker, had remained an amateur throughout his career. This enabled him to play in the 1908 and 1912 Olympic sides, on one occasion scoring eight times in a game against France. He had originally joined the Rifle Brigade when war broke out but transferred into 17/Middlesex on receiving a commission just prior to the Somme. The severity of his wound meant he would never play football again.

On the attack on Waterlot Farm the battalion were in their assembly positions by 2100 hrs on 7 August and immediately sent out patrols to ascertain the strength of the enemy opposite along with the impact of the pre-attack barrage. With visibility down to just ten yards on the misty morning that followed the Footballers attacked side by side with 1/King's. By 0520 hrs two flares indicated that 1/King's had reached and entered the German front lines – its first objective.

17/Middlesex was less fortunate. Coming under immediate en-filade fire, those men that did reach the enemy wire were either killed or captured. Throughout the remainder of the day repeated attempts were made to bomb away to the right in an attempt to link up with 1/King's but each attempt met with failure and by nightfall forty-one men of the battalion lay dead with many more wounded. Among them was the thirty-two year old Aston Villa and Bristol Rovers star F/936 Private Walter Gerrish. Reports suggest he died after losing both his legs. Alongside him lay F/1723 Oscar Linkson, the Manchester United star and like so many of their comrades they are listed on the Thiepval Memorial.

Though wounded F/653 Private Fred Keenor went on to lift the FA Cup with Cardiff City in 1927, one historian noted that although he had, 'a "terrible" shot and [was] unable to reliably run with the ball, his strength lay in his commitment to the cause and in his uncompromising tackling.' This mixed review did not prevent him captaining the Welsh national side in the 1920s.

Keenor would lose a Welsh team mate the same month when Lance Corporal Leigh Roose of the 9th Battalion, The Royal Fusiliers was killed at Ligny-Thilloy. Roose, the eccentric Welsh goalkeeper, had played for numerous league clubs including Stoke, Everton, Sunderland and Port Vale; his trait of dashing from his goal line to collect the ball anywhere in his half prompted the introduction of a rule restricting keepers to handling the ball only in their own penalty areas. Capped twenty-four times for his country he proved a very capable soldier. In his first spell in the trenches he was awarded a Military Medal for gallantry, his citation reading:

> Private Leigh Roose, who had never visited the trenches before, was in the sap when the *flammenwerfer* attack began. He man-aged to get back along the trench and, though nearly choked with fumes with his clothes burnt, refused to go to the dressing station. He continued to throw bombs until his arm gave out, and then, joining the covering party, used his rifle with great effect.

F/162 CSM Richard McFadden, the Orient striker who had broken news of the death of his friend William Jonas a few weeks earlier, himself succumbed to his wounds on 23 October 1916, he had been awarded a Military Medal for his role in the earlier Somme fighting and is buried in Couin Military Cemetery.

The battalion's Somme experience would have one last twist when, on 13 November, 17/Middlesex attacked in support of 6 Brigade's operations in the Battle of the Ancre. In thick fog the attack floundered and despite 200 prisoners being taken a new line was consolidated only just ahead of their starting positions. At that point the entire brigade numbered just 600 fit men. Amongst the day's fatal casualties were twenty-four men of 17/Middlesex and many more had received wounds that would prevent future football careers.

As the year came to a close 1917 saw 17/Middlesex busy on the Arras front. On 28 April the battalion advanced towards the ruins of Oppy Village. Formed up on a four company front in three waves, each group had a 'mopping up' party attached with Vickers machine guns and Stokes mortars offering close fire support. It left its trenches at 0425 hrs and within a short space of time the battle fell into a confused state due to the units on the left flank being pinned down in a sunken lane. Before long all four waves were intermixed as 17/Middlesex set about consolidating its position in the old German front line. Ultimately a German counter attack cut off the battalion and surrounded it, a terrific close quarter battle raged for the remainder of the day and by nightfall only one officer and forty-one wounded men reached the original British line. The history of the 2nd Division records that, 'the pity is that the details of that gallant fight on the first objective are not in existence.'

No one had returned to tell the full story. A further twenty of the original men had lost their lives, now only a few of the footballers that had enlisted remained fit and in the ranks. After a spell in the Cambrin sector 17/Middlesex ended the year at Cambrai where they saw action in the German counter attacks on Bourlon Wood. It was during this period that a fellow footballer fell whilst serving with the 13th Battalion, The East Surrey Regiment. Fred Wheatcroft had retired from the game to become a school master in Swindon but in an active career the thirty-five year old had been one of the first to turn professional and had played for Fulham between 1905–7, he had also been awarded England caps whilst still an amateur.

F/1930 Sergeant Arthur 'the Black Prince' Whalley, the Manchester United half back, was severely wounded towards the end of that year. He did recover from his wounds to play professional football for Southend United, Charlton and Millwall before retiring in 1926. He then became a bookmaker, an interesting career choice given the match fixing scandal referred to earlier.

The final action of the year led to a member of 17/Middlesex earning a Victoria Cross. Captain McReady-Diarmid of D Company led a bombing party to rescue some comrades cut off from the rest of the battalion. His citation states:

> For most conspicuous bravery and brilliant leadership. When the enemy penetrated some distance into our position and the situation was extremely critical, Capt. McReady-Diarmid at once led his company forward through a heavy barrage. He immediately engaged the enemy, with such success that he drove them back at least 300 yards, causing numerous casualties and capturing 27 prisoners. The following day the enemy again attacked and drove back another company which had lost all its officers. This gallant officer at once called for volunteers and attacked. He drove them back again for 300 yards, with heavy casualties. Throughout this attack Capt. McReady-Diarmid led the way himself, and it was absolutely and entirely due to his marvellous throwing of bombs that the ground was regained. His absolute disregard for danger, his cheerfulness and coolness at a most trying time, inspired all who saw him. This most gallant officer was eventually killed by a bomb when the enemy had been driven right back to their original starting point.

Sadly his body was not recovered and he is today commemorated on the Louverval Memorial to the Missing.

The final year of the war saw 17/Middlesex disbanded in February 1918, ending three years of active service overseas but few of the footballers remained. There was, however, one original from the Fulham Town Hall meeting of December 1914 still in its ranks – Major Frank Buckley, the battalion Adjutant. Frank had in fact joined the army as early as 1902 but had bought himself out to play professional football for Aston Villa, Manchester City, Manchester United, Birmingham, Derby and Bradford. In a successful career he was capped for England and joined the Footballer's Battalion on its creation. Wounded twice in the lung and shoulder he was decorated for gallantry. After the war he turned his hand to management with numerous clubs, even discovering John Charles whilst at Leeds. Known as the Major after the war, he finally retired in 1955.

The success of 17/Middlesex was replicated by its sister battalion, 23/Middlesex (2nd Footballer's), again raised by the Rt. Hon. Joynson Hicks MP on 29 June 1915. As part of the 41st Division they arrived in France in May 1916, in their first action on the Somme in September of the same year they famously captured the village of Flers with the aid of tanks. Though a successful attack, 23/Middlesex suffered 195 casualties including their commanding officer and F/2779 Private James Howarth, a Bolton bred labourer who had became a swimming instructor at the exclusive Lancing College in Sussex before enlisting with the battalion. They went on to fight at Ypres the following year before a spell in Italy where perhaps their most famous sportsman soldier came to prominence.

Walter Tull had initially joined 17/Middlesex Regiment in 1914. He was promoted quickly to sergeant and fought throughout the Somme campaign of the following year. In December he developed an illness often described as trench fever and was invalided back to Dover to recuperate. It was during this time that he was put forward to receive a commission, a sticking point being the military regulation forbidding 'any negro or person of colour' from becoming an officer. He spent some time at an officer training school in Scotland before – and against the odds – his commission came through in May 1917. Transferred to 23/Middlesex he went with the battalion to Italy and led his men at the Battle of Piave and in this action he displayed 'gallantry and coolness under fire' which led to his earning a mention in despatches.

When 23/Middlesex Regiment returned to France in early 1918 they arrived just in time for the German Spring Offensive. On 25 March at Favreuil, Tull again led his men in an attack on the German trenches but shortly after crossing the British line he was struck down in a hail of German bullets. Walter Tull was such a popular officer that several of his men made valiant efforts under heavy fire from German machine guns to bring him back to the British trenches. These efforts were in vain as Tull had died soon after being hit. Tull's body was never found and alongside so many featured in this book he is commemorated on the Arras Memorial to the Missing.

Born in Folkestone in 1888 by the time he had reached the age of twelve both his Barbadian father and his English mother were dead. Walter and his elder brother Edward were placed in a children's home in Bethnal Green. It was there, whilst playing for the children's home football team, that he was spotted by an Orient scout in 1908. He played in the side that claimed the FA Amateur Cup, the London Senior Cup and the London County Amateur Cup that same season and soon attracted the attention of other clubs. Tottenham Hotspur signed him after he had appeared as a trialist for the first and reserve teams. Still an amateur, Walter Tull was invited to tour Argentina and Uruguay with Spurs, signing as a professional on his return. After only seven first team games he was dropped, it has been suggested that he had received racial abuse in an away game at Bristol City. After those seven appearances for Spurs, Herbert Chapman signed him for Southern League Northampton Town in 1911 and there he remained until, like many of his contemporaries, he joined the colours. Walter Tull was a true pioneer of equal opportunities and equal access. He is widely regarded as the first black officer in the British Army and only the second black professional footballer in Britain.

Walter typified the men of the footballers' battalions of the Great War. Disbanded when no longer required by the end of the conflict, they remain among the most fascinating 'Pals' units raised during those troubled times.

Chapter 18

The 'Sportsman's Battalions'

23rd and 24th Battalions, The Royal Fusiliers

The Sportsmen

Sportsmen of every kind,
God! we have paid the score
Who left green English fields behind
For the sweat and stink of war!

New to the soldier's trade,
Into the scrum we came,
But we didn't care much what game we played
So long as we played the game.

We learned in a hell-fire school
'Ere many a month was gone,
But we knew beforehand the golden rule,
'Stick it, and carry on!'

And we were a cheery crew,
Wherever you find the rest,
Who did what an Englishman can do,
And did it as well as the best.

Aye, and the game was good,
A game for a man to play,
Though there's many that lie in Delville Wood
Waiting the Judgment Day.

179

But living and dead are made
One till the final call,
When we meet once more on the Last Parade,
Soldiers and Sportsmen all!

'Touchstone' in the Daily Mail

It was whilst challenging a group of male acquaintances for not being in khaki that one Mrs Cunliffe-Owen was challenged to raise a battalion herself. Not one to shy away from such a task, she marched the party to the nearest post office and wired Lord Kitchener the following telegram; 'Will you accept complete battalion of middle and upper class men, physically fit, able to shoot and ride, up to the age of forty-five?' The reply came swiftly; 'Lord Kitchener gratefully accepts complete battalion.'

Seizing on K of K's request and taking up the offer as a personal quest, Mrs Cunliffe-Owen then secured the use of the impressive India Room at the Hotel Cecil in the Strand for a month and with the help of a dozen retired army officers set about the recruiting process. Advertisements were placed and when applicants arrived they were assessed by the ex-officers in terms of meeting the formalities of age, profession, chest measurement, height, weight, nationality and their ability to walk, shoot and ride. With these formalities completed their application was then taken to a screened off section of the room where Mrs Cunliffe-Owen would add the final signature to complete initial enrolment. With form in hand the men would then attend the nearest recruiting office for a thorough medical examination and attestation.

This fast track service was a great help to the overburdened recruiting offices in September 1914 and within four weeks the initial battalion was raised and presented with the formal title of the 23rd (1st Sportsman's) Battalion, The Royal Fusiliers.

Training was initially undertaken in London's busy streets with physical training taking place on the slopes of Savoy Street and drill stopping the Strand traffic itself. On falling out, the men would disappear down the steps alongside the Coal Hole – they still exist to this day – before passing taxi drivers hurled non-complimentary comments in their direction.

This phase of training was short lived as within nineteen days of the ranks being filled Mrs Cunliffe-Owen had hassled and paid for a contractor to design and build a fully equipped camp in Horn-church, Essex. This progress was a far cry from the accommodation 'enjoyed' by many New Army units elsewhere in the country and the battalion, dressed in full uniform and led by a band, marched through city streets lined with cheering crowds from Hyde Park to Liverpool Street.

Her duty done, far from relaxing, Mrs Cunliffe-Owen used the overspill of potential recruits for her first battalion to raise another, the 24th (2nd Sportsman's) Battalion, The Royal Fusiliers. This unit was ready for inspection by Brigadier Kellet at Horse Guards Parade on 17 March 1915. By the time the War Office officially took over the two battalions in late July of the same year Mrs Cunliffe-Owen had supplied 1,500 fully trained men for the war effort.

What set these two battalions aside from 'pals' units being created elsewhere was their cosmopolitan backgrounds. Often it was a local community or the unity of a workplace that forged the spirit of many Kitchener units of the New Army. The multitude of back-grounds of recruits in the Sportsman's Battalions is summed up in their history when describing the occupants of a thirty-man hut at Hornchurch in November 1914:

In this hut the first bed was occupied by the brother of a peer. The second was occupied by the man who formerly drove his motor-car. Both had enlisted at the same time at the Hotel Cecil, had passed the doctor at the same time at St Paul's Churchyard, and had drawn their service money when they signed their papers. Other beds in this hut were occupied by a mechanical engineer, an old Blundell Schoolboy, planters, a mine overseer from Scotland, a man in possession of a flying pilot's certificate secured in France, a photographer, a poultry farmer, an old sea dog who had rounded Cape Horn on no fewer than nine occasions, a man who had hunted seals, 'with more patches on his trousers than he could count,' as he described it himself, a bank clerk, and so on.

On arrival in Hornchurch and escaping the hustle and bustle of London life the 'Sportsman' set about familiarising himself with the less glamorous side of soldiering. Potato peeling, coal painting, guard mounting and button stick cleaning inevitably led to tradi-tional 'grousing' from many. This was welcomed by the ageing instructor – a man who had marched with Lord Roberts at Kabul –

who now declared that by moaning they had taken a major step to becoming real soldiers.

For the first time the opportunity for organised sports arose and suffice to say that the battalion football, cricket and rugby sides were a match for all opposition given the talent within their ranks. To a degree the professional and senior amateur sportsman in the battalions were overshadowed by an incredible array of empire builders who had ventured from the four corners of the globe to enlist. Teachers from the Argentine, traders from the Yukon, tea planters from Ceylon, big game hunters from Africa and administrators from India ensured that the battalion title 'Sportsman' referred as much to the field sports of hunting and all round adventuring as it did to our modern perception of a sportsman.

One such character was Frederick Courtney Selous. At the age of sixty-three this famous author and big game hunter enlisted as a private in the 2nd Sportsman's in 1914. He was commissioned soon after and as an officer with 25/Royal Fusiliers would earn a DSO in East Africa before his untimely death in battle. This led to his adversary General von Lettow-Vorbeck sending a letter of condolence to his family and his friend US President Theodore Roosevelt to conclude: 'He closed his life as such a life ought to be closed, by dying in battle for his country while rendering her valiant and effective service.'

Selous was not alone in receiving a commission in the early days of training. Given the social demographics of the battalion it proved the biggest problem in its early days with numerous applications to become an officer being received each morning on the CO's desk. Many men felt this was the quickest way to get to France and they had a point, so whilst the Colonel continued to support worthy applications he added the rule that any man wishing to leave the battalion on commission should supply two suitable recruits to take his place. This agreement suited all parties and before long a special company – E Company, often referred to as the 'Essex Beagles' – was full of men awaiting their commission. It was claimed by those who remained in the ranks that this company did not 'parade' but 'met'. This company undertook almost all the fatigue parties required for the camp releasing the remaining men for combat training and before long original members of the Sportsman's Battalions were holding commissions all over France within a myriad of regiments and corps.

When the units were finally ready to proceed overseas they did so as part of 99 Infantry Brigade, consisting of the 17th (1st Footballer's) Battalion, The Middlesex Regiment, the 23rd (1st Sportsman's) Battalion, The Royal Fusiliers, The 24th (2nd Sportsman's) Battalion, The Royal Fusiliers and the 22nd (Kensington) Battalion, The Royal Fusiliers. The formation landed in France on 17 November 1915. Within a week the brigade make up had been changed with 23/Royal Fusiliers joining the 2nd Division in late November and 24/Royal Fusiliers following them a month later.

After a spell of trench training under supervision, 23/Royal Fusiliers took over a section of the line at Cambrin on 19 December 1915 and two days later witnessed their first gas attack on the enemy as the wind conditions suited. Christmas Day was spent in the trenches and in a marked difference from the famous cease fire and football match of a year earlier, a special bombardment of the enemy lines was arranged. This was followed by the battalion's first ever active patrol. Carried out in daylight by a party of five the adventurers located an enemy sniper position, brought back some barbed wire from their front line and got lost whilst being sniped at themselves.

By the year's end the first casualties – SPTS/426 Archie Joseph Bury Palliser from Marylebone and SPTS/1451 Clarence Wilfred Eley from Derby had been lost to snipers.

The year 1916 saw the battalion move south to take over the Souchez north sector from the French 77 Regiment of Infantry, during this period they rotated in the trenches with their sporting colleagues in the Footballer's Battalion of the Middlesex Regiment. In June, whilst at Carency, the CO Lieutenant Colonel Vernon was wounded alongside the boxer, SPTS/1731 Jeremiah Delaney. Jerry, as he was known, fought out of Bradford and had thirty-four competitive bouts to his name; his last two pre-war bouts had been fought in London with wins over Harry Stone in Stepney and Jack Denney at Covent Garden. The latter had been in February 1915 after Jerry had enlisted in the battalion. He would be awarded a Military Medal for bravery before his death on the Somme a month later.

The battalion's involvement in the Somme fighting centred largely around actions at Delville Wood on 27 July; at 0710 hrs they entered the wood and advanced to the Princes Street line. This first objective was consolidated within nine minutes and as the barrage advanced the second wave passed through and pushed forward and became engaged in a fierce struggle with a German redoubt on its left flank. Good use of the Lewis Gun section and personal dash by SPTS/375 Sergeant E. Royston led to the capture of the position. Royston turned a newly acquired German machine gun onto the fleeing defenders. He was mentioned in despatches to which was later added an Italian Bronze Medal of Valour for his gallant work before he received a commission. Later in the day a fierce counter attack saw the last of the battalion reserves being thrown into the wood before they were relieved at nightfall.

It had been a costly action with the loss of twelve officers and 276 men, over 100 of which would never play sport again.

One survivor of the action was cricketer SPTS/342 Private Andrew Sandham. Since making his Surrey debut in 1911 he had developed into a useful right-handed batsman. Despite a number of close shaves he was able to return to a full sporting life after the war continuing his association with Surrey and batting for England in Australia, South Africa and the West Indies. In 1924 he was named as the *Wisden* cricketer of the year. After a playing career that spanned three decades and featured over 100 first class centuries he coached Surrey after the Second World War as they claimed seven consecutive county championships.

Alongside him in the battalion stood SPTS/1213 Private E.H. Hendren, known to the cricketing world as 'Patsy'. Hendren was also to survive the war to become perhaps the most prolific England batsmen of the 1920s and 1930s. Starting his career with Middlesex, where he had joined their groundstaff aged just sixteen; he went on to play 833 times for his county and in fifty-one tests for his country before retirement. A useful footballer he also played semi-professionally for Brentford, QPR, Manchester City and Coventry!

The Somme battle also saw the battalion engaged on the Ancre in November; ending the year at Boom Ravine.

The 24/Royal Fusiliers also saw heavy fighting at the Battle of the Ancre on 13 November 1916. They attacked at 0515 hrs behind a creeping barrage and whilst they captured their objectives it was not without cost; mainly down to the failure of a general advance on their left flank. Among the casualties were SPTS/4183 Arthur Gilbert Decimus Dorman from Eastbourne and this loss was all the more tragic as Dorman's brother Anthony was killed on the same day with 13/East Yorkshires and both are commemorated on the

Thiepval Memorial. Alongside Dorman SPTS/3078 Edward 'Minty' Miller fell. Minty had been born in Colombo, Ceylon where his father had been the Archdeacon. A keen sportsman his loss was described by his company commander in the following terms, 'I cannot tell you how sorry I am to lose him as I had such great hopes for him.' He too is listed among the names of the missing on the Thiepval Memorial.

In 1917 23/Royal Fusiliers were spared the Ypres Salient, instead seeing action at Monchy Le Preux, Oppy Wood during the Battle of Arras and Bourlon Wood at Cambrai. Wounded here was SPTR/903 Private Herbert Temple; not exactly a sportsman in his own right, but the inspiration behind a humorous British charitable organisation formed 'to foster the noble art and gentle and healthy pastime of froth blowing amongst Gentlemen of leisure and ex-soldiers'. Known as the Ancient Order of Froth Blowers they raised thousands of pounds for children's charities in the 1920s with the majority of membership being drawn from surviving members of 23/Royal Fusiliers.

The 24/Royal Fusiliers were engaged in the battle for Oppy Wood during the Arras campaign. Attacking at 0400 hrs they initially captured their objective of the Arleux sunken road when a ferocious bombing attack opened up on their left. For his work during the action Second Lieutenant Sidney Jeffcoat, attached from 22/Royal Fusiliers, was recommended for a Victoria Cross. Jeffcoat was mortally wounded during the attack and, alas, did not receive the VC.

In the final year of the war 23/Royal Fusiliers fought ferociously during the retreat across the old Somme battlefield in March 1918, often side by side with its sister battalion 24/Royal Fusiliers. The advance to victory saw a notable action near the Mormal Forest for 23/Royal Fusiliers when the capture of Ruesnes was undertaken with minimal casualties. During this engagement – the last for the battalion – a large haul of prisoners and a number of machine guns were captured. They were relieved there by the 4th Battalion, The Royal Fusiliers; a regular battalion that had claimed the first Victoria Crosses of the war at nearby Mons over four years previously.

In the case of 24/Royal Fusiliers, few of the original '2nd Sportsman' volunteers remained when they attacked the village of Behagnies on 25 August 1918 and despite the numerous new recruits in their ranks the battle saw them take more prisoners that day than the battalion had suffered in casualties that month. This was a far cry from the Somme two years earlier when they lost seventy-five men killed in a two day period in Delville Wood. Their last casualty of the war came just four days before the Armistice when SPTS/2421 William Batrick died of his wounds at Etaples. William, a native of Peckham, joined a list of 206 men killed with the battalion whilst in France.

The disbandment of the battalions did not take place for a year after the Armistice but the Great War had taken its toll on both battalions; 23/Royal Fusiliers had suffered 3,241 casualties, 944 of them killed, received 173 bravery awards and seen 4,987 officers and men pass through its ranks. Both the 23/Royal Fusiliers and the 24/Royal Fusiliers formed part of the Army of Occupation which crossed the Rhine and entered Germany. Perhaps the last word on their history is best summed up in reflecting on the results of the brigade sports day held on 22 July 1919. 23/Royal Fusiliers claimed two thirds of every prize on offer proving that despite the impact of four years of war, they remained sportsmen to the last.

Chapter 19

Army Physical Training

The Spirit of Sport

'No efficient Army ever underrates the value of personal fitness, and sport, in various form, has always helped to this end.' These were the introductory words written by General Sir Charles Harrington in the first pamphlet of the Army Sport Control Board (ASCB) which was formed in 1918. That sentence is as true today as it was then.

Physical fitness has always been the core attribute of a soldier. Surprisingly, however, it was not until 1860 that the British Army formed an official 'School' of Army Physical training. Originally known as The Army Gymnastic Staff (AGS), it was founded by Major Frederick Hammersley in 1860 when, during the Crimean War, the general health and fitness of recruits and soldiers left a good deal to be desired. The nucleus of the AGS under Hammersley was a group known as 'The Twelve Apostles'; a dozen NCOs of great fitness, discipline and foresight. Posted to various garrisons and camps across the globe, the apostles began their work in 1861 armed only with rudimentary bar bells, dumbbells, parallel bars and lots of imagination. Gymnasiums began to spring up across the Empire and soon army physical training was an accepted facet of army life with an increase in funding to match. The importance of sport in the army goes far further than simply being about physical development, of course, helping to build self esteem and esprit de corps and also having a significant impact on recruitment and retention. One of the earliest showcases for such sporting prowess in the military was the Royal Tournament which, for decades, was held at Earls Court and Olympia.

Cramped facilities at Wellington Barracks in London were soon outgrown and by 1904 the AGS had a swimming pool and full-size gymnasium at Aldershot. Officers and NCOs attended the school for physical training and swordsmanship instruction and the skills learned were taken back to their respective units. The AGS was 170 strong in 1914 and on mobilization all ranks were immediately recalled to their original units. This hasty move was soon recognised as short sighted and these valuable, qualified and experienced instructors were soon recalled to Aldershot in order to train the huge numbers of other instructors that Kitchener's rapidly expanding New Army required. This move did not entirely remove the risks and twenty AGS staff were killed in the Great War. Some had asked to return to their units whilst others went overseas on attachment especially as bayonet instructors. They were killed on active service in locations ranging from Donegal to Basra. Army physical trainer and bayonet instructor Sergeant Wilcox killed eighteen Germans with his bayonet in the First Battle of Ypres. He survived the war but died shortly afterwards in a sporting accident.

The spirit of the bayonet has always been close to the heart of the British Army and even today young soldiers practise bayonet drill and use it on the battlefield. The command 'fix bayonets' may sound old fashioned and bizarre in a world of digital technology and 'fly by wire', but boots on the ground, with bayonets fixed is sometimes still the only tactic or option available. The 'spring' bayonet rifle resembled a life size replica of a wooden rifle complete with bayonet fitted. The 'bayonet' was however a blunted metal plunger which if jabbed into something solid, like a soldier, merely retracted in on itself. This allowed bayonet training to progress beyond the simple expedient of straw filled hay sacks suspended from a wooden gallows. Two opponents, bearing similarities to competitors fencing, were suitably clad in protective outfits complete with gloves and face mask. With the clothing and spring bayonet the two gladiators could duel with each other putting into practice skills and techniques that might prove invaluable at the front. The cut, thrust, parry and jab were all taught as was use of the rifle butt to follow up with bone crunching aggression.

As the army grew so did the need for further physical training schools and especially for establishments closer to the front lines. By 1916 a number of schools had been established at Rouen, Etaples, Le Havre, Hardelot and Flixecourt. It was advocated that the so called 'base instructors' lacked credibility and understanding, having the wrong temperament for the work needed. The same was to be said of commanders and thus the schools needed influential and inspirational men. One such commander was Captain Harry Daniels, VC, MC. Daniels had been a Company Sergeant Major during the battle of Neuve Chapelle in March 1915. Realising that the attack of the Rifle Brigade was held up by barbed wire, he had rushed forward and, whilst under machine gun fire, had used his bare hands to tear the wire away and wrench up the wooden pickets that held it in place. For his valour he was awarded the Victoria Cross. Duly promoted to officer, he was then awarded the Military Cross in 1916 for carrying a wounded soldier, again under fire, for over 300 yards to safety. His approach to bayonet training undoubtedly carried with it the stamp of authenticity and credibility that such instruction required.

Command of the School at Flixecourt was held by Colonel Ronald Campbell CBE, DSO, Legion D'Honneur. A giant of a man with fair hair, a broken nose and battered ears, he struck an imposing figure at the head of a class. Pulling no punches he worked the troops up into a frenzied state of hatred against the enemy:

> The bullet and the bayonet are brother and sister. If you do not kill him he will kill you. Stick him between the eyes, in the throat, in the chest – do not waste good steel – 6 inches is enough. What is the good of a foot of steel sticking out of a man's neck when 3 inches will do for him? When he coughs, go and find another, Kill them! Kill them! There is only one good Bosch and that is a dead one!

In his book *Memoirs of an Infantry Officer*, Siegfried Sassoon relates his experiences during his time at the Army School in Flixecourt. Although not naming Campbell he describes the sandy haired major who:

> ... spoke with suicidal eloquence, keeping the game alive with genial and well judged jokes. His sergeant assistant, a tall, sinewy machine, had been trained to such a frightful pitch that at a moment's warning he could divest himself of all vestiges of humanity and on command would adopt his killing face combined with an ultra vindictive attitude. To hear the major talk one might have thought he did it himself every day before breakfast.

189

Sassoon describes Flixecourt as, 'a clean little town exactly half way between Abbeville and Amiens.' Far from the desolation and dangers of the front, Sassoon found children playing in the street and blossoming apple trees giving welcome shade for outdoor lectures: 'I looked at a chestnut tree in full leaf and listened to the perfect performance of a nightingale ... but the lecturer's voice still battered my brain, "kill him, kill him!"'

There was another far deeper and gentler side to Campbell for which he became equally well known and it complemented the other emerging arm of work with which the AGS were becoming entrusted; that of the rehabilitation of wounded and suffering men. In fact by 1916 the aims of the AGS were listed as:

1. Developing physical efficiency of recruits.
2. Exercise of trained soldiers.
3. Restoring war worn men by physical training and games.
4. Remedial treatment in hospitals.
5. Sustaining the morale of the Army by bayonet and boxing training.

The priority remained recruit fitness training. How did the army cope with such vast increases in recruits, with varying degrees of health and fitness, and still pass out effective fit soldiers? Peacetime tables for recruit training dedicated 110 hours for fitness activity but Kitchener's New Army had this reduced to only fifty. Shortages of Assistant Instructors (AIs) at battalion level meant also that the timetable had to be pruned for their courses as well. The AGS trained 2,000 Officers and 22,000 NCOs to be AIs in periods of just twenty-one days. Facilities improved too, especially after visits to the AGS base in Hardelot by Generals Haig and Allenby. A proper gymnasium rivalling that at Aldershot was built at St Pol in France and served as the new AGS HQ. Prisoners of war helped build the gym and adjoining Nissen huts. Equipment for these growing establishments was often in short supply and had to be begged, borrowed or acquired by other means. One grant for St Pol sent seventy-five footballs, fifty sets of boxing gloves and 2,000 pairs of shorts. 'Adapt, improvise and overcome' is a well worn army motto so with little equipment and even less time, the men of the AGS organised football matches, boxing bouts, cross country running, assault courses and even swimming in lakes and rivers. None of these activities proved a heavy drain on resources or equipment but did wonders for raising general fitness levels, maintaining an aggressive spirit and restoring war weary men. It had been found that fitness levels actually dropped during sustained periods of static warfare with men confined to trenches.

Remedial treatment in hospitals was where the aforementioned Colonel Campbell's psychological understanding of men had most impact and proved most beneficial. John Gray, in his book *Prophet in Plimsoles*, described Campbell thus, 'his appearance in devastated areas was like a visit from God.' Whilst there is no mention of 'shell shock' it is clear that within the establishment there was recognition that 'war weary' men needed remedial treatment and sports and physical training proved a very valuable outlet. Campbell oversaw specialist convalescent depots focusing on orthopaedic rehabilitation and physiotherapy. An AGS school in Salonika (Greece) had, as its greatest trial, the recovery of men suffering from malaria and severe dysentery. Its PT classes had to be held early in the morning or after dusk due to the intense heat.

Boxing, alongside bayonet training, was a key element of physical training and held in very high regard in the AGS; remaining so even after it became the Army Physical Training Corps in 1920. Dozens of members of the AGS and AIs were renowned boxers including several Lonsdale Belt holders. Six were famously photographed together, Billy Wells, who hit the 'gong' for Rank films, stood alongside Pat O'Keefe, Dick Smith, John Basham, (welterweight champion), Jimmy Wilde, (lightweight) and Jim Driscoll, who was a forty year old featherweight champion. Due to his age, he had to apply several times to get into the army but when stationed at St Pol in 1917 he trained for eight hours a day and was afraid of no man in the ring. Amusingly, however, Driscoll helped run the St Pol animal stock farm and was seen at Christmas trying to catch the pet pig affectionately called O'Grady. The pig charged at Driscoll who was then chased by O'Grady for some distance across the fields. The staff at St Pol still laid on a lavish Christmas feast – without O'Grady on the menu – and invited over 100 local children and the local nuns to the dinner. In recognition the nuns provided a hand made flag for the base flag pole, upon which were added the names of the victorious winners of inter-unit sporting events held at the base. Surprising names added to the list several times were those of Portuguese units. Described in the *History of the Army Physical Training Corps* as 'awkward and ugly' they later carried off both team and individual honours in the cross country at St Pol 'despite their ugly movement they covered any ground speedily.'

One of the last additions at St Pol was the bullet and bayonet course. Speed, vigour, fire control and use of the bayonet were all tested across the assault style course but the rather hasty construction and lax safety rules lead to a number of locals complaining of ricochets; one such even wounding a French postman. A far sturdier and safer range was under construction in March 1918 when the Germans suddenly launched the *Kaiserschlacht* (Kaiser's Offensive) on 21 March. Along a huge frontage, thousands of German guns fired a rain of huge shells which fell on St Pol destroying the village and the AGS gym. A few days later with the British under enormous pressure and retreating, the AGS staff of St Pol formed a composite company under arms and marched toward the sound of the guns.

The tide of the German advance was checked without the need for the AGS Company and 'normal service' was resumed, however, the base at St Pol was not rebuilt and the staff relocated to the safer environs of Hardelot-Plage, on the coast south of Boulogne. Little remains of the AGS schools in France but evidence of its teaching methods is still to be found in the shape of the pamphlets that were written in such profusion for both pupils and teachers. Titles and content alike would certainly raise an eyebrow amongst the risk-averse 'Health and Safety' brigade of today. Take 'Bomb Ball' for example, a game featured in the 'Games for use with physical training and in bombing pamphlet – 1916'. Played on an area the size of a football pitch, with teams similar in number, it was a game, 'bringing into play muscles used in bombing and for the development of quick and accurate throwing.' The Army Schools of Gymnastics and its physical trainers had definitely played their part in the final victory by adapting methods and techniques for a very different kind of war than that which influenced the founding 'Twelve Apostles' on their return from the Crimea over half a century earlier.

Bibliography and Sources

Published works

War Hammers, Brian Belton (Tempus Publishing, 2007).
Hull Pals, David Bilton (Pen and Sword 1999).
Oppy Wood, David Bilton (Pen and Sword, 2005).
Spitfire on the Fairway, Dale Concannon (Aurum Press, 2003).
VCs of the First World War – Arras, Gerald Gliddon (Sutton, 1998).
VCs of the First World War – Somme, Gerald Gliddon (Sutton, 1994).
British Regiments 1914–1918, Brigadier E. James OBE (Samson Books, 1978).
They Took the Lead, Stephen Jenkins (DDP One Stop, 2005).
The Royal Naval Division, Douglas Jerrold (Naval and Military Press, reprint).
Men of Gallipoli, Peter Liddle (David & Charles, 1988).
Somme, Lyn Macdonald (Penguin Books, 1983).
Fallen – The Ultimate Heroes, Main & Allen (Crown Content, 2002).
The Somme Day by Day, Chris McCarthy (Brockhampton Press, 1993).
Fields of Glory, Gavin Mortimer (Carlton Publishing, 2001).
Gallipoli 1915, Joseph Murray (William Kimber and Co., 1965).
The Royal Fusiliers in the Great War, H. O'Neil (Naval and Military Press, reprint).
The History of the Army Physical Training Corps, Lieutenant Colonel E.A.L. Oldfield (Gale & Polden, 1955).
The Tanks at Flers, Trevor Pidgeon (Fairmile Books, 1995).
Race Against Time, Therese Radic (National Library of Australia, 2004).
Memoirs of an Infantry Officer, Siegfried Sassoon (Faber and Faber, 1930).
Defeat at Gallipoli, Nigel Steel and Peter Hart (Macmillan Books, 1994).
British Battalions on the Somme, Ray Westlake (Leo Cooper, 1994).
The Mobbs Own, Dave Woodall (Northamptonshire Regiment Association, 1994).
The History of the Second Division, Everard Wyrall (Naval and Military Press, reprint).
The Last Post – Death Roll of Sport 1914–18 (Field Press, 1919).
Official History of the War, Military Operations, various authors (MacMillan, various years).

Archives and Internet

The National Archives
The Imperial War Museum
The Commonwealth War Graves Commission, Debt of Honour Register, the online roll of casualties from the Great War: http://www.cwgc.org

Index